By Bicycle in Scotland

Cycle-touring on the quiet roads of Scotland

Roger Leitch

impact books

First published in Great Britain in 1993 by
Impact Books
151 Dulwich Road, London SE24 0NG

ISBN 1 874687 22 6

Designed and typeset by
Paperweight Print Production and Design Consultants, London SE24

Printed and bound by The Guernsey Press, Guernsey

Dedication

This book is dedicated to Helen Jackson for her humanity and kindness.

Acknowledgements

Quotations from various in-copyright works appear at the head of and within certain chapters of this book, and are hereby acknowledged as follows:

Chapter 1: Laurie Lee *As I walked Out One Summer Midsummer Morning* (André Deutsch Ltd)

Chapter 6: Iain Crichton Smith *The Exiles* (Carcanet Press Ltd)

Chapter 7: Tim Enwright's Introduction to Micheál O'Guiheen's *A Pity Youth Does Not Last* (Oxford University Press)

Chapter 8: Edward Thomas's 'Rain' from *Selected Poems* (Faber & Faber Publishers Ltd)

Calum Maclean *The Highlands* (Mainstream Publishing Co. Ltd)

Chapter 9: Flann O'Brien *The Third Policeman* (Harper Collins Publishers)

Chapter 10: Edwin Muir *Scottish Journey* (Mainstream Publishing Co. Ltd)

Other works alluded to are acknowledged within the text or mentioned within the *Suggested Further Reading*.

Contents

Preface

I wish to thank my publisher, Jean-Luc Barbanneau, for his guidance and support. I would also like to express my gratitude to Roger King Graphic Studios who drew the maps, to Peter Harrison and David Skinner who edited the text, and to Vicky Pearce of Paperweight who typeset it. I also owe a special thank-you to Ian Fraser of the School of Scottish Studies for his unstinting advice with the derivations of place-names, to his colleague Donald Archie MacDonald for introducing me to the Uists, and to the following who gave freely of their time and help in numerous ways: Professor JB Caird of Dundee University, Brendan Coleman, Margaret King of Arbroath Signal Tower Museum, Charlie MacFarlane of Glenfinnan, May MacPhail, the Scots poet Alastair Mackie, Joe O'Donnell, Jim Robertson and my fellow-traveller Iain Smart.

Finally, I am greatly indebted to the Scottish Arts Council for a research and travel grant which helped make this book possible.

Introduction

UNDERLYING THE WHISKY and tartan image often peddled to visitors, Scotland is a country of contrasts, a land of beautiful scenery and dramatic regional variety, embodying an age-old skein of folk-ways and traditions. There is no better way, to my mind, of discovering this diverse country at first hand than by bicycle.

Heavy traffic is the bugbear of the cyclist, but certain parts of rural Scotland are fortunately blessed with a varied network of quiet, unpolluted byways and upland tracks which allow the cyclist to weave his or her way through the landscape of its outlying communities. For me an ordinary ten-gear touring cycle opened up the freedom of the roads and provided an independence of spirit which I found lacking in faster modes of transport. A bicycle was a means to an end – a cheap and healthy way to explore my native country, free from being encased in a metal box, free from the fumes of choking city traffic and at one with the sights, sounds and smells of the land.

These journeys I have described were not undertaken to be the first, the quickest, the longest; they were for pleasure with a purpose in mind. My goal was to salvage folk traditions based on the spoken word from ordinary people. In practice there is no such thing as an ordinary life. Everyone has *their* story to tell. Partly I wished to gather information about the work of earlier folklore collectors, having been inspired by the mammoth efforts of the late Calum Maclean, a co-founder of the School of Scottish Studies. Many of the people I interviewed have sadly died. Their like will most certainly not be seen again. With them I experienced uncalled-for hospitality and the warmth of human friendship, not to mention informed opinion, moments of great integrity and laughter. I also met others on an impromptu basis, as any traveller, does and these chance meetings also added to the richness of the experience.

It would be impossible for a book of this nature to cover every area of Scotland in detail. Regretfully, I had to abandon a trip to Banff and Buchan – the heartland of spoken Scots – and I also did not reach Dumfries and Galloway, another great cycling area, to name but two.

I hope that cyclists, armchair travellers and anyone who wishes to escape the mad dash of cars will enjoy this book.

Roger Leitch
February 1993

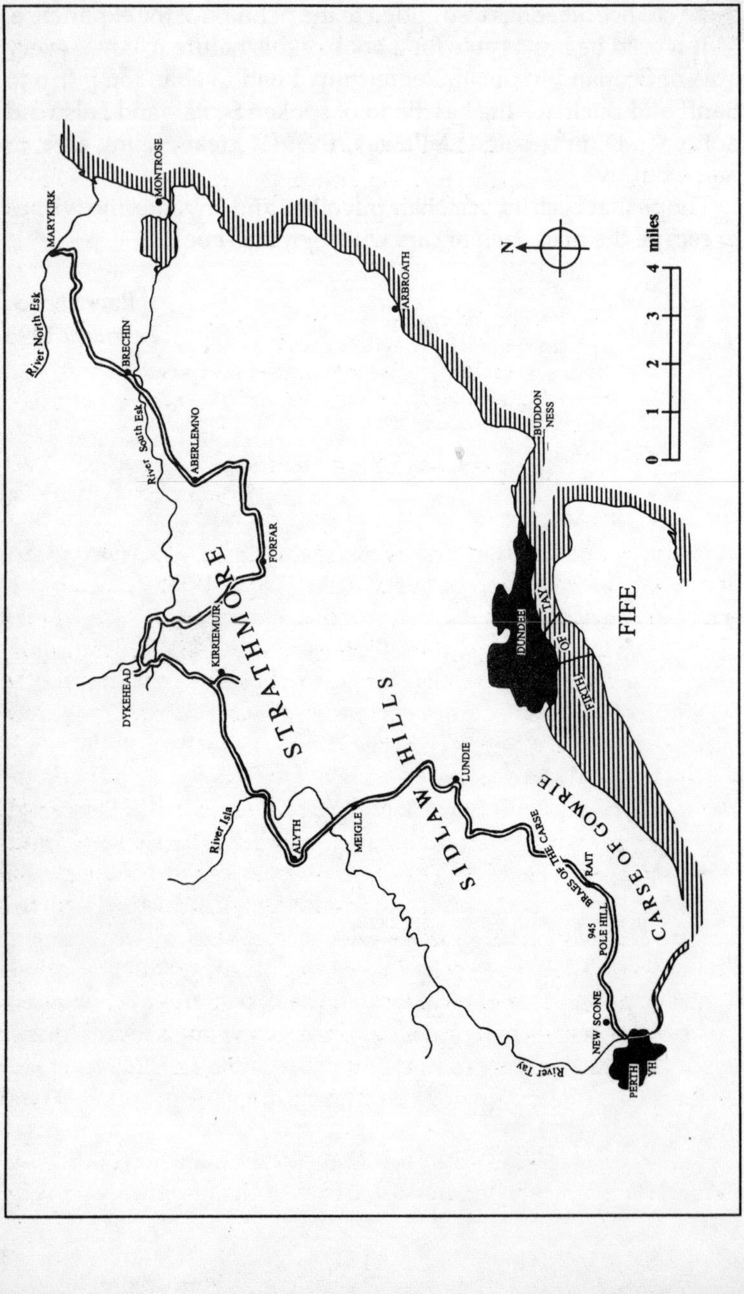

MARYKIRK
MONTROSE
River North Esk
BRECHIN
River South Esk
ABERLEMNO
ARBROATH
BUDDON NESS
N
0 1 2 3 4 miles
FORFAR
STRATHMORE
KIRRIEMUIR
DYKEHEAD
DUNDEE
FIRTH OF TAY
FIFE
HILLS
SIDLAW
LUNDIE
River Isla
ALYTH
MEIGLE
BRAES OF THE CARSE
RAIT
CARSE OF GOWRIE
945
POLE HILL
NEW SCONE
River Tay
PERTH
YH

CHAPTER 1

BY THE BRAES OF THE CARSE THROUGH STRATHMORE

> Most of the old roads have gone, and the motor car, since then, has begun to cut the landscape to pieces, through which the hunched-up traveller races at gutter height, seeing less than a dog in a ditch.
>
> Laurie Lee, *As I Walked Out One Midsummer Morning*, 1969.

AT AROUND EIGHT O'CLOCK one overcast and decidedly dreich morning in late March I arrived in the 'Fair City' of Perth at the start of a five-day cycle journey which would see me skirt the Braes of the Carse, thread my way over the Sidlaw Hills into fertile Strathmore and on to the Mearns village of Marykirk, before penetrating the heart of *Sunset Song* country – that area of east Scotland immortalised by the writer, Lewis Grassic Gibbon.

Improved communications have led to Perth being dubbed the 'City of the double 90s' – it is within 90 minutes reach of 90 per cent of the population of Scotland, strategically placed at the upper limit of navigation on the River Tay and an important hub of the national road and rail network. Unlike centres of heavy industry, Perth has never seriously undergone the effects of economic depression; it remains a bustling market town serving a large agricultural hinterland. Although its medieval heritage has been largely obliterated, some of the names of its streets and narrow vennels reveal former trades such as the glovers and skinners, fleshers, horners and ropemakers. Nowadays the main employers are whisky and glass and insurance.

As I keyed on the front wheel of my Kalkhoff touring bike in Tay Street, the river raced under the arches of the elegant 'Auld Brig' which links Perth with Bridgend. Built in the 1760s, this bridge was never designed to cope with heavy modern-day traffic and has become a bottleneck, choked with cars and articulated lorries. Little room is afforded the cyclist and I decided to wheel the red machine along the pavement to the Bridgend traffic lights. Ahead was a short spin along the A94 to New Scone, a wide and accommodating trunk route with traffic passing me only in short bursts, most of it thankfully heading in the opposite direction.

New Scone originated as a planned village, designed to replace the nucleated settlement of Old Scone which was cleared to make way for landscaped policies around Scone Palace. Near enough opposite a church, I forked right and ascended Bonhard Road, passing a string of modern bungalows, a lone standing stone in a field and finally a golf course. I had escaped the impatient world of traffic only to enter a world of fog which reduced visibility to 100 yards at most.

As I progressed, there were only fleeting glimpses of Shien Hill which lies some two miles north-east of Scone and is capped by an ancient tumulus. Directly under the shadow of this hill lies the rickle o' stanes which was once a crofting settlement with the suggestive name of Boglebee. I parked the bike against a fence bordering the Scone to Pitroddie backroad and made the half-mile detour on foot to explore this forgotten place. All that remains of Boglebee are the foundation walls of some of its rubble-built cottages, traces of drystane dykes and a disused spring. The old route from Rait and Kilspindie, formerly a green way, runs past the former settlement and is still marked on modern day maps.

The silence was audible at Boglebee as the ghosts of the past stirred a solitary tree into rustling motion. Fog swirled round the tops and curled over long abandoned walls. I checked my watch. Time to be on my way – it was 9 a.m.

Wandering back to the road I could detect the sound of a tractor working in a nearby field, and for a few moments, the drone of a distant aircraft winging its way high above me, presumably from Scone aerodrome. The fog had become a thick, impenetrable curtain and I decided to switch on my battery lights. Once more back in the saddle, a Peugeot pick-up crawled past in the opposite direction without any lights, the driver peering over the steering wheel into the void.

Approaching Oliverburn, the fog receded in one gigantic glorious sweep. Flecks of blue became visible away to the east. The steep buttress of Pole Hill towered upwards and I could just make out the remnants of the prehistoric fort which lay like some giant's grave close to the summit. I pedalled on, passing on my left the sturdy white walls of Goddens farmhouse, when I suddenly noticed a black dog come racing down the hill I was about to climb. It was haring down the centre of the road with its tail in the air, eyes seemingly fixed on my wheels. Just as I and the dog met, the mongrel reared back on its hind legs and barked ferociously while baring all its teeth.

I pedalled furiously on, and the dog gave chase for a short distance before giving up. At a cottage further down the road, a woman wearing pink overalls emerged from her front door unaware of my presence. The road surface was excellent.

At a gate opening into a field, I stopped to observe an overhead skein of geese noisily cross the sky in a flapping arrow-head. This halt had allowed the dreaded black dog to catch up with me, but this time all it did was take a casual sniff of my panniers, before trotting off back down the hill.

Mist was still lingering lower down in the Carse and the view over to the North Fife hills was incomplete. From near the entrance to Craiglochie House, I swooped down past Pitroddie Den where a dark fine-grained igneous rock known as trap was once quarried. A roadside row of low-roofed cottages which once housed the quarry workers flashed by on my left as I made the twisting descent down to Pitroddie Farm. A family called Grimmond had tenanted this farm at one time and were held in high esteem as strong men and bone setters. Bone-warming was more on my mind as I tried to pick up the pace on the level ride towards the sleepy hamlet of Kilspindie. From there, a lonely byroad with two hairpin bends rises 600 feet up the Braes of the Carse to ruined Evelick Castle, the ancestral stronghold of the Lindsays. That could wait for another day, and I pushed on to Rait within earshot of the busy traffic flying along the A85 dual carriageway between Perth and Dundee.

A raw air stung my face and hands as pheasants darted across the road in front of me and the morning stillness was shattered by flurries of activity from nest-building crows whose hoarse cawing drowned out the murmur of the traffic. Slipping down to third gear I pushed on up the short brae which leads to Kirkton of Rait, nestling in a fold in the hills at the foot of a glen. The name Rait is presumably from the Old Gaelic *rath* or *rat*, meaning 'fortress' or 'hill-fort'. Out of all the communities dotted along the edge of the Braes of the Carse, Rait has retained the most character. The compact huddle of individual houses reveals the former shape of the village, like that of a plough, with a ruined kirk at one end and a straggling line of thatched cottages to the north. The latter splendidly illustrates what a linear fermtoun would have looked like in the pre-improvement era of the 17th century.

Although described as a kirkton, Rait did not take shape around its former church, but evolved out of three distinct fermtouns. As far back as the 12th century, Rait is mentioned in old documents, and for hundreds of years was the centre of its own parish. It retains a time-warped atmosphere with its higgledy-piggledy collection of old cottages mixing with modern bungalows, a substantial farm, post-office and a former inn that is now a large dwelling house.

In 1603 there was a notorious murder committed at the old inn, when a local man by the name of John Sharp was barbarously stabbed to death. The heyday of Rait was in the 18th century when it boasted a population of 200, a flourishing flax mill, its own shoemakers, weavers and blacksmiths. Last century there still survived the old custom whereby locals gathered once a year at the inn to elect a mock group of village officials, including a local Bard. For many years the Bard was Charles Spence, a stonemason who lived in the old mill house beside the Rait Burn. His collected poems are in a book called *From the Braes of the Carse.*

For a short while I explored the village, at one stage passing a large brick shed which reverberated to the sound of welding operations, the only audible sign of life. Proceeding by a series of narrow wooden footbridges which spanned the burn at various intervals, I made my way to the post-office and bought some stamps. A young postman was having a jovial chinwag with the elderly postmistress. Back outside, plumes of blue smoke wafted up into the sky from a handful of chimneys.

I pulled the relevant Ordnance Survey map from my pocket and studied it carefully. A short cut appeared to lead out of the village by the roofless old kirk. It turned out to be a rutted cart track which I followed in low gear, weaving between the ruts and stones. At Flawcraig there was a game farm with a number of wire compounds housing partridges, young pheasants and wild ducks. It was at the old Flawcraig mill, which appears to be further into the Braes, that James Ramsay the Rait Inn murderer lived over 350 years ago. The road continued past a steep bank of trees and came to a crossroads. Here I turned left and a steep brae took me past some expensive-looking properties into the hidden village of Kinnaird, dominated by its castle. The red sandstone houses were sited at different levels on the hillside that sweeps up nearly 800 feet in a mile.

Upon leaving Kinnaird, the road over the Braes of the Carse makes a sharp U-turn and continues uphill in a north-eastward direction, parallel with the road running along the edge of the Carse, but climbing steadily away from it into the hills. Up on the hillside to the left is the site of another lost village. In the later part of the last century, Pitmiddle supported around 30 to 40 families of smallholders and was the most substantial settlement in the parish. A large wood off the B953 Abernyte to Balbeggie road still bears the name, Pitmiddle, but there is now little sign of where it once was.

I climbed higher and higher up this delightful byroad and the views across the 'model' landscape of the Carse of Gowrie became ever more impressive, a crossword patchwork of woods and fields with a lingering band of mist blotting out the Tay. Near the farm of Outfield I could hear the doleful fluting of curlews and watched as some of these marvellous creatures swooped out of the sky. Ahead were views to the north over rolling farmland and the magnificent small hill called King's Seat. The road then dipped into a bowl of arable land as I found a new rhythm and rode on towards Abernyte, for a time obscured from view by a fold in the hills.

The village of Abernyte is something of a route centre in these parts, but blink and you'll miss it. The village has one shop where I stopped for a can of juice and some chocolate bars. Old Abernyte was known as Balfour, although there is nothing to be seen of the former village. A century ago, Abernyte had a celebrated inn or howff called Cauple-Stowp and the building which housed it can still be seen at the top end of the village. *The Cauple-Stowp o' Abernyte* was a well-known local poem which extolled the virtues of its wares.

An enjoyable backroad to cycle took me below Kirkton Hill, passing Abernyte House which stands between two copper beeches at the foot of a crag looking down the valley between Tinkletop Hill and Rossie Hill. Abernyte Church lies a few hundred yards away on the opposite side of the road, adjacent to an attractive manse with wooded gardens. The well-kept churchyard affords magnificent views towards the Firth of Tay and Fife. I came upon a rare example of a flesher's gravestone with handsomely carved trade symbols which are an excellent testimony to the mason's art. There is also here a memorial to the Rev. William Ross, who was born in 1802 and grew up in Abernyte, starting his working life as a ploughboy, then becoming a joiner before studying Divinity at St Andrews University. This 'lad o' pairts' later travelled to Africa as a missionary on the same ship as David Livingstone.

Gently closing the kirkyard gate behind me, I pedalled on to Newton Cottage where an enticing road leads down to Knapp. This road is unlike any of the others in the Braes, a low-lying and winding route which goes through a wooded den with little to divert the eye, other than the beauty of the immediate surroundings. There are traces of old mills half-hidden among the trees which crest the burn and there are pleasant little cottages which seem to pop up along the roadside.

My destination was East Newton Saw Mill at the top of Knapp Den. The present mill was rebuilt in 1980 after a fire gutted the original, a former flax mill. The mill's owner was Ivan Havranek, born in Yugoslavia in 1935 and the only scythe shaft (or sned) manufacturer in Britain. Outside his workshop, Ivan told me: 'We make six different types of scythes. The most popular one is called the Perth pattern, which is y-shaped. Then we've got Long Striker, used mostly in the Western Isles or west coast of Scotland; we have Lucky Slap, the Thripplin and two different patterns for the Aberdeen area.' A pattern is the wood or metal outline of the scythe's shape which is laid on top of the base wood so that the component parts can be drawn to the correct size.

As well as sneds Ivan also produced long-handled wooden rakes used by golf course greenkeepers, market gardeners and others. Because the demand for sneds is not as great as it once was, Ivan told me he had diversified into industrial woodturning and general sawmill work. Before the mill fire, the original owners had been the Carr brothers from Coupar Angus. They started off supplying ash to scythe makers in Coupar Angus but then branched out on their own in 1926 from the present site. As Ivan explained: 'At the time I bought the business, there was one Carr brother left and although he was past retirement age, he stayed on with me for approximately three years and taught me all the details of manufacturing. There's no written document on how to make scythes; it's all been passed down by word of mouth from worker to worker.'

Thankfully, the original patterns were rescued from the fire, but most of the traditional tools and custom-built machinery was lost. Ivan still keeps close to the old methods of sned-making except that nowadays his machines are powered by electric motors.

I asked Ivan if a special type of ash was required for scythes. 'Yes,' he replied, 'It's got to be a young ash, normally about 20 – 30 years old, preferably grown in a lime soil and also in a den fairly near water so that the timber is forced and gives a long grain in the wood. We normally obtain ashwood locally and I think that's one reason why the mill was originally built here – it's the only part of Scotland with the appropriate hardwood.'

Prior to use, the ash has to be sawn to the appropriate thickness and left to season for one and a half to two years. Before I left, Ivan took me into the workshop and demonstrated the process of making a sned. Blades were generally fixed to the sneds by local blacksmiths. I warmly thanked Ivan for giving up his time and left the mill for the direction of Littleton Den, keeping a watchful eye on the tarmac for thorns in case my tyres were punctured.

Rooks were busy nesting in the Den. These are birds of long-established tribal ways and age-old customs, retaining a firm place in country folklore. Traditionally, they are said to begin nesting on the first Sunday in March and some farmers believed in days gone by that when a flock of rooks passed over their fields they cast a spell and ruined the crops.

With the morning sun beating down I cruised on to join the A923 near the old Tullybaccart Quarry. I was only on this road for just under a mile, before forking left down a real cyclist's road which gradually descends to Lundie, a charming hamlet lying deep within the Sidlaws. On the way I had time to pause and inspect a fascinating old mile post which had outlived its use as far as motorists were concerned, but still accorded the cyclist information that belonged to an era that wasn't obsessed with time and speed.

Arriving at Lundie I drew up outside the prepossessing kirk which had a green cockerel for a weather vane. This was a place not so far from the madding crowd – Dundee is only minutes away by car – yet it seemed lost to the outside world and breathed a quiet charm that was refreshing to the human spirit. After consulting my map, I struck left and found myself following a fine green road which led me by Lundie Loch with the Crags of Lundie forming an interesting backdrop to this tranquil rural scene. I could see a green boathouse on the other side of the loch and this stretch of water was a haven for birdlife which added to the pleasures of the ride. Shortly, however, the route became guttery and rutted, being more suitable for an All Terrain Bike. I was forced to dismount and push the red machine at a slow pace. What did time matter here? Offroad cycling was on the go long before mountain bikes were ever heard of and my gaze was constantly drawn to the loch and the hills beyond. The only sign of human activity was a red GPO van heading towards the hill farm of Ardgarth. The condition of the road improved sufficiently to enable me to ride between the ruts in second gear. The track curved round in a semicircle before changing character once more and becoming a narrow path which snaked its way past wild dogrose and trees. At one stage a large fallen tree blocked my way, but I was able to lift the bike over it before rejoining the tarmac on a backroad to Clushmill.

This road skirted the Round Loch which was flanked by tall esparto-type reeds that added another dimension to a constantly changing scene. At Thriepley a building had been tastefully converted with a splendidly proportioned belfry which had a striking blue-faced clock inlaid in the outer wall. There was always something different to see.

I increased my speed for a short spurt to join the A927 Dundee-Meigle road. At the top of the Glack of Newtyle ('glack' is Scots for a ravine), the vista which unfolded in front of my handlebars stretched across the breadth of Strathmore to the Angus glens and the snow-capped summits of the Grampians. Bounded on the south and south-east by the Sidlaw Hills, 'the great strath or vale' reaches from near Perth to Brechin, about 40 miles long and some four to six miles broad.

Newtyle was as dead as a kirkyard at midnight. The only signs of activity came from four territorially minded cats who patrolled Belmont Street. In the 1840s, at least 12 different trades had been practised in the village, including a large amount of textile work. Now Newtyle seemed to be nothing more than a dormitory village for Dundee. I had held out high hope of a refreshing cuppa at the local tearoom but even this was closed.

Leaving Newtyle with a thirst building up, I steered past the body of a large brown rat which had come a cropper on the road. Notwithstanding, I was able to keep down an excellent value steak pie at the Belmont Arms, an old coaching house on the outskirts of Meigle. A notice in the hall of the inn dating from last century advertised the premises along with nine and a half acres of land, plus curling pond, stalls for nine horses, loft with stableman's room over, two loose boxes, harness room, carriage house, small cattle shed, washhouse, poultry house and piggery. The present day bar had a welcoming open fire, oak-panelled walls adorned with horse collars and other memorabilia, and a range of seven draught beers, one of which went down a treat with my lunch.

The Belmont Arms overlooks the former Meigle station, its long platforms standing empty and derelict. From the map it was evident that the course of the disused railway line would have provided an interesting cycle path to Alyth, offering an alternative route to the A927.

Meigle lies near the centre of Strathmore, straddling both sides of the Perth to Forfar A94 trunk road. In the 14th century it was spelt as 'Mygghil' or 'Mygille', the first part of the word being unknown, but the generic is *dol*, meaning 'meadow' or 'haugh'. In the old village school, now a museum, is the most outstanding collection of early Christian Pictish sculptured stones in Scotland.

I chose to follow the A927 to Alyth, crossing the floodplain of the River Isla by the Bridge of Crathies. A sharp flurry of hailstones and the discovery of a slow puncture in my rear tyre greeted me on my arrival in this somewhat drab Perthshire town. Finding shelter in a nearby garage off the main street, I fitted a new tube and studied the map until the shower passed. The feature of greatest historical interest is probably the small 17th-century pack-brig which spans the Alyth Burn. Some of the houses in the old quarter are perched high up and gained by steep winding lanes.

Jock Mollinson, a retired baker who has lived in Alyth all his days, told me the reason why Toutie Street was so-called. In former times herd-tenders used to toot on their horns as they led their cattle to and from the communal grazings at 'the tap o' the toun'. Jock mentioned that the pack-brig used to have no parapets; these were only added as a safety measure about 150 years ago.

Alyth formerly had six annual fairs, two of the older being St Malogue's and Troit Fair. Others for the sale of sheep and cattle were held on the Muir of Alyth. There was also the 'Oo' or Wool Market, plus twice-yearly feeing markets held in the Square for the hiring of farm servants. At the top of Toutie Street, Jock explained how this was where cobblers, or soutars, from Forfar came to sell boots in threes rather than pairs, the idea being that the spare boot would be used when one of the others required repair.

I left Alyth by the B954 and veered second right along a backroad that took me past Shanzie and within a mile to a dramatic den which encases the River Isla as it falls from below the Slug of Auchrannie. The sides of this den were overhanging in places and it was dangerous to go too near the edge. The road gradually ascended the Kaims of Airlie, yielding good views over Strathmore as well as north to the Lintrathen and Prosen hills. Certain farms were locked away in worlds of their own, none more so than Meikle Kenny with its hill ground rising steeply to the north.

Reaching Kirriemuir proved to be a tough slog. Masses of gulls rose and wheeled in the sky above Loch Kinnordy on the western outskirts of the town: the din was incredible. Kirrie has character, with narrow one-way streets and red sandstone buildings which do not offend the eye. It provides an excellent base for exploring the Angus glens and is proud of being the birthplace of JM Barrie, creator of *Peter Pan*. I shoved some glucose sweets into my mouth as I scanned the map. My aim was to find a small whitewashed cottage off the Glamis road, home to 91-year-old Will Adam.

Smoke was issuing from the chimney as I arrived at Pluckerstone farm cottages: Will was at home. I gave a short rap at the front door and after a minute or two, Will peered round the door. Walking ahead of me with a distinctive stoop, he led me into his front room and we took our seats by the fire. I asked Will about his early days. He recalled attending Roundyhill School – half-way between Kirrie and Glamis – in the early years of this century. Once a year there was a school concert for the soup kitchen that had been set up at the school by local farmers. The kitchen was simply a tin shed housing a portable boiler which heated a diet of green kail broth, potato soup, or pea soup on a Friday. Initially this was free of charge, but then the cost of a halfpenny a lunch was imposed.

Between 1937-42, Will worked for the Glamis family as a rabbit-trapper, gamekeeper-cum-handyman. 'I spent five years with them until I found that people were dishonest,' Will said quietly as he wrinkled up his brow. 'Somebody was selling the rabbits and pocketing the money. I was asked to leave because they said I wasn't paying my way.'

A local farmer encouraged Will to branch out on his own, trapping rats and moles, the latter at sixpence an acre. 'This farmer introduced me to other farmers and I built up contacts throughout the county. I used to cycle above Alyth, top o' the Angus glens on this side, and as far down as Kinneddie at Arbroath. Then I got a motor – a wee Austin 7 in 1940.'

Will told me he started out with about five dozen two-inch gin-traps for trapping rats. He also used to snare rats in the more awkward corners of barns and suchlike. With a slight twinkle in his eye, he recalled: 'The stackyaird was their happy hunting-ground – where there was stacks sitting all winter, then ye got a heeze o' rats in. But the stackyaird is a thing that's gone.' With a touch of irony in his voice, Will told me of one incident involving some farmer's sons who had perpetrated a mindless act of cruelty on a rat by dowsing it with paraffin and setting it on fire. 'Aye, thon wes cruelty,' Will continued, raising his voice – 'But the rat involved ran into the steading and set fire to part of the farm. It was stupid, of course, but there's something of an omen there.'

I was interested to know what Will felt about modern society. 'I would rather go back 70 years than have society as it is today. I would be right in going back but in other ways I wouldn't , because this is progress. Ye have these things [tape recorders] and ye have computers – it's a terrific move forward in this existence. But in a matter o' five or ten years time there will be 6 million unemployed in this country. No need half o' them wae this advance that's been made in technology. When I meet any o' ma auld cronies, the first thing we say: "We've seen the best o' it."'

I would like to have stayed longer with this philosophical man, but the twilight was creeping into the room and I still had another five miles to go until I reached Dykehead, Cortachy. Will pulled on his bonnet and came to the door to wave me on my way.

I arrived at the Royal Jubilee Arms in near darkness, 50 miles registered on my mileometer. From the outside it was an obtrusive, somewhat ugly modern building but the staff were helpful. There were only two other guests, a couple of anglers on holiday from Norwich. I had a disappointingly tough Chicken Maryland with over-salted tomatoes, but I was feeling too tired to enjoy any meal, left the main course half-eaten and retired for a much-needed soak in an extra-long bath.

Next morning at breakfast the Norwich fishermen were moaning that the river was too dry and this was behind their failure to land any fish. They told me they came to fish the South Esk every year, as much for the whisky as for the sport. The younger of the two piped up that they'd be alcoholics if they had to stay in the area all year round. I tried to dispel their grumbles as I tucked into a full cooked breakfast washed down with numerous cups of tea.

The morning was once again overcast, although the forecast was for it to clear and be replaced by sunny spells. A short way from the hotel is the junction of two roads, one leading straight on for Glen Clova, the other forking left for Glen Prosen. I had been to the top of Glen Clova many times, but the place was becoming overpopular with day trippers and hillwalkers and now had a large car-park to accommodate the vehicles which clogged up the road. From the map, the Prosen road appeared narrower with steep gradients in places. I settled for a short ride up the Clova road to Cullow, where there was a picnic spot off the road.

Cullow was formerly the site of an important twice-yearly sheep fair. By 1884 it had fallen into decline due to the growth of larger marts such as Perth. Some interesting remarks concerning Cullow Market were made by witnesses in a famous 19th century rights-of-way case in the Court of Session regarding the use of Jock's Road between Glen Doll and Glen Callater. One of these witnesses was David Milne; he had shepherded for 24 years with David Welsh at Tullitogills who had the grazing of Doll Farm opposite Acharn. Surviving Notes of Evidence have preserved for posterity what he had to say: 'I went in 1847 for six years. The bit of the hill I had was on the south side of Glen Doll in summer and at Lammas I was in the out end, to the outside of the Doll Glen at Jock's Road. I lived for two months in the summer at the Lunkard Shieling. Sheep came down Glen Doll from the north. James Stewart came down that way with about 400 sheep from Lochaber. They brought sheep to Cullow when they failed to sell them at Castleton Market, Braemar. Not many stopped on the hill overnight. Sometimes they were put up by Welsh of Acharn – sometimes at the Doll. Sheep came down either side of the White Water – crossed the water at Craig Mellon ford.'

Jock's Road was established beyond all doubt as being a recognised right-of-way. Drovers also brought cattle from the north by that route, the alternative way by Bachnagairn being unsuitable for droving since there was a wood to go through. It was generally in April and September that the sheep droves passed through – the hoggs in April and the wethers in September. Cullow Market was two days after the Braemar market and other witnesses stated that Welsh of Acharn made all welcome, providing a free table for man and beast. Long before hillwalkers were ever heard of, packmen and tinkers also used Jock's Road, the latter collecting deer antlers with which to make horn spoons which they sold on their rounds.

After a refreshing drink of tea from the thermos, a swift downhill spin took me to Airlie where I parked the bike outside the Parish of the Glens Church and sauntered round the kirkyard. There was a queer smell like rotting dead cats or a burst sewer. The River South Esk gracefully flows through the grounds of the impressive Cortachy Castle which can be seen to good effect from the bridge nearby.

After crossing the bridge, the road twists up through woodland, where I was overtaken by a tractor towing a foul-smelling septic tank on a trailer. At Newton of Inshewan I halted for a brief chat with the farmer who was taking a rest in the cab of his John Deere tractor, complete with personalised number plates. He commented that he had been up since 4 a.m. on account of the lambing. I pressed on by Memus and once more crossed the Esk, this time by a modern roadbridge at Shielhill.

It was an uninspiring ride to Forfar by dull plantations, a tumbledown sawmill and a high-security gas installation plant which had cameras mounted above the entrance gate. At Quilkoe the Forfar bypass was in the course of construction and I had to play cat-and-mouse with fast-moving traffic, at one stage mounting the pavement for safety. I reached the busy market town bang on 11 a.m. having ridden round by Station Park, the small ground that is home to the local football team and which stands next to a cattle market.

Would there be a cycle shop in Forfar? Eventually I found one on the High Street, run by a knowledgeable enthusiast who sold me a spare inner tube and a puncture repair kit.

Leaving Forfar by the B9113 Montrose road, in a mile and a half I had arrived at the enchanting Restenneth Priory, a National Trust for Scotland property and one of only four monastic houses in Angus. An Augustinian Priory was founded here in the early 1160s and dedicated to St Peter. The Priory is on an earlier ecclesiastical site which dates from before the Scoto-Romanesque period. King Malcolm IV granted the church, chapel and lands to Jedburgh Abbey. The Augustinians were priests, not monks, and may have replaced an earlier order. This morning the sunshine drenched these ancient hallowed walls, the most striking architectural feature being the impressive Saxon-type tower with its medieval broach spire. Inlaid in the wall of the vestibule was a finely carved Pictish stone. The Priory lies on raised ground bounded to the north by the old railway in what was until shortly before 1792, the moss or loch of Restenneth, the building being reached by a causeway. The name Restenneth is possibly *Riask Cinead* – Bog of Kenneth – hence 'Restenet'.

Restenneth remains one of the jewels of Angus and I spent a

good hour soaking up the atmosphere of the place, before moving on to Reswallie where I spent the rest of the day and night with friends who lived in converted stables on the estate.

The following morning I was woken by the dawn chorus of a large brindled rooster which strutted arrogantly around the courtyard below my bedroom. The forecast seemed hopeful: drier and brighter weather would be spreading from the north-east, but it would turn cold later on. I decided to delay my start until the sun peeked through the clouds. Reswallie is a secluded spot and the place I had stayed was reminiscent of a home farm in deepest Selkirkshire.

Joining the B9113, I skirted the wooded shore of Rescobie Loch under the late March sky which sent shadows scurrying across the restless water. A wind had sprung up but at least it was dry. At a dangerous corner of the road, I passed Quarry Park Cottage, which had flat stone walls and large greeny-grey slates on its roof. Just round the bend I came to a crossroads and forked left for Brechin, eight miles distant across the hills. The full brunt of the crosswind bit into my cheeks as I slowly climbed past the entrance to Turin House. On the gradual ascent, my eye was hooked on the rugged crags which stood out near the top of the 700-foot summit of Turin Hill. From here I coasted into Kirkton of Aberlemno and parked the Kalkhoff next to a yellow joiner's van which was standing outside the church.

In the kirkyard at Aberlemno is an outstanding example of Pictish art. Standing six feet high, it is an ancient cross-slab, one side of the stone bearing a finely ornamented cross surrounded by animals; the other side depicting a battle showing soldiers in action, both mounted and on foot. This battle scene is unique among Pictish stones. It has been suggested as the famous battle of Nechtansmere when the Picts defeated the Northumbrian army in AD 685, the stone being erected some hundred years later to record the victory. At present more than half the Pictish stones are in private ownership or in museums; the remainder are in churchyards or in the open. These are scattered over the landscape from Fife all the way up the eastern seaboard to Shetland. For anyone interested in our ancient past, Aberlemno is a must.

Unfolding a large-scale map, I could see this entire area was littered with the remnants of history: sites of lost castles, prehistoric hillforts, the Mote of Melgund on Angus Hill, old quarries, a doocot...

Leaving the graveyard, I rode up a gentle brae to reach the B9134 Brechin-Forfar road where I turned left towards Henwellburn, dropping first right down a narrow road which took me to the foot of a superb vitrified fort occupying a rocky hillock, immediately east of Finavon Hill. The fort was enclosed by the remains of a massive stone wall. I doubled back to Aberlemno. Children were playing in the village school as I rode past on the Brechin road. Three further Pictish stones, encased in wooden boxes as a protective measure against the elements, stood by the roadside.

With the wind at my tail I cruised downhill, jamming on the brakes at a superb vantage-point above Hillbarns. From here I had a bird's-eye-view of the meandering South Esk and across the strath to the snow-capped Grampians. An exhilarating freewheel took me down to Netherton. While ascending the next brae my bicycle pump clattered to the ground, directly in the path of an oncoming Suzuki jeep whose driver just managed to avoid running over it. Continuing on my way with the pump secured to the frame, I entered Brechin by the Stannochy Bridge.

The best view of the precipitous streets of the old town is from the river bridge on the Arbroath road. Brechin became a royal burgh in 1641 and like all the Angus towns has its own character. The sandstone houses are hard up against the streets with gardens to the rear of the properties. I rode along Castle Street, then turned down the narrow Chanonry Wynd towards the small cathedral, now the parish church. It is largely 13th century in construction, but the foundation stone was laid by David I in 1150. Prior to this there had been an early Culdee abbey which is virtually lost.

Attached to the church is the famous Brechin Round Tower, 87 feet high and one of only two round towers of the Irish type in Scotland – the other is at Abernethy in Perthshire. Such towers stood on Celtic church sites as bell-towers, or safes. The Brechin tower dates from about AD 1000 and was originally freestanding. The elevated doorway closely resembles Irish prototypes. Crouched beasts flank the threshold, while the conical roof was added some time in the 14th century. The interior of the tower was not open to visitors.

After a short while I pedalled round to the surprisingly steep High Street and half-way down rested the red machine against the side of a grim looking building which was like something out of East Berlin. A flashy sign said 'Flicks'. I later learned that this was reckoned to be Scotland's number one nightclub at the time.

Apart from three worthies exercising a pale-faced whippet there were few people on the street. I rode along to the local library, a handsome building overlooking a tree-lined square. The librarian, Mrs Robertson, lived in a flat directly over her place of work and kindly allowed me to store the bike in her hall, while I took a look at a fascinating exhibition about the town which was in the museum section of the building. Over coffee Mrs Robertson explained that the town's modern heritage was centred on the textile mills. 'The true Brechiners still live at the bottom end of the town. At the top end the newer houses are mostly taken by incomers and professional people.'

I left Brechin by Trinity on the B966. The 'Tarnty' or Trinity Fair was formerly held on the second Wednesday in June and was a great occasion lasting three days. It attracted cattle and horse dealers from a wide area.

After turning first right along a minor road past Trinity Lodge I clicked into middle gear and set off at a comfortable pace. It was a gloriously quiet road running between beech hedgerows, which always serve to enhance a route. Strands of wispy white cloud traced their way across an enormous sky as the sweep of the Howe of the Mearns unfolded from above Brae of Pert.

Strathmore runs into the Howe, an intensively farmed corridor of land wedged between the Grampians and the Hill of Garvock. I noticed that the architecture of the farmhouses was less pretentious than those between Perth and Coupar Angus, which were characterised by baronial facades in sharp contrast to the simple utilitarian design of the cottar houses. It was perfect weather for cycling as I followed my shadow on the sun-dappled road to Logie Pert.

I understood there was an old graveyard somewhere in these parts but couldn't find it on the map. A girl who had been mucking out stables next to a rundown cottage directed me to a house whose elderly occupant would be bound to know. Soon I came to the house lying just off the road. I rested my cycle against a wall, stepped over a chicken wire fence and shouted 'Hello!' An old boneshaker lay rusting in a shed whose door was ajar. Three small kittens lay curled up outside the back door of the cottage. There was no answer to my cry, so I gave a loud rap on the door. After an interval, there was sound like the rattling of chains and out shot a lively brown-and-white cocker spaniel which was barking its head off. An elderly man followed in turn, giving me a cursory glance but more intent on yelling at the dog to 'Get ben the hoose!' He was wearing a fawn padded jacket over an old jersey and his face looked as if it had been chiselled out of rock. He wore no bonnet and had a spikey shock of yellowy-white hair.

An introduction was delayed while he brought the spaniel to heel, cursing the dog for its disobedience. In answer to my question about an old graveyard, he bellowed out directions in a broad north Angus accent: 'Strike tae yer right eftur Pert an it's near twa cottar hooses!' He repeated the command for my benefit. I remarked that not everyone these days would be so helpful and to this he gave out a hoarse laugh, exclaiming 'Aye, yer mebbe right their loon'. Before leaving I asked if I could take his photograph. He seemed quite chuffed at this unusual request, despite his initial retort: 'Ah'll brak yer fuckin camera wae yon face o' mine!'

I never did locate the graveyard. In no time at all I came to the A937 Montrose-Laurencekirk road and crossed the River North Esk by a bridge which had an attractive tollhouse on one side. The North Esk was surprisingly wide and I noticed an angler on the south bank preparing to cast upstream.

That evening in the Marykirk Hotel I feasted on deep-fried Gourdon haddock, chips and peas, buttered toast, scones and cakes: a good old-fashioned high tea. It was a homely sort of place, lacking any pretensions and frills. In the cosy TV lounge I struck up conversation with an Irishman from Donegal who now lived in Coupar Angus and was in the business of laying all-weather surfaces for tennis courts and bowling greens. He told me his grandmother had been born in 1857, about ten years after the Great Famine, and how he could recall the last of the great storytellers in the 1930s. With undisguised glee he narrated an anecdote about a group of Donegal gamblers who played cards for hens rather than money.

I left the man from Donegal watching TV and went upstairs to record the day's events in my journal. The bedroom door closed behind me with a low growl. Inside, the room was furnished in a slightly eccentric fashion, including a maroon chaise longue with a curling stone resting at one end. I was tired but content; tomorrow would bring a new adventure and I eagerly scanned the map in anticipation of some memorable cycling roads through a relatively unexplored corner of Scotland. That night the silence was broken only by the periodic rattle of trains crossing the North Esk viaduct.

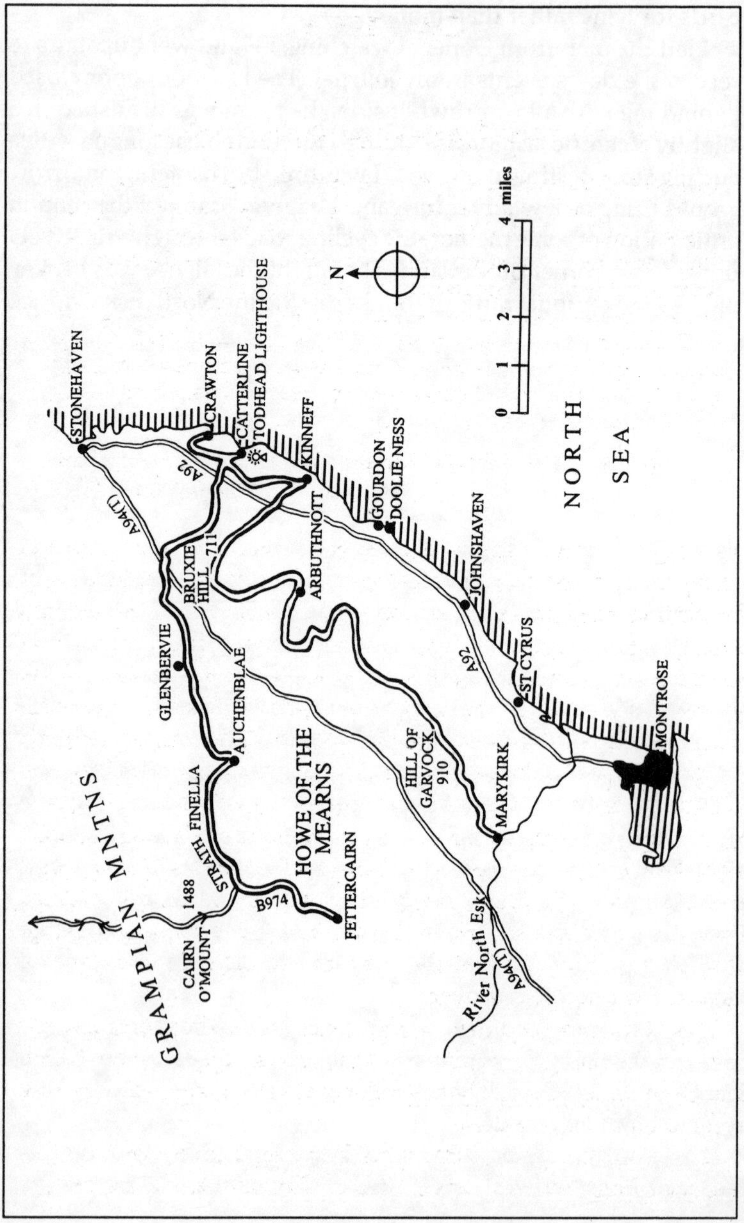
STONEHAVEN
CRAWTON
CATTERLINE
TODHEAD LIGHTHOUSE
KINNEFF
GOURDON
DOOLIE NESS
JOHNSHAVEN
ST CYRUS
MONTROSE
NORTH
SEA
N
0 1 2 3 4 miles
A92
A94(T)
BRUXIE HILL
711
ARBUTHNOTT
GLENBERVIE
AUCHENBLAE
GRAMPIAN MNTNS
STRATH FINELLA
HOWE OF THE MEARNS
HILL OF GARVOCK
910
MARYKIRK
CAIRN O'MOUNT
1488
B974
FETTERCAIRN
River North Esk

CHAPTER 2

Into the Land of *Sunset Song*

That is The Land out there, under the sleet, churned and pelted there in the dark, the long rigs upturning their clayey faces to the spear-onset of the sleet. That is The Land, a dim vision this night of laggard fences and long-stretching rigs. And the voice of it – the true and unforgettable voice you can hear even such a night as this as the dark comes down, the immemorial plaint of the peewit, flying lost. *That* is The Land – though not quite all. Those folk in the byre whose lantern light is a glimmer through the sleet as they muck and bed and tend the kye, and milk the milk into tin pails, in curling froth – they are The Land in as great a measure.

Lewis Grassic Gibbon, 'The Land', *Scottish Scene* (with Hugh MacDiarmid, 1934).

I BREAKFASTED AT 8.30: sausages and eggs served with toast, a pot of strong tea and a buttery. This last item of food seemed indicative of the fact that I had arrived in a different part of Scotland. The Mearns used to labour under the long-winded name of Kincardineshire. But it has always been better known as the Mearns – the name of the ancient Celtic province that is believed to derive from Mernas, who was given the area by his brother King Kenneth II in the 9th century.

That it might hold interest for the cyclist was something I wished to explore; between the main arteries of the A92 and A94 was a hidden upland scene, a place apart from the 16-mile-long corridor of the Howe. Most tourists flock along the Deeside trail to Balmoral and Braemar, seemingly neglecting this corner of the district. Travelling through the Howe by car had given me a somewhat blinkered picture of what the area had to offer; it was the real Mearns I wanted to discover.

This is farming country, wedged like an uncompromising fist between the rising Grampians and the broad expanse of the North Sea. Here, generations of hardy folk have, as they say in these parts, 'wrocht baith land and sea'.

It is also the area of Scotland immortalised by one of this century's finest writers, Lewis Grassic Gibbon. His classic trilogy,

A Scots Quair was his salute to Scotland. A 'quair' is the same word as 'quire', and means a set of papers or a volume. It is an angry social document, far removed from 'the scum of kailyard romance'. The first part of the trilogy, *Sunset Song*, is a flawed work of genius, first published in 1932 and written at breakneck speed in about eight weeks. The lyrical intensity of its prose has an urgency which a more polished work would have lacked.

Sunset Song records the death-knell of change for the small tenant-farmer in the second decade of this century. Change to the land, the people, and the Scots language are symbolised through the eyes of Chris Guthrie, the female central character of the story. But the land endures despite everything. For a 32-year-old writer, Lewis Grassic Gibbon (the pen name of James Leslie Mitchell), possessed remarkable vision and youthful memory. He died a week before his 34th birthday on 7 February 1934, having failed to rally from an operation for a gastric ulcer at Queen Victoria Hospital in Welwyn Garden City. In the last five hectic years of his life he produced a staggering 17 books – archaeology, biography, fiction, history and science fiction – a string of memorable short stories, and inspired essays such as 'The Land'.

I squared my £16 bill and left the hotel. There was a blustery wind from the south-west and the sky was clouding over to the north. Periodic showers were forecast.

Immediately outside the hotel is the start of Kirktonhill Road, a narrow unclassified route which twists its way upwards from Marykirk, passing the village school and a row of modern houses. Ahead lay a punishing 600 feet of ascent up the Hill of Garvock. Today it looked an ugly brute of a hill.

I dug into the toeclips for the pull up to Mains of Kirktonhill. Dismounting the Kalkhoff proved to be one of those decisions that someone else takes for you, in this case, the aptly named Straitbraes. But lo and behold, the sky was breaking up. I gave a backwards glance to progress and the view made the lead in my legs seem many pounds lighter; the entire stretch of Strathmore had unfolded behind me, while towards the coast, Montrose had been reduced to toytown scale and seemed to belong to a different world.

Nearer at hand, two tractors with giant wheels were crawling down a steep field amidst a noisy throng of gulls. I paused to light a cigarette and wondered what Grassic Gibbon would have made of these 'great machines' which he predicted. In 'The Land', he wrote:

> 'Under these hills – so summer-hazed, so immobile and essentially unchanging – of a hundred years hence I do not know what strange master of the cultivated lands will pass in what strange mechanical contrivance: but he will be outwith that ancient yoke.'

And so it is. The modern-day tractorman is cushioned from the earth, he sits above the soil, encased in his comfortable cab complete with stereo cassette-recorder.

Once more back in the saddle, I took the road through a beech wood to a T-junction, where I turned right. An empty light-blue cottage sat alone under Craig of Garvock, with the Tower of Johnston beyond on the summit top.

For a few hundred yards I coasted along this, the hill road to St Cyrus, nearly missing the turnoff after Hospital Shields which comes out of nowhere. As I approached Longleys by this narrow single-track road with passing places, there were flashing glimpses of the North Sea, away to the east. In patches, it was streaked by a shimmering scatter of diamonds, the sun vainly attempting to burst through a gun-metal grey sky. A new fluency came to the gears. Once up on the whale's back of Garvock Hill, the ride was a joy.

Down on the coast to my right, buildings were held in uniform silhouette – the outline of a needle-like spire on some curious church, the shape of a turreted keep, probably Lauriston Castle.

Pasture and scrub clung to the higher reaches on my left. Light splashed over field and furrow; comical scarecrows flapped in the wind; a red GPO van shock-absorbed its way down a rutted track to some outlying farm. These were the images that made up the journey.

It was a road without cars. It was wild. But it was never lonely. I watched an enormous square of light as it chased across the fields, illuminating a long-abandoned cottar house with a sagging roof and windows like empty eye-sockets. I came to a crossroads where the B9120 from Laurencekirk marches up the hill. There was a phone box and one or two houses. With the wind at my tail, I sped towards Tulloch and took the second turning on my right, halting to photograph an old county signpost which must have stood at least 15 feet high. The road over the shoulder of Kenshot Hill was a road apart. It seemed to crawl up to the world's edge and stop. What lay beyond? There was a halt to watch a rainbow of stunning clarity which rose out of the Mearns sky and splashed the fields with the magical colours of its gigantic arch. A pot of gold would be found at Mains of Kair. Suddenly a hare darted out from the fields and bounded along the tarmac. I gave chase. Even in top gear I could not get near his slipstream. Ears pinned back and low to the ground, Mr Hare was last seen racing across the fields in the direction of Auchenblae. A hare gone mad – or so it seemed.

I pulled up at the crest of Kenshot Hill. In the distance lay the land of *Sunset Song*, an undulating patchwork of fields. I could pinpoint the houses at Mains of Allardice on the B967 Fordoun-Inverbervie road. Arbuthnott Kirk lay hidden. The Bervie Water lay hidden. These delights were still to come.

The road to Banff farm led past a double line of gorse bushes, which would be a mass of yellow in May. The solid walls of a roofless ruin opposite the farm left an impression, but my mind was more taken up with a view of the snow-capped hills which cradled the Howe.

From Banff I had an exhilarating freewheel down past Whitefield to the Bervie Water. There were some lifelike scarecrows or 'tattie-doolies' – simply old raincoats with sock heads, but given human movements by the motion of the wind. Was it here, at the bridge over the Bervie, or at Bridge of Kair, that one of *Sunset Song*'s memorable characters met with a cycling accident?

> 'Alec himself had such lugs that they said he flapped them against the flies in summer-time, and once he was coming home on his bicycle from Laurencekirk, and he was real drunk and at the steep brae above the Denburn bridge, he mistook the flow of water for the broad road ... and went head over heels into the clay bed twenty feet below.'

Despite the chemicals, the red clay soil which hallmarks the Mearns is still the same, although the face of the land has greatly altered since Leslie Mitchell's day. The working horse has gone, the ploughmen in sodden bothies have gone, the trees which sheltered the fields were cut in wartime emergency. Large farms have replaced smaller units, the giant combines have arrived, and in May the fields are a blinding yellow with the predominant oilseed rape crop.

Even the climate seems to have changed. The distinctive seasons are not so distinctive as the picture Gibbon paints in 'The Land'. But the roads of the fictional Kinraddie in *Sunset Song* are unmistakably those of the real-life country parish of Arbuthnott. As Gibbon wrote, they can be

> 'fair blistering in the heat, thick with dust so that motor cars went shooming through ... like kettles under steam'.

I joined the Fordoun road at Townhead, passing the entrance to the Home Farm and Arbuthnott House, before arriving at the village shop and post-office. It stocked almost everything. In front of me was a middle-aged farmer and his wife who were stocking up on groceries. The farmer happened to remark that chewing gum was a lacklustre substitute for his pipe and favourite 'Warhorse' tobacco. 'I musta smoket nearly a quarter ton o' Warhorse in ma day,' he said. At which point his good lady slowly turned her head and interjected: 'Aye, did ye now? But it wasnae Warhorse that you smoked.' 'Fit wis it then?' 'Well, by the pong it was mair like deid horse!'

Just along from the post-office, and separated from Leslie Mitchell's old school by a football pitch, there now stands the Grassic Gibbon Centre. This opened in May 1992. It is a bright and airy modern building where teas and home-baking can be had in a dining area next to the interesting exhibition. As well as informative wall panels with photographs and a short text about Grassic Gibbon, there are a range of glass cabinets housing memorabilia connected with the writer, and at the far end of the room a clutch of seats for viewing the 12-minute audio-visual presentation which charts his life and provides extracts from some of his works.

The exhibition houses a few of the author's favourite books as a boy, including one by H G Wells – who inspired Mitchell; there is his walnut study table, copies of letters in Mitchell's idiosyncratic hand to the Angus poetess Helen Cruickshank, the Arbuthnott School Logbook showing Mitchell's name in the register, a few of his lesser-known books, and even a restored boneshaker of the type used by the youthful Mitchell when he cycled to such outby places as Drumtochty or Cairn o' Mount.

Of great interest are a series of typed letters from Mitchell to Chris Grieve (Hugh MacDiarmid) in which he outlines his plans for *Scottish Scene*, the 1934 book they co-authored. In one of the letters, Mitchell writes:

> 'Originally I regarded this book as (partially at least) a good method of getting rid of our spare junk. But I'm becoming really enthusiastic about it now, and think we can really make a sensation with it, if we pack in our best ... Let's show all the hangers–on a real book!'

Originally published by Jarrolds of London, *Scottish Scene* contains poems, short stories, sketches and spirited essays by the two great men of 20th-century Scottish literature. It is a rare find in second-hand bookshops and merits reprinting.

James Leslie Mitchell was born in 1901, not in the Mearns, but at Hillhead of Segget in the Aberdeenshire parish of Auchterless, the third son of Lilias Grassic Gibbon and James Mitchell. His father came from Insch in Aberdeenshire and moved with his wife and family to the farm-croft of Bloomfield, a few miles north of Arbuthnott in 1908. Young Mitchell was championed by his second teacher at Arbuthnott School, Alexander Gray, and progressed to Mackie Academy, Stonehaven. Here he developed a deeply rooted contempt for his teachers and became extremely unpopular with the Rector, whom he later pilloried as Sammy Dreep in his semi-autobiographical novel *The Thirteenth Disciple* (1931).

He left Mackie Academy after only one year to take up a post as a junior reporter with *The Aberdeen Journal*, then moved to Glasgow to work on *The Scottish Farmer*, where he was dismissed for falsifying his expense accounts. At the age of 18 he joined the Royal Army Service Corps and served in the Middle East. He was discharged in May 1923, then tried to live as a freelance author. 'For six months,' he wrote 'I nearly starved to death. In the end I joined the RAF about the same time as T E Lawrence.'

In August 1925 – after a holiday in her company in their native Kincardineshire – he married Rebecca Middleton. His six-year engagement with the RAF came to an end in 1929 when he embarked on his chosen path as a full-time writer.

Mitchell had published six other books under his own name before *Sunset Song* exploded on the scene. Reviewers in the couthie local press branded it an outrage. There is no agrarian cosiness in *Sunset Song*. Now living in the leafy suburbs of Welwyn Garden City, Mitchell gave great play to his imagination by including a warts-and-all picture of the thinly disguised Kinraddie. In his novels and short stories he made little effort to temper real-life gossip and scandal which had circulated round the Arbuthnott firesides of his youth. He wove often cruel caricatures of real identifiable people into his works. This gave them authentic realism and delighted more general readers, but gave grave concern and offence to some of those who found themselves or their relations transfixed on the printed page. The ministry were exposed to ridicule and Mitchell took swipes at the fisherfolk of Gourdon, the 'poverty toffs' of Stonehaven, as well as many others.

Against the above background it is little wonder that Mitchell's return forays to his native Mearns were at times uncomfortable. His parents were in many respects ashamed of their son's role as a writer of 'horrible' books. They kept them on a shelf with the covers hidden by brown paper wrappings. Mitchell and his *real* Mearns had become 'the speak of the place'.

About opposite the Arbuthnott School, a narrow road curls down to the kirk, crouched in a hollow by the Bervie Water like some sleeping toad. This is not a place to be rushed. The church is a gem. This is the kirk of Kinraddie in *Sunset Song* with its medieval tower, narrow stained-glass windows at the rear, gravestones lying higgledy-piggledy under the shade of the yews and its solid brown doors. The church is dedicated to the memory of St Ternan who, it is believed, was born to a Pictish family in the Mearns in the first half of the 5th century AD.

I parked my cycle outside the kirkyard and went inside the church for a look. As Gibbon wrote, 'the real kirk was split in two bits, the main hall and the wee hall ... and the pulpit stood midway'.

Directly behind the pulpit is a 13th-century coffin-slab which has a Celtic cross, a sword and two blank shields carved in low relief. The older part of the church was dark, being lit by what natural light could penetrate its narrow slit windows. The carved old pews could be seen, on which sat two heavy leather bound Bibles and a communion plate. There was a profound atmosphere of peace.

Outside, the silence was broke only by birdsong. Two oyster-catchers with their bright orange bills sang in unison, flying from gravestone to dyke.

In a corner of the churchyard is a fitting grey granite memorial to James Leslie Mitchell and his wife Ray. It takes the form of an open book, on one side being written the words:

THE KINDNESS OF FRIENDS, THE WARMTH OF TOIL, THE PEACE OF REST.

Next to this stone stands another to the memory of Mitchell's parents and brothers, George and John.

I walked the short distance down to the ruined mill which stands below the former manse, overlooking the Bervie. Swallows were darting overhead as I selected a comfortable spot to have my sandwiches.

From Arbuthnott Kirk I continued my journey, up to the main road then first left and along the Reisk road which leads past the strange-sounding farm of Gobbs. The next dwelling on the left is Bloomfield. It sits on the rise of a brae immediately off the roadside. Now modernised, it was here that young Mitchell spent his formative days, indulging in his passion for books, cycling, and exploring the ancient sites of the past. Bloomfield is the Blawearie of *Sunset Song*, despite the fact that Gibbon gave it three storeys and positioned it near a loch and standing stones which are to be found elsewhere. The beech trees have gone and the incongruous march of electricity pylons now straddle the Reisk road beyond Bloomfield. But it is still 'coarse land and lonely up there on the brae,' with its 'whorling mists' and the 'blatter of rain'.

A raw wind had sprung up. The swiftly changing light had a primeval quality. As I cycled away from Bloomfield I could hear the wild magic of the curlew's call, when suddenly a whaup glided over Bloomfield's slated roof and landed in a nearby field. There was no mistaking the whitish rump and slender down-curving bill. Its call epitomised the spirit of wild lonely places. Some things do not change. Bloomfield shall forever be Blawearie.

I passed the sign for Hareden, roughly scrawled in black paint. It was here that Robert Middleton lived, the father-in-law of Leslie Mitchell, and his inspiration for the congenial Long Rob of the Mill in *Sunset Song* who 'never had a thought of what Kinraddie said of him'.

I rode under the sizzling buzz of the power-lines and headed towards the coast by those other places of the sunset: Bruxie Hill, Barras, and the bewitchingly named Moor of Auchendreich. Shortly I arrived at Roadside of Kinneff. There was a brief flirtation with the A92 before I made my way past Slains Park and down the hill to Old Kinneff.

The area from the Roadside of Kinneff to the historic Old Kirk and the sea-coast around is the setting for Gibbon's unfinished novel, posthumously titled *The Speak of the Mearns* (Ramsay Head Press, 1982). The Mearns countryside is here enriched by the constant presence of the sea, a feature that Gibbon worked into his writing:

> '[T]he sun had gone down saffron behind except for some tint on the verge of the sea, it was sleeping in a little foam of colour and far away on the dying edge of the white wings of the Gourdon fleet went home, you stared and stared at it all, at the quietness that was rising a dim wall in the east, creeping up the sky and overtaking and drowning in blood the lights behind the fisher boats.'

It is a quiet road, a road which journeys back in time, that leads to Old Kinneff Kirk. Here, time-slipped gravestones almost topple into the neighbouring field, and it is only fitting that such an enchantingly peaceful spot should also be a place of romantic legend. And what a fine story it has.

The church one sees today was largely rebuilt in 1738 and is an excellent example of a substantial T-plan Scottish kirk. The earlier church was most notable for having been the hiding place for the Honours of Scotland – the crown, sceptre and sword – that were smuggled out of Dunnottar Castle during Cromwell's siege of 1651. The most popularly known version of how this was done tells that the wife of the Kinneff parish minister, bringing bundles of flax from the Castle, had the crown concealed under her apron and the sceptre disguised as a distaff. Another version relates that the crown jewels were lowered down the Castle rock to an old fishwife who, 'on pretence of gathering tangles' on the seashore, hid them in her creel and carried them off.

Near the seaward entrance to the adjoining manse can be seen a dwelling that has been converted from a castellated doocoot or pigeon-house. From here, a secret-looking path wanders round to some ruined cottages perched on top of the cliffs. That is all that remains of the small but prosperous fishing settlement of Shieldhill, which had 12 fishermen operating from it in the middle of last century. Their boats lay in a tiny cove at Crooked Haven, reached by a path that wound its way down the precipitous cliffs.

In the space of a mile, there existed no fewer than four castles. The crumbling walls of Whistleberry Castle – Gibbon's Maiden Castle in *The Speak of the Mearns* – can still be seen at a vertiginous site high above the tides which crash against the rocks.

Under a hazy sky I pedalled north and made the slight detour to Todhead Lighthouse, where field meets cliff and sea horizon. The foghorn which 'moaned all hours' in *Sunset Song* is no longer – strangely missed by local people. Out in the North Sea was a passing container ship and an oil rig in tow.

I arrived at Catterline in the early evening light. A more enchanting spot on the east coast of Scotland is hard to find. Perched on a wedge-shaped bluff of land, a jumbly row of old fishermen's cottages peer down on a delightful harbour, rocky stacks and the omnipresent lunge of the waves. Little wonder it has been the haven for artists of the calibre of Joan Eardley, one of the most prodigious Scottish painters of the 20th century. Eardley was absorbed by the place: the form of the village and its environs, the enormous Mearns skies with their variable weather and, not least, the elemental energy of the sea. Such aspects haunted her imagination and gave rise to some of her finest paintings, one of which she gifted to the villagers and it still hangs in the Creel Inn.

I stayed at the old schoolhouse, a short distance out of the village. After tea, I cycled back into Catterline as the beam of Todhead's light illuminated sleeping fields. Earlier I had arranged to see Louis Adam, a man in his late seventies originally from Johnshaven.

Louis was one of the hardy breed of men who had formerly worked at commercial salmon fishing off this wild stretch of coast. He joined the Montrose company of Joseph Johnston and Sons in 1924 and worked the bag-nets for over 50 years. 'The season lasted from 16 February to 16 September. There used to be a hundred salmon fishers left Johnshaven in the 1920s. Usually there were six men in a crew and it was mostly rowing cobles in these days, although Catterline had a motor coble from about 1912 – a Kelvin engine that started on petrol but ran on paraffin. The bottom of the coble is flat so that you can pass over the nets without destruction.'

I asked Louis if it was a dangerous craft to work in such hostile waters. 'You could be knocked away from the net during a heavy swell, and it's been known for cobles to go down when they were weighing an anchor in heavy weather. If you didn't slacken your block and tackle, you'd take the boat under. But it's different gear they use now: all synthetic and plastic. It's child's play now compared to when I was a young man. We worked with steel wire moorings and chains and heavy barrels as floats. The nets were all cotton. When you'd a wreck you'd to cut everything loose and it just went down, whereas now everything comes to the surface because it's so light.'

Salmon fishermen who worked rock stations were paid one shilling a week extra because it was heavier gear they worked with, and deeper water meant heavier nets. The wage for a crewman in 1928 was £2, with a shilling bonus for the rock men. For Louis, the enjoyment of the job was being out in the open air with the camaraderie of the men. Like many a place along this coast, Catterline had a bothy for the salmon fishermen. The little white-washed building still sits down by the harbour but it is no longer in use.

With a thoughtful smile, Louis recalled: 'When I came here in '28 there was four of us living in that bothy with paraffin lamps, an open fire, one wooden bunk and a two-tier iron bed. Willie Davidson cycled to work from Kinneff and they cried him 'Bunter' for a byname. Harry was the skipper and he came from Bervie, along with Willie Milne and James Paton. I was from Johnshaven and the other crewman was Hector Taylor from the village here.'

There was lots more reminiscing and the evening with Louis passed quickly. I cycled back to my digs and wrote up my notes in an enormous lounge heated by a wood-burning stove. Snow had fallen overnight. After breakfast I pedalled back down the slushy road to the village, where the scene was reminiscent of Joan Eardley's *Catterline in Winter*. This was to be her last major landscape, painted in the afternoon light of a bitter day in January 1963.

Clad against the elements with gloves, woollen hat, scarf and anorak, I rode on to the dramatic 'heugh-heid' setting of Crawton, a couple of miles up the coast. Crawton is on the doorstep of Fowlsheugh, one of the largest seabird colonies on the mainland of Britain. It was a wild day. Huge frothy rollers crashed into the rocks and standing out here on the heights, it was hard to imagine how the fisherfolk survived such a place. One of the old-time tenants had the dubious privilege of collecting eggs from the nesting grounds on the cliffs.

In 1850 Crawton was a small but prosperous village which could boast 23 houses and a school. Up to 30 fishermen were employed by 12 boats that plied the coast with creels and lines. The village lacked a harbour but was blessed with a natural pier-like rock formation which jutted into the sea, north of the bay. It was here the fishermen landed their catch that was then gutted, salted and sun-dried by their womenfolk, who also sold it in the neighbourhood.

Shortly after the turn of the century, the fortunes of Crawton declined dramatically. There was no longer a market for sun-dried fish. Families moved, some to Stonehaven and Gourdon taking their boats with them, others to join the steam-drifter fleets in Aberdeen. By 1927 the soul of the village had withered to extinction. Houses fell into disrepair and were demolished to provide building stone for Dunnottar Estate. Only a few gaunt ruins remain, although new houses have been built close by.

I left Crawton and its decaying cliffs speckled white with gulls. My eyes started to water with the cold as I rode the backroads by Barras and Bruxie Hill. I made a short spurt along the dangerous A94, then I turned right by Temple of Fiddes to the village of Drumlithie, referred to as 'Skite' in *Sunset Song*. This old-world weavers' village is often thought to be the setting of Segget in *Cloud Howe*, the second part of his trilogy. But Gibbon interwove differing aspects of each of the Mearns towns and villages into his sequel to *Sunset Song*, so Segget cannot be pinned down to any one place.

In the centre of its main street, Drumlithie still has the isolated steeple built in 1777 as a bell-tower to summon the weavers to their labour. But the power-loom put an end to all that, and by 1878 only a single hand-loom weaver remained.

I pedalled on and into Glenbervie. As Gibbon reminds us in *Cloud Howe*, the Mearns is also the country of the forefathers of Robert Burns. The quiet kirkyard of Glenbervie is dotted with the graves of Robert Burns' ancestors and reveals their farming connections with outby places such a the old 'Bralinmuir', West Kinmoth, Hawkhill, Clochnahill, and Elfhill to the north.

As I rode under the shadow of Droop Hill, I could see an enormous black cloud come lumbering over yesterday's ground. The lonely looking farm of Brawliemuir lay ahead. Robert Burns' great-grandfather lived here and its general appearance made an ideal Blawearie in the TV production of *Sunset Song*.

Once more I crossed the Bervie Water as I swept down from Brawliemuir. Consulting the map, I noticed it marked 'Paldy Fair', a great four-day cattle market in former days when beasts were driven on the hoof over the Craigincrosse Mounth from Banchory.

Shortly I arrived at Auchenblae. It too reached the zenith of its prosperity from weaving, and provided Gibbon with fruitful background for *Cloud Howe*. Today, a sleepier place is hard to imagine.

I whizzed down the steep main street, passing an abandoned mill with an inlaid wall-clock that told no time – there was a dial, but no hands. That clock spoke volumes for the place.

Moving slowly up a narrow backroad on the west side of Luther Water, all peace was shattered as a large timber-lorry came thundering by, virtually shaving my right pannier. Forestry Commission woodlands blanket Strathfinella Hill and the lower Grampian slopes. Above this, peat-covered moors reach up to the hill summits. The route curled round and through the delightful Glen of Drumtochy, where I passed an enormous Episcopalian church. It was a route well known to the young Leslie Mitchell, as he wrote in 'The Land':

> 'I cycled up the Glen of Drumtochty today. It was very hot, the heat was caught in the cup of the Howe and spun and stirred there, milkily, by little currents of wind that had come filtering down through the Grampian passes. In the long, dusty stretches of roadway my shadow winked and fluttered perspiringly while I followed in a sympathetic sweat.'

What a contrast to my own journey, with snow dripping off the trees, a growling sky, and shuddering blasts from a cruel wind which went whistling through the glen. For Grassic Gibbon, the hill-lands were more than a purple sea of heather. They had the quality of transcending time and took him back to the remote past and its people. They were constant in a changing world blighted by war and human poverty.

From dark Loch Saugh, the road twisted to the right before I plunged down to Clatterin' Brig and the old military road which leads to Fettercairn. There, I took some time to explore the village square with its solid sandstone houses with outside stairs and ancient market cross. An ell-groove can still be seen on the shaft of the cross. On Fair days travelling chapmen had their measuring sticks tested against the groove to ensure uniformity. The cross is reputed to have come from the lost village of Kincardine.

My trip to the Mearns had come to an end. It had been eventful, quiet, where no two roads were the same: the Mearns has a great deal to offer the cyclist. I will never forget that weirdly beautiful ride along the back of Garvock Hill, one I would gladly have extended long beyond the time it lasted. Nor shall I forget Arbuthnott Kirk, the solitude, the peace, and the curlew which swooped over Bloomfield: '*That* is The Land out there...'

OS 66, 73, 74

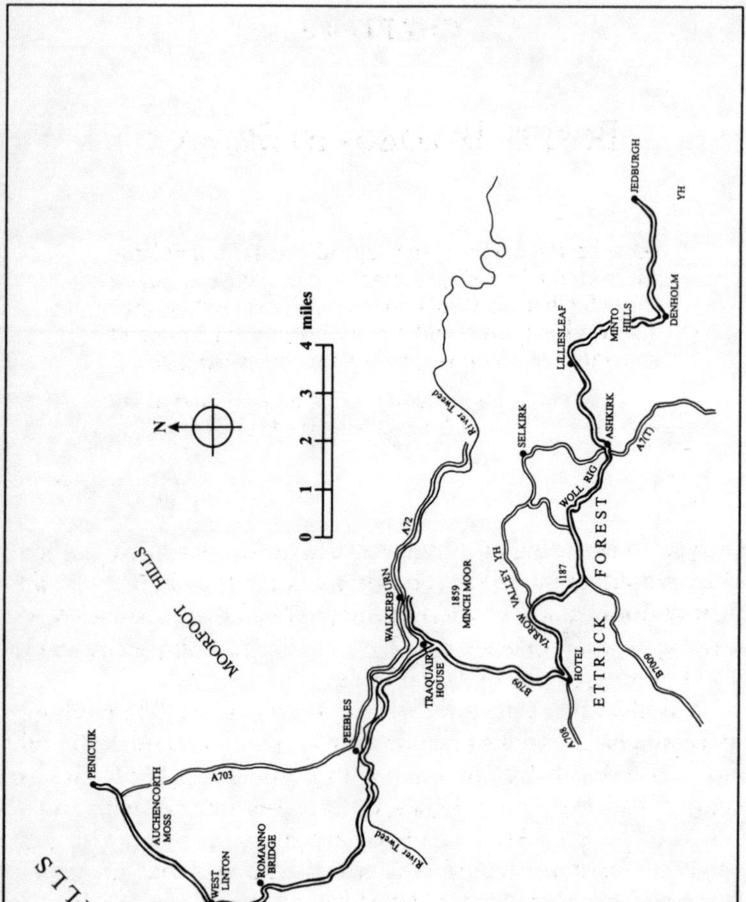
N
0 1 2 3 4 miles
PENTLAND HILLS
MOORFOOT HILLS
PENICUIK
AUCHENCORTH MOSS
A703
WEST LINTON
ROMANNO BRIDGE
1481 MENDICK HILL
River Tweed
PEEBLES
TRAQUAIR HOUSE
WALKERBURN
A72
1859 MINCH MOOR
B709
HOTEL
A708
YARROW VALLEY
YH
1187
ETTRICK FOREST
B7009
WOLL RIG
SELKIRK
ASHKIRK
A7(T)
LILLIESLEAF
MINTO HILLS
DENHOLM
JEDBURGH

CHAPTER 3

Border Byroads to Berwick

> All wheelmen who wish to spend a delightful holiday far from the 'madding crowd' of excursionists, cannot do better than visit the Borders or Galloway, where they will find exquisite and varied scenery, historic and romantic associations, good roads, and cheap hotels.
>
> James Lennox, *Cyclists' Road Book & Guide to The Scottish Borders and Galloway*, 1898

This was to be the big one, five weeks in the saddle and a journey which would see me follow some dramatic roads in the Borders, all the way from Penicuik to Berwick-upon-Tweed, then an east-west crossing of Scotland from Stonehaven to Oban, followed by some island-hopping in the Outer Hebrides.

I loaded the bike early one morning in late August 1984. Nothing vital could be overlooked for such a lengthy trip and the Kalkhoff was well and truly loaded down with sleeping-bag, bivvy sack, a length of karrimat, spare clothes, waterproofs, tool kit, maps and a couple of paperbacks. I sacrificed a camera on account of the weight, a decision I would later regret. The load was unevenly distributed towards the rear of the bike: not the way to do it. Rear-mounted panniers have more capacity but the addition of small front panniers help spread the load and affect the handling of the bike less. I made do with what I could afford. Besides, Thomas Stevens (the first person to cycle round the world in the 1980s) made do with a spare shirt and a .38 Smith and Wesson.

It was just turning eight o'clock as I wobbled out of Penicuik, south of Edinburgh. A morning haze hung over the Pentlands and there was only a light refreshing breeze. The A701 was fairly busy with commuters heading for work in the city as the road twisted round a tree-lined bend out of the town. Shortly I forked first right for the narrow road which runs across Auchencorth Moss and Harlaw Muir to the charming Tweeddale village of West Linton.

Roughly six miles in length, the moor is a wide and spacious tract, whose changing moods lend it a special atmosphere. Free from the cut and thrust of busy traffic, it is an excellent spot to view the graceful contours of the Pentland Hills to the west. Occasional sheep wander onto the road, which is flat and straight and timeless in its own way. Coal, iron, limestone and blue clay were formerly extracted from the moor; stone was also quarried at Deepsykehead and Marfield, farmers coming from as far away as Annandale to collect the white sandstone that was used for sharpening scythes in the days before carborundum was ever heard of.

I was glad of this easy opening ride. The road surface was excellent and I was passed only by the occasional vehicle. Upon nearing Deepsykehead I spotted a figure in the middle distance, bending and straightening in front of a gap in a dyke. Leaving the bike by the verge, I strolled over the field towards where the man was working. The stillness was punctuated by a 'tap, tap, tap', the sound of metal on stone.

The man was John Paul, a drystane dyker from Eddleston near Peebles. He was fair-haired and had a wiry frame, by no means a colossus, whatever the popular perception of a dyker might be. Speaking with a slight stutter, John told me he had been contracted by a nearby farmer to completely rebuild a line of double dyke which had deteriorated due to old age. He had to start at the 'foond' [foundation] and build the dyke up to its eventual height of four feet six inches. Horizontally placed stones held the dyke together and were known as 'bandstones'. The heart of the dyke comprised small stones which were closely packed to form a central core and the wall was finished with a tightly pinned 'cope' – vertical stones.

'You must have an eye for the stones and know which ones to pick up and where to place it,' John said.

'You're using blue whin [stone]?' I tentatively enquired.

'That's right,' he replied, 'It's the hardest stone around this district and it wears very well with the weather. Lower down near West Linton it's sandstone and it crumbles.'

John was reusing stones from the old dyke, so I asked him where the earlier dykers had obtained their stones from. 'Well, a lot of it was land gathered or from the river beds. And for dykes on the hills – they made small quarries on the top and took the stones down to the dyke by a horse-drawn slype [a wooden platform without wheels, used as a kind of sledge]. They always came down the hill, never up. It's always been the horse and slype that I've heard tell of.'

John's grandfather worked as an estate dyker at Barns Estate near Peebles in the early 1900s. He left there to work for an extra shilling a week on Stobo Estate. John recalled that his grandfather's wage was 19 shillings a week, whereas he was being paid £6 per yard, with extra money for gateheads and features such as a 'lunky' – a hole set in the base of a dyke to give passage for sheep. In one yard of completed dyke, John would have to lift about one ton of stone, which worked out at about five tons in an average working day. Dykers in John's grandfather's day had worn knee-pads – for rolling large stones up their legs – and leather aprons for gathering small stones used to fill the heart of the dyke.

'You can't build dykes in frost and snow,' John added.

'If you build them in frost they're liable to slip when the thaw comes. You've got to work longer in the summertime to make up for lost hours in the winter. And another thing – a dyke running up the hill will always stand straight, whereas one running across the hill is liable to slip to the bottom side.'

'Did dykers take on other kinds of work?' I asked.

'When I started, we used to follow the threshing mill round the farms and this helped to make up the wages. But these days are all gone now. Some dykers also did a bit of fencing in the wintertime.'

John went on to say that his dyker's hammer had once belonged to an old practitioner of the art, a man called Nimmo from Innerleithen. It weighed about 3½ lb., with a tempered steel head inserted into a 12-inch wooden shaft. 'I use the blunt end for breaking the bigger stones, and the pointed end is for splitting. If the head is tempered right it will last long enough, but if it's too soft, the end bashes up; too hard and it chips. Local village blacksmiths used to make them, but now it's nearly impossible to find the right tradesman.'

It was from the quarries at Deepsykehead that stone was obtained by the masons building Drochil Castle. According to tradition, these masons introduced stone-carving into West Linton. The village's craftsmen became the chief gravestone-carvers in Peeblesshire.

I left John to his stones. There was a delightful spin from the edge of the moor, down into the conservation village of West Linton with its narrow, twisting main street. I found a tiny tearoom in the appropriately named Teapot Lane where I demolished some chocolate fudge cake. The countryside beckoned and although West Linton was an interesting village, I cut my exploration short. I pedalled round by the village green where the Lyne Water glides gracefully by, then branched off and along a quiet sideroad leading through lush country around Bogsbank.

As I neared Romanno Bridge the morning haze cleared to reveal the white disc of the sun. Round the first bend of the B7059, ancient cultivation terraces climbed up the hillside in a series of grassy steps enclosed by a thin horseshoe strip of woodland. Adjacent to the road and near a former bridge, I passed the one-time tollhouse at Romanno. It is a small rubble-built cottage with ashlar dressings. Road tolls were abolished in Scotland in 1883. Usually a barrier known as the tollbar prevented those who had not paid the appropriate toll from passing. In 1832 the Romanno tollbar derived more than half its revenue from cattle droves passing through on the way to England.

I swung over a bridge across the Lyne as the road began to climb. The roofless ruin of Newlands Kirk stood enshrouded in tranquillity beside a former Georgian manse, reputedly the oldest manse in the county. On my left, the Lyne was a constant companion as I leisurely wheeled my way along this delightful byroad which has a charm all of its own. Shortly over to my right, I passed the lichen-encrusted walls of Drochil Castle, and in no time at all, I reached the A72 Peebles road.

At Five Mile Bridge I rounded the longest continuous corner in Scotland, directly under the remains of a Roman fort. I rode on past Hallyne with its squat little church. In a nearby field there were ponies, foals, and a donkey all grazing peacefully in a group. The Lyne Water was now on my right, and a few hundred yards before it joins the Tweed, it is spanned by the majestically arched Beggars' Path Bridge. Two stonemasons were busy renovating one of the arches, and it was pleasing to see that the local authority put such faith in its old bridges, because they are very much a feature of the roads in this part of the country.

Further on, I passed a sombre black sign advertising the Black Barony Hotel; the spooky illustration conjured up an image of Dracula's castle. After a few miles, I forked right and under a railway bridge on the road leading to Kirkton Manor. This was John Buchan territory and I thought of the hill-loving author out pacing the moors in his stout tweeds and shapeless hat. The noise of passing traffic on the A72 was now reduced to a distant murmur. Rather than go round by Cademuir Hill (the subject for one of Buchan's early sketches in *Scholar Gipsies*), I took a sharp left over the hump-backed Manor Brig which was built in 1702. I rested contentedly against a parapet and listened as the wind whispered to the chattering water. Trout darted out from stones in a deep pool below.

The aptly named Sware Brae proved to be a formidable climb but rewarded with a stunning view back towards the Tweed, meandering in all its glory through a pastoral landscape peppered with trees. Not far from the crest of the hill is a car park which offers a splendid panoramic view of Peebles, the old forest of Glentress, and the Shieldgreen Kips. There followed a fine airy descent into the town.

I headed straight for George Pennel's cycle shop, situated down a quiet pend at the east end of the busy High Street. I was about to rest the Kalkhoff outside the shop, when there was a sudden crash like the sound of breaking glass. 'Have your false teeth fallen out?' quipped George, as he poked his head round the door. One of his young assistants had just dropped a bottle of milk further up the lane. While I waited, George fitted new pedals and toe-clips to my cycle. Due to the weight in the rear panniers, the Kalkhoff's folding stand had proved to be ineffectual in supporting the bike, and this was removed.

Back in West Linton , the local butcher had given me the name and address of a retired gamekeeper who now lived in Peebles. I found Peter Ward in a sheltered housing complex not far from the Old Town. Peter was keen to talk about his keepering experiences on various estates in Peeblesshire. His father had been a forester at

Nether Urd Estate and used to cut the hair of all the estate workers, including Old Henry, the gamekeeper who had taught Peter how to snare rabbits. Old Henry kept five dogs and gifted one to Peter when he was a boy.

'Well, that dog wis just ma shadow. I went everywhere wae it. And I also acquired a jackdaw and a cat. Believe it or not, these three enemies used to all go with me together – the jackdaw, the dog and the cat. I used to often go to the shop on ma bike for messages and I'd take the jackdaw on the handlebars. He used to slip off so I tied a handkerchief round the handlebars so as it would get a hold. People were amused at me flyin along on ma bike, an this jackdaw. I used to lift it an throw the bird into the air, cycle as hard as I could – but it would just swoop down an land on ma shoulder.'

After a pleasantly nostalgic half-hour in Peter's company, I left and headed back to the High Street where I withdrew some funds from the bank and bought a piping hot steak pie from a local butcher whose line of customers stretched onto the street.

I left Peebles just as the church clock was chiming noon. It felt good to be leaving the bustle of the town behind as I picked up a steady pace on the B7062, a delightful byroad which tails the Tweed until it rounds Kailzie. I cruised past Kirkhope Church and on to Cardrona with its ivy—clad cottages and pristine white farm: a lovelier setting was hard to imagine.

In his book *Tweeddale* (1948), Will Grant writes:

> 'At Cardrona was the Standing Stone (the old name for Cardrona Farm), the shaft of a wayside cross pointing the way across the ford of Tweed (The Crossford). This was the highway from the North of England and the Borders to the church and monastery of the Holy Cross at Peebles.'

Close to the ford at Old Howford, I rested by a moss-covered roadside dyke to have a quiet smoke. In sections the waters of the Tweed were like a mirror, interrupted by miniature whirlpools, sun-dappled and hypnotic to the eye.

The stretch of flat but twisting road from Cardrona to Traquair is a joy to ride – a classic cyclists' route. Soon I arrived at the 'steekit gates' of Traquair House, which claims to be the oldest inhabited house in Scotland. There is a romantic tradition that the Bear Gates were closed on the order of the fifth Earl of Traquair after the last person to pass through them was Prince Charles Edward Stuart in 1745.

I rode into the grounds. It was not that busy. In the sultry atmosphere of a walled orchard complete with tearoom, courtyard and parading peacocks, I sipped a refreshing glass of the extremely potent Traquair Ale which is brewed in the nearby tun-house. It was bliss. But I couldn't linger because I wanted to track down a character who lived on the other side of Walkerburn. Sunlight flickered and danced on the road as I took my leave of Traquair.

I caught up with Joe Hall outside his roadside cottage under the forested slope of Bier Law. Joe was born at the head of the Leithen Water in 1908. In a booming voice he told me that his father had been a shepherd all his days. 'An that's the way Ah got tae ken aboot moles. A shepherd did a lot o mole-killin an he made his ain traps, half-barrel traps fae lengths o ashwood.'

Because moles rarely surface they have created a certain mystique around their activities and Joe looked upon these shadowy creatures with a certain amount of fondness and respect. 'They're damn fly customers! Take new Duffus traps. Ye've tae pit them in a burn for aboot a week afore ye can use them. Tae tak the smell aff them, ye see – the smell o the factory. Aye, ye've got tae be fly for Mr Mole.'

'Are there any secrets to setting a trap in a mole's run?' I enquired.

'Ye've got tae have it thorough blocked up, no light showin – na, na. Ah've seen us catchin moles in the summertime an no being sae parteecular because a lot of thae mole runs are opened up in the summertime wae sheep trespassin. But in the wintertime, always bury your trap well and *Firm! Firm!*'

I asked Joe what happened to the moles in fields adjacent to the Tweed when the river burst its banks in flood. Raising his spectacles above his eyes, Joe gave a grunt as if to say 'you've not caught me out there, son'.

'It has no effect on the mole because he's one of the best swimmers that ever was. He can swim in a flood and be quite safe.' With undisguised glee, he continued: 'Ah've seen them comin through water. By Christ they can go! They're sittin straicht up an doon, no lyin flatways; see thae wee feet ... Aye, water is no object to a mole. But a pig cannae swim! Did ye ken that? Ken why? It cuts its throat. Its clits gets intae its thrapple.'

'How do you recognise the runs?' I asked.

'That's eh – a kind o secret o the business. It just comes tae you. If you're a molecatcher, you know – you have a look – gaun forrid tae a drain or a burn an you know he's making for that water. Follow the molehillls an ten tae one, if a mole's runnin for water he's on a main run. He's paddin that run often in a day, an ye can follow that run. Ye see the mole – he's wan o the drouthiest animals there is.'

At which point, Joe sauntered off to his wooden shed.

'Christ, there's ma auld game-bag – look! An this is ma gibble, ma mowdie-spade. If ye can jest dig a hole the exact size o the trap, it's half the battle. You dig a great big wide hole an ye've aa this tae fill up on each side, an that gives Mr Mole a clue that there is somethin gaun on here: they're fly. Ah mind o Wee Johnny Leeman. He killed a mole for a woman, an he jest went in through the gate, right forrid an set the trap. "By God," she says, "How did ye ken that run wis there?" "Aye," he says, "Ah smellt it!" That wis Johnny Leeman for ye.'

'Who was he?' I tentatively asked.

'The auldest mowdie-catcher that ever I mind o. He went on horseback when I wis a laddie. He came from Oxnam [a hamlet in Roxburghshire] and he went on horseback aa the way from Oxnam richt up intae Leithen Water. That's easy 65 years ago. He killed aa the moles roond aboot the ferms. Then sometimes, if he wis away up in the country, he got intae digs wae a shepherd or whoever wis there, got his horse fed – jest like the doctors when they came to a birth away up intae burn-heids an thae ootlandish places. If a doctor knew he wis gaun tae be catched in a snowstorm he wid want tae bide aa night. Oh, that wis common in thae days.'

Joe paused while a name from the past came back into his mind. 'Ellis, John Ellis from Eshiels, this side o Peebles. He wis a bit o a wag: a worthy! But a true professional. A lot o thae auld mowdie-catchers, ma father usetae tell me – they got a basis o payment for so much an acre. We got so much a week, or so much for the job, but thir auld boys hed so much per acre.'

All this talk had given Joe a thirst and he decided it was time for his pint. I left with the distinct impression that I had encountered a genuine worthy in Joe . He was the sort of man one doesn't meet every day. I pedalled back to Traquair village. A couple behind a tall hedge were earnestly discussing the merits of their trimming, completely unaware of my silent progress. I cycled on past a sweet-smelling orchard, a group of confabulating farm hands and a caravanette with its windows down and pop music blaring.

Thumbing through the gears, I began the long haul up the 'Paddie Slack' [Paddock Slack] on the high road to Yarrow. A narrow bridge with high parapets marked the end of Tweeddale and the beginning of Ettrick and Lauderdale District. Here, the B709 reaches a height of 1,170 feet, involving 600 feet of ascent. The road was constructed by French POWs and the surrounding landscape was a mixture of bracken, heather, rough grazing and young plantations. My shirt was soaked with sweat by the time I reached the summit of the pass. There followed an exhilarating freewheel as I plunged down the other side to the Yarrow Valley, a mid-afternoon haze obscuring the views further afield.

At the Gordon Arms Hotel, I was given a south-facing room overlooking the beautiful Yarrow Water and surrounding hills. In the Autumn of 1830, it was at this very spot that Sir Walter Scott and James Hogg, the Ettrick Shepherd, parted for the last time.

James Hogg was born in Ettrick in 1770. From the age of six he worked as a herd boy and had little in the way of formal schooling. In the last decade of the 18th century he shepherded in the Yarrow Valley, before managing his parents' farm in Ettrick. Hogg met Sir Walter Scott, who encouraged his writing and subsequently arranged for the publication of his verse. After a spell of farming, during which he went bankrupt, Hogg moved to Edinburgh to concentrate on writing. He founded and was editor of a weekly called *The Spy* from 1810–11. In 1816 he inherited the farm of Altrieve Lake in Yarrow and lived there for the rest of his life. He wrote fiction, plays and verse but his masterpiece is a book called *The Private Memoirs and Confessions of a Justified Sinner*. It is a complex and powerful novel, remarkable for its psychological insight. Hogg interwove traditional folk material into other works such as *The Brownie of Bodsbeck*, *The Three Perils of Man*, and his short stories which seek to convey the manner of traditional oral storytelling. He died on 21 November 1835 and is buried in Ettrick.

I wallowed in a steaming hot bath as the 40 miles of pedalling gradually eased out of my legs. There was time to enjoy an old-fashioned high tea with freshly caught Yarrow trout on the menu. Yes, it had been a good day.

Over breakfast next morning there was talk of motorways and heavy traffic from a travelling sales rep seated at the next table. His journey had been a far cry from the route I had taken and the one I had in mind for today. I was bound for the Ettrick Valley and from scrutinising the map, I had the choice of two routes. One would take me up by Altrieve to another famous inn at Tushielaw; the second was a genuine hill road that climbed up from Yarrow village to nearly 1,200 feet on Witchie Knowe. I plumped for the latter.

The wind was blowing directly against me as I pedalled down the A708. After my first brae with only one mile on the clock, I was overcome by a feeling of utter fatigue. Thankfully, it did not last. I was deep in the heart of ballad country, and many poets have praised the district – notably Wordsworth. On my right for the entire journey down the valley was the gently flowing Yarrow Water. At Yarrow village I came to a signpost at a junction which indicated the Ettrick Valley was three and a half miles distant across the hills.

The Forest of Ettrick originally embraced the valleys of three rivers – Ettrick and Yarrow which met south of Selkirk, and Tweed, into which they flow. The forest was known in early times as *Ecclesia de Foresta* or *Rectoria de Foresta.* The monks of Dryburgh Abbey were granted the patronage of the kirks of the blessed Virgin Mary in Ettrick Forest. It is disclosed in the Exchequer Rolls which date from 1264 as 'a Royal forest, well replenished with wild boar and other game'. In the mid–15th century it reverted to the Crown to become a favourite hunting ground of the Scottish kings. After Flodden, James V gave the surviving souters of Selkirk freedom to cut down as much wood as was needed to rebuild their town. Freebooting led to more destruction and Ettrick in due course became a vast sheep-walk.

I crossed the Yarrow Water and embarked on an horrendous climb up the twisting hill road to Ettrickbridge, known locally as 'The Swire' [a steep pass between hills]. It was single track with passing-places. I soon dismounted and pushed the red machine up the brae. After trundling over a cattle-grid, the unfenced road became a mass of cow and sheep sharn. Near the summit (1,187 feet), a solitary car crawled past in low gear, the driver giving me a cheery wave. A light mist hung over the tops; it had been a brute of a climb.

My brakes became poker-hot as I negotiated some tight bends on the dramatic descent through a smirr of rain. Apart from some curious sheep, I saw grouse and a hovering kestrel. Down below on my left was an empty drystane stell, a circular dyke forming a sheep enclosure normally 20–40 yards in diameter and with a three-foot entrance on the lee side. In many parts these structures are no longer used, being swallowed up by forestry. Yet experienced hill men swear by their advantages in providing shelter for their flocks during rough weather. Their design apparently creates an air flow that is most effective in conditions of swirling snow.

At the foot of 'The Swire' I checked that nothing had fallen off my machine, before heading into Ettrickbridge to purchase a carton of juice at the post-office. At the bottom of the village the Ettrick Water gushed down a series of rocky shelves into deep murky pools.

After two miles I forked right for the Woll Rig road to Ashkirk. It was another punishing slog up to Hartwoodmyres, a name that would sound at home in a Conan Doyle story. There were rustling fields of golden barley whose splashes of colour broke the uniform grey of the dripping mist.

I crossed the 1,000-foot contour just below Grain Hill. By this stage the hill had altered character and was unfenced with bracken and whin breaking up the moorland spaces. Near a bleak expanse of undulating moor, a sign said 'Outer Huntly'; Outer Space would have been more appropriate as the narrow ribbon of tarmac was shrouded by mist and had an other-worldly atmosphere.

At Woll Rig Farm a young farmer was tending his sheep in some faulds. I stopped to ask him about his way of life up here on the hill. 'I wouldn't swap this job if you offered me three times the money,' he said with a smile. I left him contentedly working his Cheviots and Blackfaced ewes, and scooted down a steep brae away from the farm.

Ashkirk was a disappointment. It was boldly marked on my

1925 OS map, but contained only one shop and a petrol station. The main A7 cut past on one side, a particularly fast stretch of road holding little joy for the cyclist as cars raced by at up to 100 mph.

The little-known Borders poet, Will Ogilvie, spent the last 60 years of his life writing at his home, Kirklea, Ashkirk. He was born at Holefield Farm within half a mile of the English Border on the B6396, east of Kelso, in 1869. His farming parents sent him off to Australia when he was 19, and he worked on sheep stations in the Bush for 12 years. There he wrote a series of Bush ballads and had other works published. Devotees of Ogilvie regard his work as being on a par with Rudyard Kipling and he has never received the acclaim he deserves. Will Ogilvie died in 1963. A main topic of his material was horses, and he had published 20 collections of verse and one book of prose, *My Life in the Open*, copies of which are becoming scarce.

I was more than glad to leave the A7 drivers to their motoring madness and followed a quiet backroad to Lilliesleaf, just over four miles south-east of Selkirk as the crow flies. This linear village has a timeless rustic character. At the Cross Keys the landlady said it would be safe to leave my bike outside without a padlock and chain – and it was. I quickly downed a refreshing pint and a filled roll while making small-talk with a couple of builders from Lasswade who were the only other patrons in the public bar.

A short distance further down the village street I saw a sign advertising coffee outside a gunshop (of all places). The jovial owner was talking 'gun-speak' to a sales rep. The shop was a veritable warren of paraphernalia for the killing game. Apart from guns there were ear muffs, pigeon flappers, roe whistles, fox snares, decoy ducks, predator calls, the ubiquitous green wellies and something called an 'original ferret locator transmitter collar': even the lowly ferret had entered the age of the microchip. High on a wall was mounted an automatic rifle that was said to have been owned by a member of the Hitler Youth Movement.

I drained the last of the coffee from my plastic cup and left. A new-found rhythm came to my cycling legs as I coasted along the deserted road, passing golden fields, stubbly green knowes, clusters of broadleaved trees, narrow shelter belts and secret-looking woodland tracks. A solitary tractor chugged past me on an uphill stretch before Standhill, where the course of a former railway line was now a delightful green way. Since leaving Yarrow I had not encountered another cyclist.

The Minto Hills appeared as a mist-enshrouded lump, but the actual village of Minto oozed charm and boasted a fine kirk. The drizzle drove me on as I passed below the incredible location of Fatlips Tower, high up amidst tree-covered crags. Consulting my map, I realised I had made a navigational error and was forced to backtrack to Denholm, cursing the rain as I went. I did not stop in Denholm, which has a rugby pitch on the village green and is divided in half by the busy A698, another crazy road. Traffic came in waves of spray, and certain drivers paid scant heed to my safety. Relieved and alive, I turned first right and rode up past Spital Tower to Bedrule; given a blue sky, this beautiful hamlet could easily have adorned a chocolate box.

As I crawled through Bedrule, a tractor pulling a high-topped load overtook me at a snail's pace, followed by a bus. By this time my legs were beginning to feel like jelly and it took the last of my reserves to reach Jedburgh.

The county town of Roxburgh is situated in the valley of the Jed Water, a tributary of the Teviot, within 10 miles of the English Border. I sped down Jedburgh's steep main street which was thronged with shoppers at the start of an August bank holiday weekend.

My aim was to contact a retired shepherd who I had first met on a visit to the town when the famous 'Jeddart Baa' was taking place in the main street. This traditional game of handball is played each Candlemas between the Uppies and the Doonies. Shop windows are boarded up lest they be broken by the stramash, involving scores of youths and men, desperately attempting to smuggle the ball up to the opposing end. The custom is reputed to date from before the Reformation and to have originated in the Scots playing with the heads of their slain enemies. In the mass rolling maul, there don't seem to be any rules; it presents an ideal opportunity for the town's menfolk to settle old scores.

At an off-licence I bought a half-bottle of whisky. After asking some locals, I eventually found Kit's home in a council estate at the bottom of the town.

Kit Smith sat by his coal fire and held out his empty glass, somewhat bemused that I should have cycled all this way to see *him*. What could he recall of his first job?

'In 1928 I started herding at Greenlawden, just aboot a mile oot o Greenlaw in Berwickshire. Cameron was the farmer and he came from Inverness. There would roughly be aboot three hundred acre o hill and the other nine hundred was arable. I got seven shillin an six for the seven days. Six of us usetae hire a car for thruppence an go off tae a dance. A packet o Woodbine cost tuppence ha'penny an a pint was a penny ha'penny.'

Kit told me that before the winter storms, old railway carriages were taken out to the stells and filled with hay, to ease the job of feeding the flocks. It took about six horses to pull each waggon out. Herds were involved in stooking the hay. 'We get a lot o wind from the west in this country an aa the stacks had to face west. A lot o folks used Hume Castle an the Eildon Hills as landmarks when they were stookin. If it wis a bad harvest, wet weather, ye built the stacks on each side o a stone dyke. They built what they caad soo-stacks – big long stacks. To keep yer sheaves aff the damp, we usetae build the bottoms wae bracken; some used thorns. Very often we'd tae help wae the harvest an other work such as repairin dykes.'

Kit described the herd's year in some detail. He stayed 13 years at Greenlawden, then moved to Hoselaw near Yetholm, Ladyrig out from Kelso, and finally Kersheugh, three miles from Jedburgh, where he worked for 25 years. He reminisced about marking the sheep with red keel, feeding them in the winter drifts of 1947, the lambing at the end of March, clipping in June, and lamb sales in July when the sheep were taken by train to St Boswells, Hawick and Lanark. 'Did any of the older herds have their own cures for diseases which afflicted the sheep?' I asked.

'Well, the remedy for worms was a teaspoonful of turps to a wine glass o milk. After that, they used bluestone an nicotine.'

I left Kit with his whisky about 10 p.m. and headed back to my bed-and-breakfast. The bed was about a foot too short and sagged in the middle. A wooden board prevented me from extending my big feet out from under the bedclothes, and to add to my discomfort, I was woken in the small hours by the persistent hooting of an owl.

A clear blue sky raised my hopes of a good run next morning. After recharging my batteries with a fine cooked breakfast, I took my leave of Jedburgh by a minor road not far from the old railway station. The day was benign. I began with an assault on a steep brae that took me along a tree-lined road through gently undulating countryside. After about two miles, the Eildon Hills came into view, and what magnificent hills they are. A fast downhill stretch brought me to the point where my route crossed Dere Street, the ancient Roman road which here ran as straight as a rule. This was leisurely cycle touring at its very best. Tall hedges flanked the road, reminiscent of a Devon lane, and there was not a car in sight.

Shortly, I came within earshot of the A968 near the village of Crailing. My vague route at this stage was to make for Roxburgh. I swiftly pedalled across the main road and headed for Nisbet, another glorious spot, basking in sunshine. A green girdered bridge spanned the Teviot as a tractor at the other side halted to allow me free passage over its narrow width. Swans swam up-stream on a sluggish stretch of the river. At a junction, I passed by stables where a man was whistling as he took fresh hay over to his animals. A horse in a paddock was undergoing training and the village gardens were a riot of colour.

Pheasants darted across my path into the roadside under-growth. Some of the fields had been recently harvested; the straw was tightly baled into squat, yellow cylinders, like giant cotton-bobbins strewn across the fields. A short distance from Roxburgh, one of the giant combine harvesters came lumbering down the entire width of the road like some latter-day dinosaur, the driver perched aloft in his glass eyrie. I took to the top of the verge to let the monster pass. The road curled into Roxburgh. On my right was an impressive railway viaduct. The village had only one shop, a post-office located in a shed.

This present village should not be confused with the medieval royal burgh of Roxburgh, which was a centre for minting the king's coinage. The site of the old burgh is between the Teviot and Tweed, close to Kelso; all trace of it has gone. Perhaps this is not surprising when one considers that the ordinary medieval houses were of timber construction with thatched roofs, giving rise to a severe fire hazard. This is graphically illustrated by a laconic entry for 1207 in the Melrose chronicle: 'a large part of Roxburgh was accidentally burned'. By the 16th century it had become totally ruinous.

As I left the village three riders on horseback were trotting down the road; there was still no sign of a fellow cyclist. At Roxburgh Barns I joined the A699 and renewed my acquaintance with the Tweed. Here, it graciously complements the truly magnificent Floors Castle, built by William Adam in 1721 and later added to by the Edinburgh architect, William Playfair.

I crossed the Tweed into 'Kelsae' by Rennie's splendidly classical five-arch bridge. The toll-keeper's house looks like an elegant cottage but when viewed from the other side, can be seen to have three storeys. Kelso was described by Sir Walter Scott as the most beautiful, if not the most romantic, village in Scotland. This Saturday, there was nothing romantic about the through-traffic; huge juggernauts trundled along the cobbled street, vying for space with buses, cars, vans and motor bikes. I left them to it, and wandered into the grounds of Kelso Abbey, founded by David I in 1128 and destroyed by Hertford in 1545. The Abbey walls rise in aged and mute splendour – the mood and pulse of those centuries of monastic Scotland certainly beats strong in memory here. This was King David's favourite abbey, one which housed an order of Tironensian monks and whose remnant splendour attracted artists such as Turner and Alexander Naismith.

Kelso has a number of interesting and unexpected buildings, such as the octagonal parish church (known locally as 'the mustard pot') and the Turret Museum, the oldest house in the town. I left the Abbey and headed into the centre. An evangelical group were singing hymns and preaching through a loudspeaker in the Square, which is dominated by a splendid Georgian town hall with rusticated windows and Edwardian embellishments. In a nearby wine shop I stocked up on soft drinks. One fastidious customer was going through the motions of buying a case of wine. In terms of atmosphere, Kelso by day is not unlike a polite Edinburgh suburb.

I was glad to leave the exhaust fumes behind me as I moved upcountry to the lovely village of Stichill. Here I had a short talk with a retired councillor who pointed out a monument down at Ferneyhill, adding that it was erected in memory of a local poet whose name I didn't catch. Up by Hume Farm the going was hard and sweat was pouring from my brow. A maniac driving a black BMW shot past me at a ridiculous speed, his three kids dancing about in the back seat.

I crossed into Berwickshire. The countryside was characterised by rolling prairie-type fields and many of the tractors boasted new registration plates, evidence of farming prosperity. The ruins of Hume Castle shortly came into view; it sits on a 730-foot hill with the village of the same name tucked in behind it.

I was on the last leg of my journey to Duns. To avoid the main routes, I plumped for a secondary road leading up from the Blackadder Water past Eastfield. An old waulkmill was visible on the horizon, just down from Redbraes Castle. At a crossroads I joined the B6460. There followed a fine straight stretch for two miles; the machine was moving well in top gear and I was eating up the tarmac. Not so fortunate were the various animal casualties who lay splattered at intervals along the way. These included a recently killed crow, numerous pheasants and a wood-pigeon.

I took an interesting detour by Fogo, passing a ruddy-faced tractorman who had just couped some bales onto the road. A short distance from Fogo there is a beautiful stretch of the Blackadder Water. I halted at a bridge over some deep pools and guzzled a small bottle of Lucozade.

Caldra was a magnificent example of farm architecture. The sun radiated off the stonework and new buildings harmoniously merged with old. From here, a rollercoaster stretch of road led me into the idyllic village of Gavinton. I cruised along a deserted road to Langton Mill, where there was an exhilarating splash through an old cobble-stone ford. And so, on a baking hot afternoon, I crawled into Duns.

For a holiday weekend the town was surprisingly quiet. Only a scattering of pedestrians moved along the streets, some licking ice-cream cones, others sitting on benches in the square. Duns is the county town of Berwickshire, drawing from a wide catchment area for educational, social and trading purposes. The town was originally built on the dun that rises to the north. Destroyed by the English in the mid–16th century, a new town was founded below the hill, originally guarded on three sides by a swamp.

During the late afternoon I found accommodation in the Black

Bull Inn. Up in my tiny room that evening I could hear the strains of an accordionist rising from the public bar below. It was almost relentless. But this was nothing to the hysteria created by Saturday night revellers who seemed to charge down Black Bull Street on their rounds of the various pubs. As I wrote up my journal, their loud banter and foul-mouthed cries travelled upwards to my room.

'C'mon Jimmy yer no gaun hame yet!' [sound of broken glass]

'Ploo's the next top lads!' [charge of the mob]

'Wilson fer fuck sake come back!'

'Jim's a fuckin stirrer!'

'Fit them in the bull laddie!'

'By the knackers thirs nae whores in there!'

Eventually I got to sleep. Sunday morning came – still, blue, promising a perfect day. The ghosts of the previous night were sleeping off their hangovers. As I pedalled out of the town a little after 9.15 a.m., I passed the time of day with a street cleaner who was busy sweeping up a small army of scattered chip pokes. There was no-one else around.

I swung down a long hill which bordered a housing estate. The Blackadder was crossed by a small bridge near an old mill as I cycled on one side of a high estate wall which would nearly have done justice to a prison. The name 'Mungo's Walls' flashed by.

After two miles I came to a junction and the hamlet of Sinclair's Hill. There was a line of high-roofed cottar houses, and above one was perched a puzzling red-legged stork. I continued through a fertile plain known as the Merse. At Blackadder Bank an old windmill stood in a field, its blades motionless. I rode on by Pistol Plant Wood, then stopped at Sunwick to chat to a farm worker who was sitting outside an enormous grain-drying shed. He was a contented man, pleased with the weather and the extra overtime he was putting in. He told me that Sunwick was an 800-acre arable farm which provided employment for four men plus two extra hands at harvest time. 'The machine we've got does everything,' he added in a quiet way. There was a helicopter parked in the next field and the new farm extension told its own story. This was a prosperous part of Scotland but it retained an atmosphere of feudalism. The high lums of the attractive farm cottages were a convenient distance from the aloof and imposing farm mansions.

Close to the Border, I passed through the village of Paxton, which had a decidedly anglicised feel with its red-tiled houses, rose gardens and the contrasting architectural styles of its two churches. A group of people were standing beside their expensive-looking cars, indifferent to my progress on two wheels. Soon I came to the A699 and a sign with the St George's cross and the word 'ENGLAND'. Across the Tweed lay Northumberland. I rode by Gainslawhill Farm and over the Whiteadder Water by a tasteless modern bridge.

A long sign announced 'Borough of Berwick-upon-Tweed': I was in England on a Scottish journey. Suddenly I found myself at the A1 Berwick by-pass, my 1925 map well out of date. The A1 was thankfully quiet. I dismounted for the climb up a hill and following my instincts found the older road which led into Berwick, giving a fine view of the railway viaduct and a fleeting glimpse of the sun-bleached Northumbrian coast. I had arrived at the station with half an hour to spare before my train was due. I bought a ticket to Stonehaven for £7.90 with my student railcard. The bike travelled free. As I wheeled it along the platform, I had just passed a sign at the bottom of some stairs which read:

THIS STATION STANDS ON THE SITE OF THE GREAT HALL OF BERWICK CASTLE. HERE ON THE 17TH NOVEMBER 1292, THE CLAIM OF ROBERT THE BRUCE TO THE CROWN OF SCOTLAND WAS DECLINED AND THE DECISION OF JOHN BALIOL WAS GIVEN BY EDWARD I BEFORE THE FULL PARLIAMENT OF ENGLAND AND A LARGE GATHERING OF THE NOBILITY AND POPULACE OF BOTH ENGLAND AND SCOTLAND.

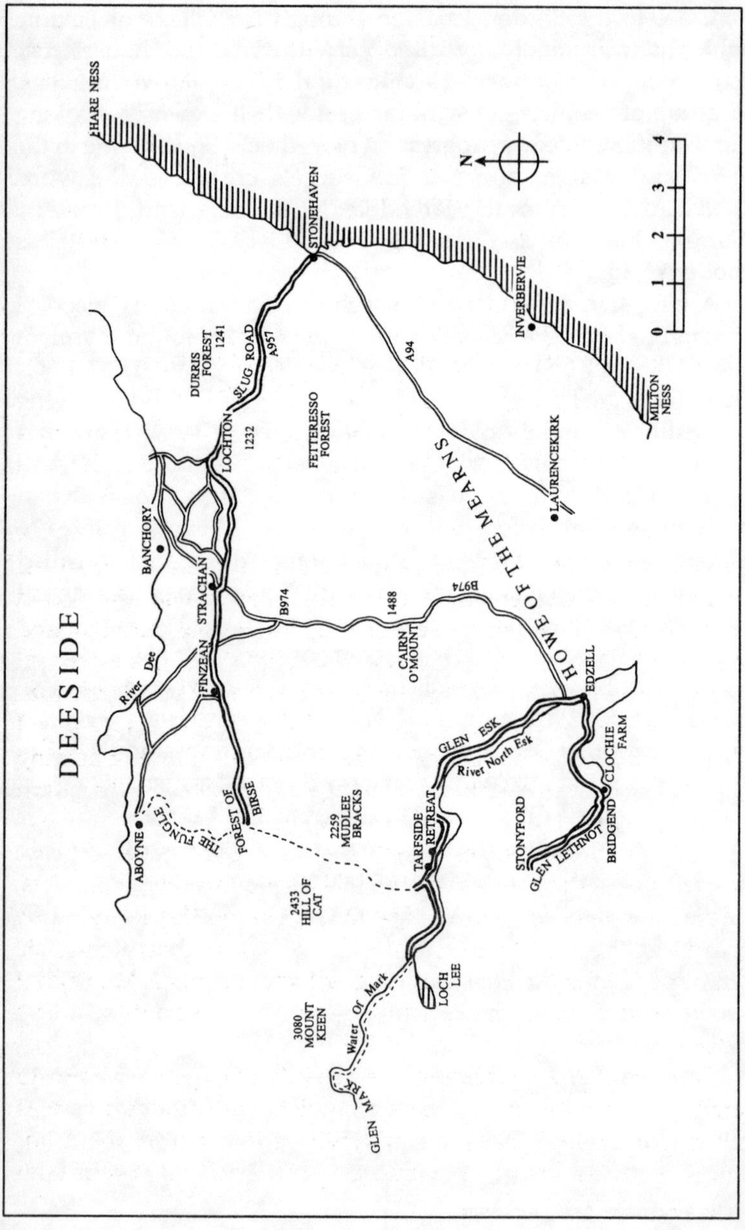
DEESIDE
HARE NESS
STONEHAVEN
N
0 1 2 3 4
INVERBERVIE
MILTON NESS
DURRIS FOREST
1241
SLUG ROAD
A957
A94
FETTERESSO FOREST
1232
LOCHTON
LAURENCEKIRK
HOWE OF THE MEARNS
BANCHORY
STRACHAN
B974
1488
CAIRN O'MOUNT
River Dee
FINZEAN
EDZELL
GLEN ESK
River North Esk
CLOCHIE FARM
FOREST OF BIRSE
THE FUNGLE
ABOYNE
2259 MUDLEE BRACKS
TARFSIDE
RETREAT
STONYFORD
BRIDGEND
GLEN LETHNOT
2433 HILL OF CAT
LOCH LEE
Water Of Mark
3080 MOUNT KEEN
GLEN MARK

CHAPTER 4

'STEENHYVE'*, BIRSE, GLENESK AND LETHNOT

> Life is like a road; you hurry, and the end of it is the grave. There is no grand crescendo from hour to hour, day to day, year to year; life's quality is in moments, not in distance run.
>
> Stephen Graham, *The Gentle Art of Tramping*, 1931

THE INTERCITY 125 rolled across the viaduct and pulled up at the station. I was desperately seeking the guard's van and found it, no thanks to the mute guard. Unshipping the panniers and sleeping-bag, I upended the Kalkhoff and lifted it aboard. At Torness there was a five-minute halt. The train's intercom sputtered into life: 'Ladies and gentlemen, this is the guard speaking. I do wish to apologise for the delay. This is due to engineering problems and we shall proceed as soon as possible.' So the guard could speak after all.

Torness nuclear power station sat like a giant piece of Lego, towering above the cranes and the construction workers' caravans. In the distance beyond Barns Ness lighthouse the May Island came into view, followed by the stark rocky wall of the Bass Rock. The train sped along the East Lothian coast and entered Edinburgh. I could make out people climbing Arthur's Seat like ants scuttling over a molehill.

Between changing trains at Waverley Station there was time to grab a cup of coffee and a cheese sandwich. The Dundee train was filled with holiday-makers, arty types returning from the Edinburgh Festival and a motley contingent of football supporters who

* The local name for Stonehaven

drank beer and mouthed obscenities about a rival team. I sat opposite a woman whose face was hidden by *The Sunday Times;* a pair of children by her side gorged potato crisps like locusts as the train rattled over the Forth Bridge. Rusting hulks lay in the shipyard at Inverkeithing; a funfair was in full swing at Burntisland as I watched a greyhound trying to outpace the train. I scribbled notes on the back of my ticket and tried to take a short nap, before disembarking at Cupar.

The main street of the county town was congested with traffic. It seemed all roads led through Cupar. A large banner high above the road heralded Cupar as 'The Tartan Town', which seemed slightly ridiculous.

Sunday was in effect a rest day with an uneventful ride to Newport on Tay where I would stay with friends before heading north. Few Scottish counties have so many types of milestones and wayside markers as Fife. The surviving milestones are to be seen at intervals along the former turnpike roads. I followed one, the 'great road through Fife' (A91–A92) and about a mile east of Cupar passed a splendid cast-iron milestone, three feet high with a slightly convex curve on its face. In bold black lettering it gave the distances to Pettycur (the old ferry point near Kinghorn), New Inn, Cupar and Newport. A short distance north of St Michael's Inn there was another sign – 'To Newport & Dundee Ferry' – which gave no mileage, only the direction indicated by an outstretched finger from a clenched black hand.

Next morning I left Newport with the intention of catching the 8.52 Aberdeen train from Dundee. On reaching the Tay Road Bridge the rush-hour traffic was heavy and a strong crosswind added to my difficulties. About half-way across my chain-set became taut, forcing me to a sudden halt. My rear mudguard was caught in the back spokes; the holding nuts had somehow become loose and dropped out. I had no other option but to try and manhandle the fully laden machine over the iron railings which border the central pedestrian walkway. This was easier said than done. Cars were hurtling down the fast lane at up to 80 mph. My first attempt was a hair-raising failure. I waited for a gap in the traffic. In a swiftly executed move I threw the panniers over into the walkway, lifted the Kalkhoff over the railings, and jumped over myself.

Mightily relieved, I limped into Dundee Station having managed to get the bike moving in second gear. The connecting roads and busy roundabout were no place for a cyclist. I rushed through the doors of the station and down a corridor, only to see my train pulling away. The next northbound train was over an hour away.

I left the Kalkhoff at the inspector's kitchen on the platform and made my way to Halford's where I bought a packet of the appropriate sized nuts, screws and washers. Back at the station I undertook some of the necessary repairs. The machine seemed none the worse.

On the journey north I browsed over a map, plotting my intended east to west crossing of Scotland: Stonehaven, Birse, Glenesk, Lethnot, Glenisla, Strathardle, Strathtay, Loch Rannoch, Rannoch Station, Dalmally and finally Oban. From Birse to Glenesk would involve some 'roughstuff' over the hills, and Rannoch Moor would be negotiated by train to Tyndrum. On the map it looked an exciting route.

Stonehaven seemed a prosperous town, near enough to Aberdeen to take advantage of the oil boom. It still retains one of only a handful of fire ceremonies dating from pagan times which are still current in Scotland. Each Hogmanay on the stroke of midnight, a fireball-swinging procession sets off along the main street to bring in the New Year. It is a colourful and exciting spectacle to watch.

Upon checking my bike before setting out, I discovered that a rear mudguard spoke was loose. My first impression was that it might need soldering but fortunately I found a friendly mechanic who managed to fix it after some difficulty. It had been a fiddly job but the young mechanic refused all talk of payment. Close to the garage I purchased a small transistor radio which would come in handy for weather forecasts. I made my way along a backstreet and up a brae which gave me a fleeting glimpse of the steely-grey North Sea. Overhead, rain was threatening but I thought the wind might keep it away. I pushed on by Mackie Academy where some boys with blue legs were playing hockey. A new bridge carried me over the as yet unfinished Stonehaven bypass.

The machine was moving sweetly and I soon arrived at the start of the Slug Road (A957). Ahead of me was a lone cyclist plodding his way up the hill. The Slug Road is immortalised in Grassic

Gibbon's *Sunset Song* as the route which John Guthrie and his family took when flitting from Aberdeenshire to the Mearns. With all their belongings piled on a horse-drawn cart, theirs was a frightful crossing one January when the weather was 'smoring with sleet'.

I butted into the wind, the low gears in play, steadily climbing until I reached the summit of the hill at 750 feet. There followed the luxury of a glorious freewheel on the fast descent. Dense, eerie forests straddled the road on either side, but beyond Spyhill there unfolded a splendid vista of lower Deeside. With both brakes screeching I slowed for the left hand-turn along a minor road at Blairdryne. There followed another punishing climb up to a Y-junction near the farm of Standingstones. A quick scan of the map showed two sets of stone circles within one and a half miles of here, the first at West Mulloch being fairly close to the road. This quiet road dipped and twisted along through woodland, passing occasional houses before dropping down to the Water of Feugh where it joined the B974 Cairn o' Mount road.

Strachan (pronounced 'Strawn') was a mix of old and new. I continued through the village without stopping. The most striking aspect of this road was the distant view to the south-west of the snub-nosed hill of Cloch-na-Ben. A hand-painted roadside sign made a comical diversion: 'Tractor Lawn Mowing – For a Canny Wee Price. Feughside 655.' At a shop-cum-post-office I bought a banana, some chocolate and a bottle of wine. Earlier I had halted to speak to an old man who was hirpling along the road, a brindled terrier by his side. In a soft Deeside accent he gave me directions for Finzean (pronounced 'Fingan') and Haughend, my destination. When I asked him if there were any historic connections hereabouts, he mentioned the site of an old inn at Cuttiehillock on the old military road from Fettercairn.

I was now on a single-track road and only once had to draw into the verge in order to allow two cars past. Drystane dykes skilfully constructed from large stones criss-crossed the countryside in geometric patterns. Most of these Deeside dykes were built in the 'Age of Improvement' (1770s–1870s) during which the rural scene underwent a remarkable transformation, including the displacement of many people from the land.

I passed a sawmill, a weaver's craft workshop, then bore left by a mill, crossing a wooden planked bridge; here lay Haughend. A man in his early thirties approached me from beside a line of tall, pink granite walls. He was wearing overalls and had a weather-beaten complexion with sharp eyes and a few days' growth on his cheeks and chin. We introduced ourselves. I had just met Robin Callander: master-dyker, bee-keeper, local historian and publisher.

Robin told me he had been dyking since 1975 and had a degree in ecology from Aberdeen University. 'We arrived at Haughend to find an abandoned croft that hadn't been lived in for thirty years. The majority of the ground was exhausted and lying derelict, consisting of grass and bracken together with a fair amount of bedrock above the surface.'

The old Haughend had at one time 14 acres of arable land and supported four dwelling houses in the three acres which Robin now owned. These had been laboriously transformed into vegetable plots sheltered by magnificent drystane walls which Robin had constructed himself. Some idea of what the old houses in Birse were like is provided by Robert Dinnie, writing in 1865:

> 'In the interior of the house the divisions were composed of furniture – box beds, presses and doors which divided the general apartments. The floors were composed of clay and some were laid with natural faced stones. Very few of the farmers' houses at this time had joisting, lofting or ceiling but were open to the top of the roof. The fireplaces had no chimneys or vents ... but what was called a back stone, of five [feet] in height, was built into the gable wall and the fire placed before it. The smoke went up the side of the wall and out at a large wooden "lum" or chimney top, with an opening 2 feet square...'

At the time of the Old Statistical Account in the 1790s, there was not one slate-roofed farm house in Birse. Buildings were built in the drystane method and had turf roofs. The population of the parish numbered 1,253, of which there were three masons, two quarriers, six meal millers, three shoemakers, five blacksmiths, ten weavers, ten tailors and four travelling pedlars. In all, the people kept about 300 apiaries during the winter 1791–2.

In the evening I took a stroll out to see Stanley Moyes, a craftsman in wood who lived opposite the old Finzean bucket mill which was in the course of being restored. 'I don't mind people coming to look round the mill,' said Stanley, 'but my main aim is to see the place working: making buckets again.'

The mill began operating in 1853 and continued to turn out buckets under the expertise of several people, among them a man named Willie Brown, until 1974. In the years before the Second World War, the mill produced eight different kinds of tubs. They had a variety of uses, for everything from carrying water and food for hens to holding dye for tanning leather. After 1945 there was a drop in demand but the buckets and tubs revived again due to their use as containers for growing shrubs and plants.

Stanley showed me the kiln house which was used for drying the Scots pine and red cedar, the base material of the buckets. He told me most of the pine was windblown and came from neighbouring estates. In 1983 Stanley was involved with others in restoring the timbers on the 13-foot diameter waterwheel, as well as rebuilding a weir and wooden lade.

On a gloriously sunny evening I returned to Haughend. That night I slept under the pine-panelled eaves of Robin Callander's delightful cottage.

Come early morning, the skylight in the roof was filled with a brilliant blue portion of sky. The morning was benign, the day alive with the natural colours of stone, hill and trees. It would be perfect for cycling. Over a breakfast of fresh brown bread and delicious heather honey, I chatted away to Robin and his girlfriend. The journey ahead would involve crossing the hills to Glenesk by one of the historic Mounth passes and I was keen to make to most of the day.

Astride the bike I consulted the OS map and plotted my route. The narrow road wound its way past the red corrugated-iron roof of the bucket mill and slipped quietly into the Forest of Birse. Shafts of sunlight squinted through a breathtaking variety of trees: birch, hazel, oak and Scots pine. The only vehicle on the road was the red van of the postman who was making his morning deliveries. The road dipped and disappeared, swung round the foot of crags, trees and blind bends. All the time I had for company the chattering Water of Feugh as it tumbled along a rocky course close to the road. On a morning such as this, the Forest of Birse road ranked as one of the most delightful cycling routes I had travelled.

Shortly I came to an old rectangular well-trough, fed by a trickling spout that was part of a shotgun barrel. A pink granite slab had the following words carved: 'Erected by Peter Brown – Pail Mill 1904 – since 1853'. The same Browns that had worked the bucket mill further downstream.

At Ballochan, a remote hill farm at the end of the road, I came upon the farmer scything grass in a field. I pulled up and he came over, a stockily built man wearing dungarees, a bonnet on his head and deep-lensed spectacles. 'This is a real hill farm, ' he said in answer to my question. 'Last winter there, we were cut off for a fortnight. Three times the plough had to turn back.'

I commented on the sharpening stone sticking out of his back pocket. 'We called them brodes in Morayshire,' he added. Our conversation turned on old and new ways of farming in these parts. He told me that all going well, the farm would be connected to the national grid next year. He worked the farm on his own, whereas four men had been required in former years. This man seemed content with his lot. He did not smoke or drink and relished his independence.

After puzzling over the exact route which would link me with the Fungle, an ancient way from Aboyne to Glenesk, I set out along a rocky cart track below the farm. It led me through a field with a gate, then over a narrow concrete bridge that was only about two-and-a-half feet wide. From here on the track was extremely rocky and pitted. I continued over the Burn of Allanstank after passing a direction post which revealed I was on the right route. Ahead I could see the rough surface of the track wind its way up the slopes of Gannoch.

After some time spent wheeling the bike through deep, stony ruts, I came to a wider section of hill country where the track became a single footpath. The meaning and origin of the word 'Fungle' are uncertain. This Mounth pass to Glenesk was at one time known as the Cateran Road, an indication that it not only had its share of legal cattle drovers but was also a route used by cattle thieves. In October the drovers would have been passing through such Grampian passes as this, bound for the last of the trysts before the snow smored the route, and the burns froze with winter's severity.

Today, the hills on either side were characterised by their bare brown flanks, intermittently broken by patches of purple heather. As I wheeled the red machine along the path, heather tugged at the pedals and forced me off line. It was decidedly rough going but worse was to come.

I stopped for lunch. Tea from the flask tasted like nectar and the sweet taste of heather honey on bread revived me for the daunting climb up between Hill of Cat and Mulnabracks. Patches of grey cloud went scurrying over the tops and directly overhead were the white tracers from a jet, high up in the sky.

I climbed slowly, conserving energy. The footpath seemed to peter out down from the summit of the pass. It was then I met up with him. He was a youngish man, tall, with a thick crop of black hair. On his back was a small rucksack and a monocular dangled from a cord round his neck.

The red bike must have seemed alien in such surroundings. The walker informed me that he was returning to Aboyne, but more importantly he confirmed that the path disappeared for a time on the highest section of the pass. He suggested I should pick my way to the right of a narrow cleft and cast me a doubting glance about the wisdom of negotiating the peat hags with a fully laden cycle. At this stage I had my doubts as well.

It became increasingly difficult to wheel the bike once I reached the upper section. I adopted the fresh tactic of unloading it and carrying the machine on my shoulder for up to 50 yards at a time, returning for the panniers and sleeping-bag. This method involved covering twice the distance but was the only option if I was to make the crossing.

I made a number of these double climbs, carrying the machine being less arduous than bringing up the luggage. With the former I was able to wedge the portion of karrimat under the cross-bar of the bike and thus pad my shoulder. One particular section involved a sharp climb through knee-high heather and furze, while at another point on the way, I squelched across a marshy tract and felt the cold sensation of my feet submerged in water as the ground gave way beneath my weight. The top of the pass eventually arrived and the land evened out at just under 2,000 feet. My efforts were rewarded with a fine view. Back down the way I had come, I could see the fertile land above the Feugh give way to the higher forested slopes of Birse and the Deeside hills beyond. The Glencat track was visible and I could also see a section of the Fungle as it snaked its way across the hill to the west of Brackenstake.

As I made the last of my return trips, it was evident that certain large boulders had the purpose of waymarking the route which at times disappeared into the hollows. Once I gained firm ground it was also possible to cycle. At 1,800 feet this provided a sensational feeling of complete freedom since there was not a proper road in sight.

The rolling hills of Angus lay ahead. I dismounted to watch the play of light and shade, caught by the lonely spell of this mysterious high domain. I thought of the times when this very pass witnessed the clandestine traffic of whisky smugglers and their ponies loaded with kegs of the illicit spirit, making their way in a shadowy line for the Lowlands.

Shortly I came to a series of drystane cairns marking the track. At this point the route merged with the Firmounth which crawls up from Glen Tanar by Craigmahandle and over Tampie (2,363 feet).

In one of several grouse butts I took shelter from the wind and lit a cigarette. My pocket radio gave excellent reception on VHF but there was only some inane quiz game when I had hoped for music. Shafts of light pierced through the clouds and lit the Glenesk hills – a fusion of differing shades of brown.

A few turns of the pedals and I was able to free-wheel down the track which was not as rough on this side of the pass. Due to the load, the Kalkhoff had its own mind about the rate we should travel and neither of my hands ever left the brake levers. I hurtled down towards Shinfur. The name means wind-cast and was certainly appropriate in today's conditions on the hill. Below Shinfur the Burn of Tennet joins the Water of Tarf which flows into the North Esk down from Tarfside. The Tarf is a beautiful upland water-course with its own individual character.

I came to a padlocked gate forcing me to hoist the bike over a low fence. The track on the other side was relatively free of stones allowing an enjoyable passage down to Tarfside, partly along a green way. The route skirted a small wood and crossed over the

Tennet by a wooden bridge, before becoming a stone-strewn track. This provided cycling all the same, although the enjoyment was taken out of it by the need to keep a wary eye out for potholes and rogue rocks.

Glenesk is rich in minerals. Gold is reported to have been abundant in the Tarf, especially at Gracie's Linn (the spot where a woman of the same name drowned). Frequent violent floods are believed to have washed away many of the deposits.

St Drostan, a former abbot of Donegal, is regarded as the patron saint of Glenesk. Local place-names retain this association – e.g. Droustie, Droustie's Well, the Kirk of Droustie and Droustie's meadow. Side valleys of Glenesk such as Glen Tennet, Glen Effock, Glen Lee and Glen Mark were populated as late as the early 19th century.

Tarfside consisted of a few houses, a church and a hall, a tiny post-office and a black shed – formerly a tearoom – which sold soft drinks, crisps and sweets. The owner was a lady of about 80 years of age. I arrived to find her dolefully gazing out of a window. She seemed glad of having somebody to muse with, and told me that her grandfather had been a shoemaker in the glen. I left and bought some stamps for postcards. In no time at all, I arrived at The Retreat, a former shooting lodge which now serves as the Glenesk Folk Museum complete with tearoom and shop.

The museum was under the care of Agnes and Ross Robertson who also did bed-and-breakfast. Ross, a retired gamekeeper on the Dalhousie Estate, had recently suffered a stroke which had left him paralysed down his left side. Despite this, he retained a marvellous sense of spirit and had many amusing anecdotes to relate about his days on the hill.

Ross and Agnes had formerly lived at House of Mark, an old manse just over a mile from Loch Lee at the head of Glenesk. Part of Ross's beat had taken in Glen Effock. I asked him about the changes he had seen in his time.

'On Invermark Estate they bulldozed 50 miles of road so that they could get the Land Rovers into the hills. But when I first came it was all ponies. We had eight garrons at Invermark and they lived out all winter unless it was really coorse weather, when they'd be stabled. Their coats used to thicken up about the time of the stags and by winter they'd a really good coat.'

In the winter of 1957–8, Ross told me he had obtained an eaglet for a lady falconer. She trained it and when fully grown, the bird had a wingspan of seven-and-a-half feet. Ross also provided me with the names of a couple of old-timers who lived up the glen, adding that they were fast becoming a dying breed.

After supper I was allowed to look round the fascinating little museum at my leisure. It was divided into a series of small rooms and its treasures included a magnificent set of 18th century bagpipes made form laburnum, deer horn and walrus tusk. There was also the copper head of an illicit still, a rudimentary tinker's anvil and a beautiful Edwardian-style doll's house. Many household implements and items had been collected locally and these included an original heather pot-reenge, numerous spurtles and branders, a stone mould for cruisie lamps, thraw cruicks (for twisting straw rope), a flail and a tapner (a large curved knife with a hooked tip for lifting and tailing turnips).

There were also some fascinating photographs. A portrait of the famous Deeside fiddler, James Scott Skinner – 'the Strathspey King' – contrasted with an old photo of Geordie Duncan, one of the glen's molecatchers. The latter was standing with a gnarled old walking-stick, wearing a shapeless hat, waistcoat and bulging knee-pads over his trousers. Opened in 1955, the Glenesk Folk Museum is a lasting testament to the late Greta Michie, a native of the glen who instigated much of the collection.

There was enough to do in Glenesk to keep me occupied for weeks but I only had a few days. The following morning I perused the small archive of books and papers. I came across an illuminating inventory of farm stock belonging to William Duke, a tenant of Migvie in November 1876. The value of various ploughs, harrows and a long list of other farm implements amounted to the grand total of £27 9*s*.9*d*.

That afternoon I called on the oldest surviving resident in the glen. Elizabeth Davidson was born in 1897 at Dykeneuk, a short distance up the glen form Tarfside where she was presently living. Elizabeth was nearly blind and her hearing was impaired, but this was no handicap to her memory of former times. The house of her birth was thatched with sprots and had a wooden lum. For generations

Elizabeth's people had been joiners, making cartwheels and fitting shafts onto various tools being just two of the types of work they undertook. But demand fell away after the Great War when Dalhousie Estate started employing their own joiners. In 1910 Elizabeth moved to West Migvie, the next farm down the glen from Dykeneuk.

Back in The Retreat I had seen a photograph of 'the Four in Hand' – the last stagecoach used in Scotland, which ran form Edzell to Loch Lee and also to the Glen of Drumtochty via Clatterin Brig. It was withdrawn from service in 1930 and I asked Elizabeth if she could recall what it was like.

'Aa ma life Ah can mind o the Four in Hand. Manson wis the name o the man that ran it an he wis awfie pompous. A lad wae a trumpet horn sat at the back an tooted his horn at the corners. We aye heard him at the corner o Migvie. Oh, it wis quite a thing the coach. Thir were braw horses and the number depended on the number o people comin up the glen, but my goodness, the big coach wis generally full. It wis a great service an ye wid hear the clatter o the horses feet an the rumble o the coach o'er the gravel road. The road noo has nae stour like it use tae be in the auld days. In the dry weather the coach use tae raise the stour aff the road.'

'Can you recall any of the old characters in the glen?' I asked.

'Ah can mind o Willie Gless [Glass] who wis at the mowdies. He wis an odd mannie, wise in some weys but queer in ithers. He wis a hermless character though, an he passed awaa early in the century. When we were gaun tae school we saw him at Tarfside. His hair wis unkempt an he lookit odd – that's whit he wis. Efter his mither died he lived by himsel and when he wisnae workin at the mowdies he pu'd neeps, gaithered tatties, took a hairst – jist odd jobs that he could get.'

I took five pages of notes from Elizabeth before returning to The Retreat. Browsing through some of the old scrapbooks, I came across a description of a 'gaun-aboot buddie' who regularly visited the glen. He was called the Blind Fiddler and for 40 years before he died in Kirriemuir Almshouse in December 1916, he had travelled all over by Braemar, Invermark, Glenshee, Strathardle, Dunkeld and further west. In Glenesk he and his two collie dogs would sleep in old quarries at Glen Effock and Inchgrundle.

The Blind Fiddler was described as being a very tall man with a handsome weather-beaten face and an eagle nose. His blue eyes had a far-away look in them that gave him the appearance of a man who had visions. He always wore the kilt, a Kilmarnock bonnet cocked jauntily on his head, and on his feet were a pair of enormous boots like shoes of fortune that tilted upwards at the points. Over everything he wore an old Highland cloak and a fiddle case dangled from his chest. He walked with his head held high, tapping the road with a stout stick as he went along. Also in his possession was a very heavy tin box which he told the curious 'held some things for makkin sovereigns'.

Some people said that he and his dogs ate and drank out of the same wooden coggie. His real name was John MacGregor and he was supposed to have been blinded after a quarry blast. A woman is said to have turned her back on him and that was why he took to the road. In conversation he talked of the hills, the mist, the silence and the lonesomeness, and he was expert in quoting ancient prophecies. He reputedly played the fiddle before Queen Victoria on Deeside and would tell people: 'But for the doggies, I wadna be here. Often when I'm far from shelter I dig a hole in the snow and lie down in my cloak, and the doggies snuggle round my neck. The snow covers us up but we dinna mind, for the three o us are cosy and warm thegither.'

I thought of the Blind Fiddler and his dogs tramping over the time-worn Mounth passes where there is little in the way of shelter from the winds of space. It must have been a decidedly rough existence he led. How much of what I'd read was romantic illusion, and how much was fact? Many such gangrels have tramped into folklore, their stories forgotten, save by a very few.

I left the room which was as quiet as a cloister and cycled back up the glen to Tarfside. Once more I called in at the shed-shop where Tibbie emerged from behind her dark counter to give me a packet of sweets and a certain amount of quizzing as to how I'd been spending my time in the glen. I told her I was keen to see Whitestane, the old cottage where Willie Glass the molecatcher used to live. She told me to follow the track past Milton Cottage and it was just beyond where the Burn of Calanach flowed into the Milton Burn.

Leaving my bike beside a tied gate, I proceeded up to Whitestane on foot. The cottage, now in ruins, was situated at the edge of a small clump of trees not far from the burn. The walls were best preserved at the north gable end and showed the drystane style of construction to good effect. At the other side were a number of bee-skeps. Rather foolishly I approached too near and had to beat a hasty retreat as an advance party of bees from the swarm started buzzing round my head.

Whitestane had been part of the thriving clachan of Arsallary, now a sheep farm. The first edition of the six inch map for the area reveals other dwellings at Dykefoot, Garthead, Stonywell, Badabay, Kirny, Burnside and Braidlees. A number of these houses were in close proximity to old limekilns and as I later read, this was one of the centres of Glenesk's illicit whisky trade. It was still a flourishing concern in the early part of last century but gradually faded out when legal distilling was sanctioned by the government in 1823. Without the whisky there was no longer a livelihood for most of the people, and so Arsallary witnessed a decline in its fortunes.

Cycling on the way to Dalbrack, further up the glen, I scattered legions of flies which were teeming round the corpse of a car-flattened hare. The bridge at Dalbrack was impressive and Elizabeth Davidson had told me it was a tremendous spot to see the North Esk in times of spate. I noticed part of the coping stones on the left-hand parapet were missing. Below, the river tumbled down a time-eroded gorge in a peat-brown cascade. The action of the water created curious circular pot pools in the rock, while the opposite side was exceedingly deep and slow-flowing.

Prior to 1764 there had been no road suitable for carts in the glen; everything came in by packhorse. By 1790, statute and privately-organized labour had so improved the situation that carts were in common use. From Dalbrack a former packhorse route known as the Whisky Road or Priest's Road crosses to Stonyford in Glen Lethnot by way of 'Chapmans Holms' and the Clash of Wirren. This route was a continuation of the whisky-smuggling trail from the Aberdeenshire and Banffshire Highlands which crossed Deeside and over by Mount Keen to the upper part of Glenesk. But other types of people also used the route which was the nearest and most direct way to the Lowlands from Deeside. Migrant harvesters from the Tomintoul area walked in their bare feet by this same way in order to reach the great 'Taranty' or Trinity Fair at Brechin. Place-name evidence also preserves the fact that this was a common route for travelling chapmen, the predecessors of packmen, whose height of prosperity was the 18th century, long before there were any country shops. These chapmen came on foot or by horse, bringing a range of merchandise such as linen and dyes, and other minor luxury items to the outlying glens. The name, the Priest's Road, came about because it was also the most direct route for the Episcopal minister of Loch Lee travelling to his second charge at Lethnot.

A regular traffic in cattle certainly used the Mounth passes in the first half of the 17th century and later – the Glen Tanar to Glenesk route was one of 11 such droving ways linking Deeside and the South.

From Dalbrack I made my way back up the twisting single-track road and down to West Migvie. The farm was uninhabited and showed signs of neglect. Part of the garden dyke had crumbled away and the wooden sun-house was contorted into that awkward twisting stage prior to complete collapse. I had the distinct feeling that one strong gale would be enough to bring the structure down. In the back yard an old cheese press lay discarded, and there were numerous rusting hulks of other bygone farm machinery: old ploughs, a Wallace's mower and reaper, as well as a circular ring of stathel stones which once would have supported corn stacks.

Further round, a sheep was dozing inside the entrance to an old limekiln and nearby were a couple of tattie pits with stone-built openings reminiscent of Skara Brae in Orkney. These pits are believed to be unique to Glenesk. They were introduced around 1760–70, approximately at the same time as free-standing limekilns were built. According to Elizabeth Davidson, they were used until about 1910, the potatoes being covered with straw then clods of earth. All in all, I felt as though I had stumbled back in time and come across a ghostly agricultural museum rather than a present-day farm which had not long been vacated.

The first drops of rain splattered on my notebook as I made my way over to a roofless outbuilding. An old black boot lay propped up in a wall nook, while its partner lay laceless on the ground amongst a scattering of acorns. It was an image of great pathos.

Where was the one-time wearer of those boots now?

The clouds overhead scowled down at me and there followed a skarrach. I decided it was time to leave this place of the past and head back down to The Retreat. After my evening meal, I cycled back up to Tarfside, this time to call on Sandy Stewart, a retired gamekeeper of 82. Sandy was a tall, thickset figure of a man with a brick-red face and kind eyes. His voice was clear and slow, if a trifle hesitant with strangers.

'I started keepering in 1924 on Lord Dalhousie's Millden Estate,' he explained in his quiet way. 'My beat stretched up the Turret on the south side of Mount Battock, over by the south side of the Tarf by the Burn of Berryhill and then between Drumgreen and Whigginton, over by the tops of Wirren, Craigangower and Bulg – all over two thousand feet. A keeper's pay wisnae very big at that time but ye got vermin money: a shillin a head for weasels and hawks, five shillins a time for foxes, a shillin for hoodie craws. The money was always a help and gave you a wee bit o encouragement to do your job. It was all grouse and partridges with a few black game as a sideline; no river work.'

In 1930 Sandy went to Hunthill, Glen Lethnot, and stayed there for 17 years before returning to Glenesk. For the first two years he stayed in a bothy with another man who looked after the pony and did orra-work. When he married in 1932, Sandy moved into a cottage, and latterly the keeper's house at Stonyford. There was no water supply in the cottage at Blackhaugh, nor electricity.

'We carried the water in a pail from a freshwater spoot fifty yards away. It wis far enough when it wis snowin an it could be pretty wild up the head o Lethnot in the winter, but it wis water worth goin for. Paraffin lamps hung frae the ceiling an we'd the tilly as well. I did my ain butcherin. We generally bought half a pig locally an salted it in a big barrel for a month. If an egg could float on the top, that meant the brine in the barrel wis salty enough to put yer pig in. I sometimes did venison. At the time o the war I usetae strip the fat off the stag's intestines, take it home an melt it down for cooking fat. We survived!'

I asked Sandy if keepers were supplied with special clothing for the hill. 'Twice at Hunthill we got a tweed suit: plus-fours. The Dalhousie tartan had a blue-green stripe running through a dark herring-bone twill. It was supposed to be a cloth that wasn't easily detected on the hill. But my dress was mostly the proper dress – the kilt. I wore it summer an winter. Wet snow apart, I never felt cold in it. An I'd ankle-length leather boots on my feet.'

Time flew by talking to Sandy and it soon was the end of another enjoyable evening.

There was a glowering sky overhead next morning and a dank mist enveloped the hills. I planned to pedal up to the head of the glen and explore neighbouring Glen Mark because I was keen to find 'Bonnymune's Cave' [Balnamoon's Cave] which Elizabeth Davidson had mentioned in our talk. This is one of innumerable fugitive lairs used by proscribed Jacobites after the Forty-Five rebellion. The cave was marked on my OS map but I had heard it had a small opening and was difficult to find.

The rebel laird, James Carnegie of Balnamoon (an estate to the north-west of Brechin) was hunted by Royalist troops and forced to take refuge in the wilds of Glen Mark. Here he evaded his pursuers for a long time, though many of the local inhabitants knew of his hiding-place. But despite being offered heavy bribes, none would disclose Carnegie's place of refuge. According to the story, Carnegie was an Episcopalian, and the local Presbyterian minister was said to have told government troops the approximate area he was hiding in. One cold, wet day the rebel laird, dressed as a poor hind, was drying himself in the ingle-neuk of a nearby house when a party of Campbell Highlanders arrived in search of him. The farmer sized up the danger of the situation, urged the soldiers to take some refreshments and gruffly ordered the seeming hind to go and clean the byres and make room for the strangers. This ploy gave Balnamoon enough time to reach his cave in the hills. He was later caught but released due to a legal technicality, and lived quietly back at Balnamoon thereafter. By all accounts he was something of an eccentric figure, with his passion for the Episcopalian faith matched by his fondness for port wine.

About noon the rain stopped and the clouds partly receded. I journeyed up the glen and followed the rough track which leads to the ruined kirkyard at Loch Lee. The old kirk looked a forlorn site. This one-time parish had been a self-sufficient world, with its own weavers and shoemakers amongst the former inhabitants.

Within the kirkyard lies a gravestone in memory of the Dominie-poet of Loch Lee, Alexander Ross (1699–1784), author of *Helenore,* a narrative poem in Scots which Robert Burns described as 'precious treasure'. Ross was born in Kincardine O' Neil, moved to Loch Lee in 1732 and spent 52 years of his life in that remote community. He died at Buskhead, in the house of a relative, having gone there to live after the death of his wife.

I pedalled back to the 16th-century square keep that is Invermark Castle, its gaunt granite walls a reminder of the days when the caterans came over the Mounth to plunder the fat cattle on the Esk grazings. Here I left the bike and proceeded on foot by a track up the west side of the Mark to Cowiehillocks Plantation. It was a fine sheltered spot to unscrew the flask and have some tea. Ahead I could see the track known as the Ladder which winds its way up and over the shoulder of Mount Keen, the most easterly Munro in Scotland.

A narrow sheep-walk took me round by the south of the river into the throat of Glen Mark and I came to the remains of the Gripdyke, built long ago to keep Highland cattle from venturing down to the lower pastures of the glens. Close by this rugged spot, three cataracts drop down to Whyte's Pool on the River Mark. This was the location of a tragic accident on 27 October 1820, when two young shepherds drowned at the spot while gathering in their flocks for sale at Cullow Market. The point where they intended to cross the Mark is so narrow that almost anyone can make the leap; but on this fateful occasion the sloping rocks were wet with spray and extremely slippery. One of the shepherds made the jump in too casual a manner and was swept down into the pool. His brother jumped in to rescue him but both were lost under the swirling eddies of the river.

After some searching I came upon the narrow entrance to the Balnamoon's Cave marked on my OS map. It has a frontage wall that is man-made, consisting of flat stones, above which there is a heathery top. Although quite close to the path, the cave can be easily missed. I squeezed inside to face a massive back wall of natural rock, evidence of a fireplace and recent occupation. It was impossible to stand upright in the cave, but it would sleep up to five people in relative, albeit damp comfort.

Without giving too much away, the view from the entrance of

this cave looks directly over to the scree on the Craig of Doune. A more convincing bolt-hole, with a view straight down the glen, lies higher up in the crags above. Entry to this second cave – which has an even smaller opening – necessitated an eel-like crawl at right angles, before it opened out into a commodious chamber whose sloping floor was the natural bedrock. Inside it was as dark as the Earl o' Hell's waistcoat but completely sheltered from the wind. The narrow beam from my torch was not enough to dispel feelings of claustrophobia, and I was relieved to wriggle back out into the open. That said, this second howff remains a more convincing fugitive's refuge. It blends in totally with the natural lie of the land, offers a commanding view of the glen from its opening, and is the more difficult cave to find since it is not marked on any map.

With the light beginning to fade, I made my way back down the glen and rode down to The Retreat, content with the results of my explorations. I settled down for my last night in the former shooting lodge. My bedroom window faced west to the distant rocky buttress of Craig Maskeldie, now blanketed by the evening sky.

There had been a downpour overnight. I slept through it all. After a light breakfast of scrambled eggs on toast I stepped outside to find the Kalkhoff dripping wet. I was sorry to be leaving Glenesk because it is a fascinating place, but at least the weather was holding as I set off down the glen. After a short distance I was overtaken by the Robertsons in their Renault, hooting as they passed. At Millden, several cars were parked outside the lodge and smoke drifted skywards from another building by the roadside. I had the feeling that the seasons were changing and could feel the rawness of the day on my hands.

Further down the glen on the opposite bank of the North Esk is Holmhead. A family who lived here formerly had to cross the river to the road by a wire bridge suspended from two trees. A pulley system was used for taking food over to their side of the river and there was quite a knack in crossing such bridges. A short distance away are the remains of a deserted settlement at Dalforth which boasted a cobbler's shop at one time. Glenesk was full of such places; this, the glen of rowans.

Apart from a slight stiffness in the gears, the red machine was performing well and it was an enjoyable easy ride down to Edzell.

The first building which came into view had a high V-roof and I could just make out the word CAFE. Across from a football pitch there were a large number of cars and lorries, as though some sort of outside market or show was taking place. I rested the bike against the outside of the cafe which had sun-bleached confectionary boxes and plastic ice-cream cones in the window. It was a bluebottles' Eldorado. Inside, the shop was like a dark church. Two leather-jacketed youths were playing snooker on a full-size table whose suspended panel light broke the gloom. It was 9.45 a.m. The elderly shopkeeper seemed to pop out from nowhere. I bought some cigarettes and in a slow Scots-Italian voice she took ages to count out every single penny of my change from a £5 note.

Edzell with its broad main street looked a one-horse town. In a small general store I bought some rolls, an Arbroath Smokie, a tin of salmon, cheese, soup, fruit, chocolate and a bottle of whisky. Safely stashing these in my panniers I headed round to where I'd seen the gathering of vehicles. A sheep sale was in progress and the verbal jousting of the auctioneer could be clearly heard. The sheep were being driven through various gates by men waving sticks and arms in a wild flurry of movements. One of the handlers behaved and looked like a scarecrow on amphetamines. Other, more subdued characters with hawk-like faces and slanted bonnets were engrossed in their own clandestine conversations, seriously puffing away on pipes and cigarettes.

Resting the bike by a gate, I entered the small oval-seated arena where the main auction was taking place. The auctioneer was barking out the bids received from the punters seated round the ring. 'Another good lamb – never seen a cabbage in its life,' quipped the auctioneer as his figures shot up at a rapid rate. The noise of the sheep was incredible, so I ventured out for some peace and quiet. In one of the outside paddocks a man the size of the Incredible Hulk with tattooed forearms was furiously cursing some obstinate animal which refused to be ushered through an open gate.

After consulting the map, I pushed off towards Lethnot by an unclassified road that took me past Edzell Castle. The L-plan sandstone tower-house overlooks a walled parterre garden whose architectural devices are unique in Scotland and give Edzell Castle a distinctive place in the history of European Renaissance art.

The road climbed above the West Water and further round at the farm of Newbigging, there was a fine outlook over the Howe of the Mearns. I continued down a steep brae, arriving at my previously arranged destination – Clochie. The Robertsons had told me to phone the farmer of Clochie, Sandy Strachan, since they believed he had a vacant cottage for a weekend let: he had. The cottage had just been left by a group of tattie roguers who were working on his farm. I tried the farmhouse door but nobody answered, except for the fierce low-pitched growl of an old collie with marble-coloured eyes.

About mid-afternoon a fawn-coloured Rover pulled up outside the row of cottar houses where I was waiting. Out jumped the smiling figure of Sandy Strachan, who apologised for being late and produced a Yale key from his jacket pocket. The lock was slightly stiff, but after a few minutes of trying, the door budged open and we proceeded inside.

Sandy collected some mail addressed to the former occupants before showing me round. The concrete floor of the kitchen was half-covered with tattered linoleum and one of the windows was boarded up. To his credit, Sandy had described the place on the phone to me as 'basic', but all I needed was a roof over my head, and at least the cottage wasn't damp. One of the mustard-coloured doors led to the toilet which was as warm as a snow-hole. The sitting room was furnished with sticks of furniture and a long sofa. There was an old TV at one side.

I slotted my last 50 pence in the electricity meter. The TV didn't work, nor did the fridge. Tea was a cold Smokie and a glass of water. From one of the windows I could see the outline of the ancient Caterthun hill fort. Later that evening my supply of electricity expired, mostly eaten up by an electric fire.

I lit a candle and retired to the flea-bag with a book of short stories by the great Russian writer Maxim Gorky. Pre-Revolution Russia swarmed with tramps, vagabonds and pilgrims, and this soulless cottage was doubtless a palace compared to their lot in life. There is probably no better tramping story in literature than Gorky's *My Travelling Companion* which he wrote in 1894. I blew out the candle. The pinhead of light from the wick seemed to take ages before it disappeared, leaving me engulfed by the darkness.

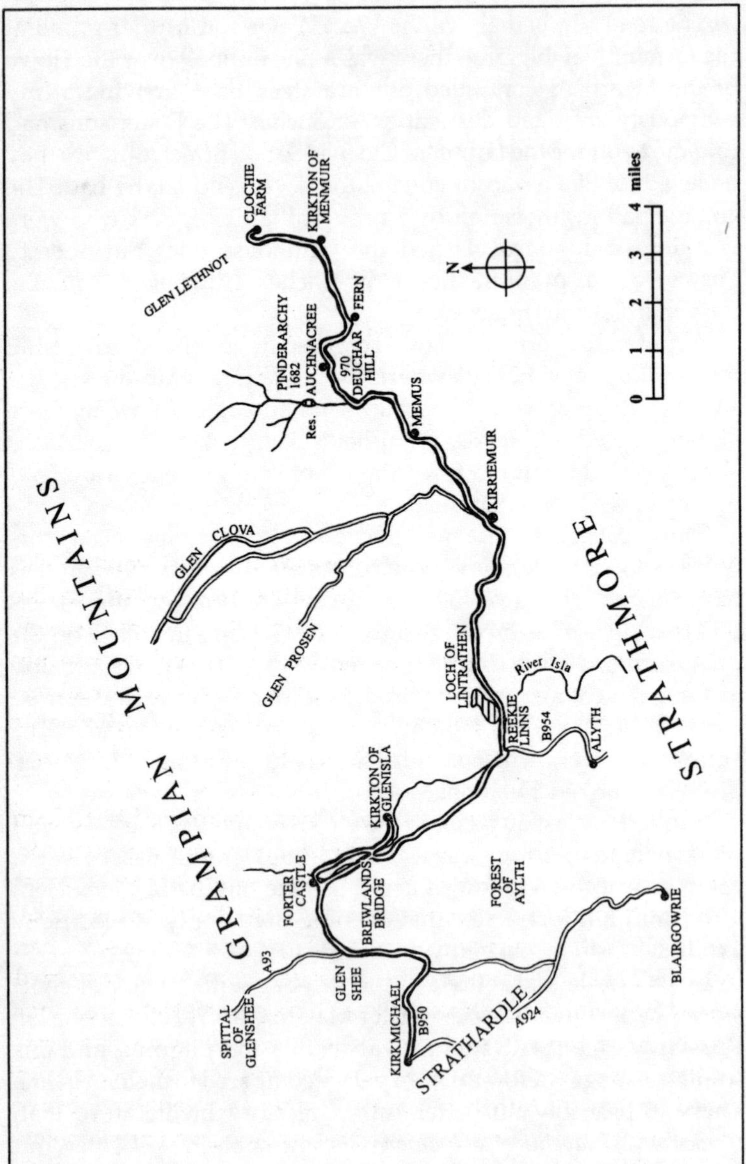
GRAMPIAN MOUNTAINS
STRATHMORE
GLEN LETHNOT
CLOCHIE FARM
KIRKTON OF MENMUIR
N
0 1 2 3 4 miles
PINDERARCHY 1682
AUCHNACREE
970 DEUCHAR HILL
FERN
Res.
MEMUS
KIRRIEMUIR
GLEN CLOVA
GLEN PROSEN
LOCH OF LINTRATHEN
River Isla
REEKIE LINNS
B954
ALYTH
KIRKTON OF GLENISLA
FORTER CASTLE
BREWLANDS BRIDGE
FOREST OF AYLTH
A93
SPITTAL OF GLENSHEE
GLEN SHEE
KIRKMICHAEL
B950
STRATHARDLE
A924
BLAIRGOWRIE

CHAPTER 5

Pedalling West: Lethnot to Oban

'Slow and easy goes far in a day' as Moleskin Joe once said!

Patrick MacGill, *Children of the Dead End*, 1914.

After a sound night's sleep I awoke to find a miserable wet morning. Wriggling out of my sleeping-bag, I dressed in the spartan bedroom, dowsed my face and hands in ice-cold water, then cycled the few hundred yards down to the farm. I was warmly received by Mrs Strachan who cooked me a princely breakfast which greatly lifted my sagging morale. Seated at the kitchen table I noted the names and origins of the Clochie fields, Sandy having produced a large-scale map dating from 1924.

Sandy explained he had come south from Aberdeenshire to farm Clochie in 1941. He was keen to discuss older farming methods. 'One of our wet weather jobs was rollin up spartie [esparto] grass into a round baa. This was used for keeping the thatch on the stacks. The thatch was usually wheat straa and came in bunches. Ye had twaa thatchin ladders an worked in pairs. We used whit they caad bosses for ventilation but also to keep the stacks upright. Yer stack was built on top o a ring o stathel stanes that were like large mushrooms. They helped keep the vermin out.' We were later joined by Sandy's father-in-law, from whom I noted a number of north Angus dialect words for certain farm tools and implements.

Sandy then telephoned an elderly lady who lived at the foot of Glen Lethnot and arranged for me to pay her a visit, having explained that I was interested in hearing about life in the old days. I left the farmhouse about noon and pedalled off into the rain. There was a steep, winding ascent from the bridge over the West Water and the glen hills began to rise on both sides with mist creeping along the tops.

On the track up to the house, small, loose stones crackled under my tyres. I parked, unhooked my notebook, and rapped on the door. An old lady answered wearing a brightly patterned apron. Her face was deeply lined and she had a thin moustache above her top lip. I explained who I was and what I was doing, and she gingerly invited me inside. In her front room I was told to take a seat by a sideboard with a loud ticking clock. The lady asked once more what I wanted to know. I told her again. It was becoming clear that her contribution was going to be short. And it was. I asked her about her earliest memories of life in the glen but it was like pulling teeth to obtain more than two sentences from her. I managed only 13 lines of notes before she made a rather lame excuse that she was expecting visitors. On at least three occasions she referred to an old book about the history of the glen and told me I would find all I wanted to know in its pages. She became rather thrawn-gabbit when I replied that it was her own version of the past in which I was interested and I decided there was little merit in prolonging my stay, so I thanked this rather stern customer for her time, and left.

It was the first and only occasion on the entire trip when I was to experience rejection. Despite the horrid weather I decided to push on to the upper reaches of the glen. Lethnot is a much barer and lonelier glen than Glenesk, and is the least well-known of the longer Angus glens. The present-day road is narrow and runs in close proximity to the West Water. Higher up on the other side lies the course of an older road which was part of an ambitious plan to build a carriage route to Lochlee in Glenesk. This older route only runs so far up the east side before it stops. On Thomson's map of 1825 there is a route clearly marked running from 'Dikehead' up the east side of the glen, over the Priest's Road to upper Glenesk and Glen Mark. This map also shows that upper Glen Lethnot was populated to a much greater extent than it is today. Settlements no longer marked on modern maps included Achrie, Whirleston, Redholes, Glascorry and Blindderg Haugh.

By now well and truly soaked, I rode as far as Stonyford before deciding that it was not worth the extra effort to reach the head of the glen. In olden times there was no bridge at Stonyford, just a rough and dangerous ford which was impassable if there was the slightest rise in the level of the water. The safest route was undoubtedly down the east side of the West Water. Long ago two young men were drowned at Stonyford when attempting to cross the ford under swollen conditions. It was this sad event which led to the building of the bridge.

Under a leaden sky I cycled back down the glen, determined to find the abandoned graveyard of Navar. I followed a farm road to Lichtnie, and from there wheeled the bike down a track by the side of a trickling burn. Within a round cluster of trees there was what I took to be some form of monument in ruins.

This was all that remained of the old Navar Kirk. My so-called monument was the ruined belfry. It lay amidst a mangled network of dead roots. The intensity of the storm was exaggerated by the eerie souch which moaned through the trees. Large droplets of rain fell on my head and anorak as the tree tops swayed to and fro. On one side of a jungle of nettles were seven moss-covered tombstones that leaned over at awkward angles, one lying flat on its face. It was just possible to decipher the date '1791' on the back of one of the stones. There was something grotesque about this place. It was the last place on earth to be in the howe-dumb-dead of night. Never have I experienced such an intensely forbidding atmosphere as I did here.

Later I discovered that this was the burying-place of a legless beggar called John Gudefellow who died in 1810, just up the road at Tillyarblet. He travelled the locality on his hands and stumps, playing on people's charity and superstitions, ferociously demanding food and clothes at his various ports of call. The farmer at Tillyarblet is credited with giving him a handsome burial.

I headed back to the cottage to dry out my clothes. The brakes on the Kalkhoff had lost their bite and fast descents called for caution in the treacherous conditions. A couple of drams helped revive me and I snuggled into the sleeping-bag for warmth, grateful for the company provided by the radio. The downpour continued all that afternoon, unrelenting in its intensity.

In the early evening I returned to the farm house to pay for my stay, but Sandy generously refused to accept any money. His wife gave me a pint of milk for the morning and we all had drams out of my bottle. The couple waved me off as I stepped into the gloaming. On the way back to the cottage I passed a jet-black bull who looked up like an angry colonel whose game of billiards had just been interrupted. This was £3,600-worth of Aberdeen Angus and he knew it!

Rain continued through the night, pattering on the slates as I tried to get some sleep in the stuffy room. I awoke to the sound of birdsong and sunlight streaming in through the thin curtains. I turned over in the sleeping-bag and listened to the morning news. Since leaving Penicuik I had not read a newspaper.

After a few nibbles of some leftover cheese washed down by milk, I tidied up, assembled my load and left the key in the lock as instructed. I pedalled past the old manse, picking up speed on the descent past the caravan site. Round the next bend, rowan berries shone a pillar-box red in the morning sunlight. Fenceposts and hedges cast shadows across one half of the road. It felt great to be on the road again, experiencing the true freedom of two wheels.

I thumbed down the gears for the tortuous climb up by Burnfoot, when the loud blast from a bird-cannon rudely interrupted the morning silence. As I gradually made progress up the brae, the view behind unfolded to reveal a glorious patchwork of fields, woodland, and the marvellous distinct hues of brown and purple on the Lethnot hills. I dismounted to try and take it all in. Back down in the distance I could just make out the blue door of the cottage where I'd stayed. Farms nestled against the back-sheltering hills, lines of dykes marched across the fields and a noisy craws' parliament held session in some high trees. Over to my left I watched the flight of a sparrowhawk as it made a gannet-like downward plummet into a field. The White Caterthun lay dark and silent below a passing cloud, the perfect contrast to the sun-dappled fields.

I continued the haul up the brae as a pair of young heifers started head-butting each other in a nearby field. The oval-shaped mound of the hillfort on the White Caterthun came into sharper focus, while further along the ridge a pencil-thin tree broke the skyline. At the top of the brae there was a long and unexpectedly gradual descent to Kirkton of Menmuir, with the fertile corridor of Strathmore beyond. Near Shanford, a gang of tattie howkers were hard at work, their blue-grey bus parked inside the field.

At Balquharn I turned right and laboured up a bewitching, narrow backroad to Afflochie. Set against moory hills, this sheep farm lies in a little world of its own at the foot of two bare glens, that of the Cruick Water and that of the Paphrie Burn. The road twisted up and round to Auchnacree where a clutch of interesting buildings, some with crow-stepped gables, lined the road. The road was forever changing character and provided an enchantingly quiet run.

After passing through woodland, I dropped down to a small, narrow lochan sheltered by trees. Ducks swam and the occasional plop of fish catching flies could be heard. I dismounted and sat on a grassy bank overlooking the water. Not one car passed; it was bliss. Back in the saddle, I continued past Glenley, across a bridge over the Noran Water, then forked right for Glen Ogil, one of the secret glens of Angus.

At what I took to be a keeper's cottage, there was a gate that led to a magnificent woodland trail which threaded its way past towering Douglas firs, birch, rowans, the occasional yew, horse-chestnuts, a glorious copper beech, larches and Scots pine. In early summer the contrasting shades of green are broken by an explosion of colour from lilac and yellow rhododendrons. Tall ferns lined the spongy track in places, as I made my silent way up to the reservoir. This resembles a Highland loch rather than any man-made creation. A tiny tree-topped islet broke the dark expanse of water, while over to my right, part of Eastside Wood had been felled. For a short distance a road of sorts continues round the reservoir, before climbing up through the trees to lonely Mochrie.

Back on the tarmac once more, I viewed the twin guardians of Glen Ogil – St Arnold's Seat and Pinderarchy. There was time to follow a rough potholed track which terminated at two cottages not far from the Falls of Drumly Harry. Here the Noran Water makes a spectacular descent through a deep, tree-choked chasm. In parts it is overhanging and care must be exercised when walking near the edge.

Below the strange-sounding farm of Goynd, a branch road leads to Glen Quiech. I continued down to Memus and enjoyed a quick pint at the Drovers' Inn. This cosy hostelry used to be the local post-office; the remains of an authentic drovers' watering-hole can be found at Cleikhem, near Kirkton of Airlie on the western side of Kirriemuir.

A jovial middle-aged man was sitting at the bar reading a newspaper and sipping a Bacardi and tomato juice. Original stone flags provided part of the flooring; a black-leaded range complete with swey occupied the fireplace; wall shelves with books made an attractive alternative to the ubiquitous jukebox. I was tempted to linger but decided to press on for Kirriemuir.

The antics of a galloping horse broke the boredom of what was an uninspiring ride to the red town. There were quietly prosperous dwellings on the outskirts as I whizzed down a steep, bumpy road into the heart of the town. I visited the bank and eventually found a shop which sold maps. The Thrums Hotel provided an excellent piece of brisket served with potatoes and cauliflower.

The sameness of the building stone gives Kirrie a uniform atmosphere. Some of the pubs looked uninviting dens but there were some interesting crooked wynds. The playwright and novelist, James Matthew Barrie was born at No. 9 Brechin Road in 1860, the building now being under the care of the National Trust for Scotland and serving as an intimate personal museum to the famous writer. Barrie's father was a handloom weaver, like the occupants of many of the other houses in the road. Most of his stories of the town, which he called 'Thrums', came from his mother, whose life he told in *Margaret Ogilvie* (1896). Thrums is a technical term in weaving. It means the fringe of threads left on a loom when the web is taken off.

Barrie's characters are rather stereotyped and his writing lacks the urgency and lyricism of Grassic Gibbon. As a result of a stern upbringing, Barrie had a solid respect for the Kirk. The old weavers' houses were two-roomed 'but-an-bens', one room serving as a kitchen, the other as a loom-shop. Perhaps off the kitchen there would be a small bedroom and a low-roofed attic reached by a ladder from the hard earth floor. In 1811 when handloom weaving was about at its height, the population of Kirriemuir was under 5,000.

Barrie wrote about the Auld Licht Kirk in Bank Street (demolished in 1893), from which he took the name of his first collection of sketches *Auld Licht Idylls* (1888). In 1872 after two years in Forfar, the Barries settled at the ivy-covered Strathview (now modernised) but it was the cottage opposite that became known as the House on the Brae of *A Window in Thrums* (1889). Barrie also included reference to the town's poorhouse, which was where the Blind Fiddler passed away. It opened in 1872 as an almshouse for vagrants, lunatics, homeless children and the elderly. Originally the building had been a farmhouse. When I passed, the place was unoccupied and neglected, with boards across the windows adding to the grim exterior.

With the sun on my back I left Kirrie by a quiet backroad that stretched out under Culhawk Hill. A strong north-easterly took the enjoyment out of the ride and it was head down all the way to Kirkton of Kingoldrum. I took a breather in the local post-office where a postman was complaining to the owner of 'being aye oot o pooch'. Their debate over the correct amount of change was spiced with banter. I chipped in that stamps had just gone up in price – 'cheap at half the price,' retorted the postie with a laugh, as the wind howled outside the shop.

As I struggled along the B951 the farm of Greenmyre appeared on my left. One of the tales concerning the Blind Fiddler has it that he was found unconscious here one bitterly frosty night. Both his dogs lay dead beside him and in his pockets was a sum of money amounting to £50. Whether this was true or not, no one knows.

The gently rounded foothills made a beautiful backdrop to the Loch of Lintrathen, a popular trout loch. A minor road skirts the loch by Bridgend of Lintrathen which comprised a few houses and a church. Until the late 17th century, a thriving market used to be held here each November, attracting drovers, horse-dealers and travelling merchants from as far afield as Badenoch and Strathspey. Later the market moved to the Kirkton of Glenisla.

At Bridge of Craigisla the River Isla thunders down the Reekie Linns, the clouds of drifting spray giving the waterfall its name. The Isla is one of my favourite rivers, forever changing its character; dramatic, graceful, powerful, secretive, superb. It is born in the wild heights of the Caenlochan and Canness glens, having a relatively short life for a river of its size, before it merges with the Tay near Kinclaven.

I struck off for Milnacraig and the narrow road which follows the Burn of Kilry before rising up to over 1,000 feet between Druim Dearg and Knockton. It was a punishing ascent and I was vowing to give up smoking. Snow-poles lined the open, unfenced road which can be a wild and lonely crossing in winter, offering little protection from the elements. If anything, it is a road of solitude; timeless as well as testing. But the climb had been worth it. The panorama was not the kind of prospect that can be appreciated with a glance from a passing car, but required a long, slow pivoting look from the roadside. The blustery wind billowed out my jacket and flattened the surrounding grasses. The rich farmland of Strathmore faded into the afternoon haze. Windswept and treeless, the voice of the moor was my companion. I was content; tired but free.

Sucking a couple of glucose tablets, I pedalled on before the thrill of the descent down to Bridge of Brewlands. From here it was an easy ride to the Kirkton. It felt as though I was back in a different world. Tonight I would have the luxury of a hotel bed and bath. I wheeled the machine into the car park and rested it against a wall. Tea and scones awaited inside, the perfect end to the day's journey.

The School of Scottish Studies had supplied me with the name and address of the oldest surviving resident of Glenisla. This was Elizabeth Graham, born in 1898 at Dalvanie in the Folda district of upper Glenisla.

Next morning I rode back up to Bridge of Brewlands, taking the narrow road which wriggles its way above the east side of the Isla. The morning air was bracing and the glen looked at its loveliest. Elizabeth's cottage lay back off the road at the foot of Glen Beannie. Seated by the fire, she explained that the house had been built in 1870 by three men: a mason, a shepherd and a roadman. I asked her how long her people had been in the glen.

'My father told me that my great-grandfather was born in 1787,' she said. 'He was one of the great whisky smugglers, by trade a meal miller so he'd plenty of grain to make whisky. They used to smuggle it on ponies as far as Arbroath.'

Elizabeth then produced a most intriguing family heirloom – a long blackthorn stick with an iron tip. One of her forefathers had taken it from an excise man after a fight and Elizabeth told me it was used for puncturing kegs to drain off the illicit whisky. Later I read that such a weapon was known as a 'searcher' and was used for piercing holes in illegal stills made of tin rather than copper.

Further back in history, Elizabeth told me that monks from Coupar Angus Abbey used to spend the summer months at Burnside of Dalvanie. The ruins of their tiny monastery can still be seen at the waterside. For centuries most of Glenisla had belonged to the abbot of Coupar Angus. The tenants paid rent to the monks and had each to supply a hunting dog when it came to a wolf hunt. Family tradition has it that the monks came to the glen by way of Kilry, where a boy called James Graham saw to it that they were provided for.

I asked Elizabeth when Gaelic had last been spoken in Glenisla. 'Gaelic was spoken in upper Glenisla long after it died out further down. My granny could speak it and my father had quite a lot of Gaelic words. And I can remember an old school-teacher who had Gaelic when I was young.'

Elizabeth went on to mention how there had been quite a lot of journeying to Glenshee and vice-versa. People from Glenshee used to work at the Glenisla clippings, and Elizabeth's father used to walk to the Braemar Gathering by the Monega hill path, the highest right-of-way in Scotland, crossing the mountains at 3,200 feet immediately to the north of Glas Maol. 'There was far more people in the glen than there is now,' Elizabeth recalled. 'There were Duncans, Grewars, Stewarts, MacIntoshes, Robertsons, Gows, Grants and Simpsons. Forty people lived in the clachan of Dalvanie at one time. The smiddie was down at Claypotts opposite Doldy, and the souter was called Carr and he lived next door to the smith.'

I wondered if Elizabeth could recall anything about the Blind Fiddler.

'He was known all over but he was about done by the time I saw him. Many a bowl o broth we've given him. He was a lovely speaker in a real Highland way and although he'd plenty of stories to tell, he tended to keep himself to himself. He was a university lad they said. I mind his dogs never liked men but were alright with women. He was taken ill two miles down the road at Doonie and had a bag of gold on him. The farmer took him to the poorhoose in Kirrie and they later gave him a decent burial.'

Despite having both feet amputated, Elizabeth was a resolute character with a fine sense of humour. She told me that she spent the winters with her housekeeper in Kirriemuir. Most of the day was spent jotting down her memories of life in the glen and I was well and truly spoilt with lashings of tea and home baking.

After the evening meal back at the hotel, I retired to the small low-roofed public bar where I met two young Englishmen who were undertaking a tour of Scotland on their motor bike.

With a packed lunch and the thermos filled, I set off next morning to cross into neighbouring Glenshee. The wind of yesterday had dropped to a refreshing breeze. At Brewlands the creak of my bike sparked some caged dogs into howls of protest. I was content to move at a leisurely rate; there was nothing to be gained by hurrying. Occasionally I glanced at the milometer as the tarmac slowly glided under the wheels. Near Doonie an enormous brown toadstool sat in wiry grass beside the verge; then a weasel with its back arched hurriedly skipped over the road in front of me. Across the river the pattern of small fields was broken by shelter belts, farm buildings and a scattered line of white cottages. Behind the small, deep-set windows I wondered how many of the houses were simply holiday cottages since there were no outward signs of life.

On my left the craggy shoulder of Mount Blair fell sharply to the road. Grey scree and scattered lumps of bedrock replaced whin and heather. Long shadows stroked the hills of Folda, while the more distant tops stood out below a broken fleece of cotton-wool clouds. The road wound its way through a sparkling cluster of birches, then Forter Castle came into view. At a seat-shaped rock by the roadside I stopped for a cup of tea, lit a cigarette and listened to the sounds of the glen. Hardly any cars passed. A yellow, watery sun filtered through the trees, illuminating ferns and casting patterns on the tarmac. The Isla rushed over a series of rocky platforms in its unhindered journey down the glen. I drank in the surroundings, the magic of it all, wishing for nothing more in life. Today, Glenisla looked at its best, contrastingly beautiful in every direction, near yet so far from the madding crowd.

Fifteen minutes passed but it could have been a lifetime. What did time matter on a day such as this? I had no train to catch, no factory hooter to obey, no piles of correspondence stacked on any desk; life is enriched by such moments and freedom could be more than just a word.

Today I promised to take life as it found me. There would be no plans, targets, miles to meet. I did not know where I would stay and nor did I care. To journey was more important than arrival or destinations. I had no one to see, no deadlines to meet; I would be a free spirit.

Back in the saddle I headed away from beautiful Glenisla. The field dykes around Balloch had been built with large stones and, despite the ravagement of many winters, stood tall and straight without any signs of slippage. In contrast, those which bordered the road where showing signs of neglect and had been superseded by fences. The approach of placing a new fence down one or both sides of a decaying dyke has become universal since the end of the 19th century, when fencing wire first became available as a cheap and quick alternative to dyking. Fencing is nowadays no longer cheap. A properly repaired dyke will outlive several generations of wire fence, only requiring maintenance, never replacement. A dyke of natural stone is aesthetically more in keeping with the environment and provides valuable shelter to stock, as well as a habitat for lichens, mosses, and wildlife.

Nearing the top of a fairly steep brae, I saw what appeared to be a massive green-and-white kite hanging in the wind: it turned out to be a hang-glider. There were three of them in all, two of them grounded. As I passed, one of the bearded fliers shouted 'Hello' and gave me a cheery wave which I returned.

Once through some Forestry Commission land, I curled round a bend and was met by the glorious view of the white-turreted Dalnaglar Castle and beyond, the high rounded tops of the Glenshee hills. From my viewpoint on this single-track road, I could see vehicles racing along the A93 to Braemar. I emerged at Lair, where the A93 twists into a dangerous left-hand bend. A sign advertising Glen Isla pottery announced: 'A fifteen minute detour takes you to the most scenic and least expensive pottery in Scotland.'

I should have taken a turn-off for the low road which goes by Mount Blair Lodge and Westertown, emerging on the Glenshee road near a school down from Dalnoid. Instead I toiled with the roller-coaster A93. The present road roughly follows the line of the former military road that extended 100 miles from Coupar Angus to Fort George. It was constructed under the supervision of Major William Caulfeild between 1748 and 1757. Military roads are often termed Wade Roads. In fact General Wade had a relatively short time supervising the construction of military roads in Scotland – 1724–40. In 1732 he appointed Caulfeild as his Inspector of Roads. Until his death in 1787, Caulfeild was responsible for nearly 900 miles of military road, compared with 250 miles that can be credited to Wade.

Near Dalnoid a Spanish coach-driver swung right across my path, giving me an insane wave as he did so. Shortly I gladly left the A93 for he B950, a relatively quiet road. I rode at one stage through the dust-covered environs of an ugly lime-works and on to Kirkmichael. There is no longer a youth hostel here, which was a pity because it offers attractive touring country.

I stopped at the first hotel and enjoyed a glass of beer with my lunch outside in the garden. It was a scorcher of a day. Upon checking the red machine before I left, I saw that the rear tyre was flat. After a struggle, the spare inner tube was duly fitted, something of a triumph for I cannot claim to be adept at such tasks.

The road to Ennochdhu nudged the River Ardle and was littered with animal corpses, including that of a hedgehog. At the post-office I was able to stock up with chocolate bars. There followed a series of blind summits up through Glen Brerachan but the zigzagging climb was now well within my capabilities and I proceeded to pick up speed on the flattish moorland section of the route. Away to the west there was a glorious view of the Ben Alder range, before I plunged down to Pitlochry on a gradient of 14%.

Pitlochry was swarming with coach-parties of tourists who idled their way along the main street. It was a real tourist honey pot and every third shop seemed to stock knitwear, tweeds, and whisky marmalade. The main street was chock-a-block with traffic, so I decided to beat a hasty retreat to search for a place which would make a suitable bivvy for the night. Accommodation seemed to be over-priced and at a premium.

I had a nerve-wracking three-mile ride along the A9 to the Pass of Killiecrankie. The new section of this road which was being built high above the pass was not yet complete. A 30 mph speed limit was supposed to be in operation on the old road, but more than once I'd to take to the verge for safety as giant articulated trucks went roaring by, followed by a line of cars. My OS map did not extend into this area, so I relied on my instincts to find a suitable patch of greenery hidden by trees some distance back from the road. Bike and panniers were brought up to the spot I had chosen in separate journeys. For a while I dozed under the trees, the drone of traffic gradually tailing off but never quite ceasing. With the money I would save on accommodation I decided to treat myself to a good meal.

There was an hotel within walking distance of my camp, so I set off down through the trees and back along the road. Several expensive-looking cars were parked outside and the place looked a posh joint. From behind the bar, the proprietor gazed over his half-moon spectacles and in response to my enquiry if they served bar suppers, blurted out: 'Yes, I suppose we can fit you in; table for one is it?'

I took my seat, feeling sure that my hiking boots would not have gone unnoticed. The proprietor revelled in patronising his well-heeled clientele, every so often shouting out instructions to his kilted slaves to 'be more careful with the food!' I was busy scanning the menu when a well-dressed man and his lady entered. 'We've a table reserved in the name of Montgomery,' he announced. 'How do you spell that sir?' questioned the proprietor rather sheepishly. 'Are you serious about the spelling of a name like Montgomery?' retorted the well-dressed man in a louder tone of voice, adding that he was a descendant of a certain Field Marshall. 'Yes of course sir, my mistake – what's your tipple?' replied the proprietor straightening his back.

Another customer who had been posing at the bar and boasting about his high-performance Audi to another business man, suddenly detected a chip in the rim of his glass. At this, the owner nearly did backward somersaults in an effort to apologise for such 'an unheard-of oversight'.

At a nearby table, a Mancunian patter merchant took the fork from his mouth and praised the gods for 'one of the finest steaks this side of Tokyo'.

'Are you here for the fishing?' he enquired, catching my eye.

'No' I replied, 'I'm here for the cycling.'

'On a bike!' was his astonished reaction.

Conversations tended to dwell on such things as what one did to 'earn a crust', as an accountant put it to his captive audience at the next table. It was all a bit like cats marking out their territory. The man who'd complained about the chipped glass was now bragging about a recent holiday in Greece: 'The fish was first rate but the salads were a trifle on the oily side.' I finished my dessert, 'A Tipsy Laird', paid the bill and left.

Back in the woods I had a good chuckle to myself about the pretentious theatre I had witnessed. 'On a bike!' I thought to myself and laughed out loud. I got into the bivvy sack and watched the stars until I nodded off.

Breakfast was a cigarette. I had no stove so couldn't brew up. It didn't seem to matter; the morning was mine and the weather looked promising. Bathed in morning light, Pitlochry appeared less vulgar. There were fewer people on the streets. I wolfed down a hot pie, then bought a Rumanian checked shirt for a little over £6 – in a chemist's of all places.

A secondary route above the west bank of the Tummel was my choice of road to Logierait. It was reached by a descent that led me past the Pitlochry sewerage works. The scenery would surely improve – it did. Once I was over the Tummel I came to an extremely narrow road which twisted its way through a tunnel of trees that offered welcome shade from the hot sun. I was in an exhilarated frame of mind.

Upon winding my way up a small hill, I suddenly saw a green heap lying immediately off the road in a small space amidst some trees. A head of hair and a red beard became recognisable; it was a fellow-cyclist who was sleeping rough. I was just about to pedal past when a high-pitched voice enquired if I'd like a cup of tea. I pulled alongside the tousle-headed young man who was by this time sitting up in his flea-bag. He thrust a smoke-blackened pot in my direction with the request that I fetch some water from a nearby spout.

The petrol stove flamed into life and our brew was soon concocted.

'Ferocious burners, these stoves,' he remarked as the water was bubbling up. A large plastic container resembling a child's pail in size was handed to me. 'Sweeteners?' he asked. I nodded and a couple of pellets plopped into the pail and his own disgusting-looking mug.

It turned out that my host was something of a contemporary knight of the road. Ex-army and now a mature student studying outdoor activities at Bangor in North Wales, the young Englishman sat cross-legged on the ground and proceeded to regale me with some of his previous adventures. He told me of his time in Jamaica, and in South America, and in the Sudan. He had lived in caves round the coast of Knoydart, he told me, all the time speaking in a hushed voice as though he were inside some sacred temple. Did I know that it was best to take an ex-army machete to Mozambique because the local ones were too long in the blade for chopping coconuts? Foreign hammocks were not advisable and water should be boiled in large quantities for purification purposes. On he went about bandits on camels in the Sahara, wigwam-dwelling 'new age' gypsies in Wales, and alternative society on the island of Lismore. A thought crossed my mind that maybe he'd sweetened our tea with LSD. At any rate I told him I was headed for Rannoch. He piped up that he might head that way himself; I thought not if I can help it – and changed the subject. 'Ye know them whippets [racing cyclists] mate,' he interrupted. 'They do a hundred an' twenty in a day. Me, I settle for sixty.' I did not wish to become embroiled in any discussion about mileages, so I thanked him for his hospitality and proceeded on my leisurely way.

The road curled round above the Tummel and the Tay, followed by a sharp descent into Logierait. A man with a small terrier on an enormous rope-lead was hovering outside the public bar of the Logierait Hotel. 'Ye got the richt time on ye lad?' he shouted.

I drew up and told him it was 10.50 a.m. 'See this dug, it's a fucking braw ratter!' I did not doubt it, but the man's language grew tiresome, every second word being an oath, be it in regard to the licensing hours, the miners (who were on strike), or the rats which his dog went after. I bade him cheerio and pedalled on.

Just along the road was the fascinating kirkyard of Logierait. The kirk itself was built in 1805 but it is the graveyard which holds more in the way of interest. There are some finely carved stones, including an early Pictish cross slab which stands near the entrance to the church. For a long time this stone lay in the burial ground of the Stewart Robertsons of Edradynate. Close by are two fascinating stones. One depicts the sacrifice of Isaac, and the other, the tombstone of a farmer, is an Adam and Eve stone complete with a serpent coiled round the trunk of an apple tree.

Behind the whitewashed kirk lie three heavy iron-ribbed mortsafes which protected coffins in the days of the body-snatchers. Once bodies had sufficiently decomposed to be useless to the snatchers, the mortsafes were lifted out of the graves by block and tackle. In the terrace behind the church there used to be the sacred well of St Ched's, but according to tradition it dried up when the market of the same name ceased to be held in the village.

The Gaelic name of Logierait was *Bal-na-Maoir*, the Town of the Officers of Justice, dating back to the times when the village became the seat of the Regality Court of the Lords of Atholl. In the back of the hotel garden lie the foundation stones of the one-time prison, and Rob Roy is said to have been imprisoned there in 1717, only to escape after one night's confinement. I left the kirkyard and headed along the A827 until I reached the entrance to Ballechin. A rough road curves round at right-angles to the surviving wing of the notorious Ballechin House, which was demolished about 1963.

In 1873 the laird of Ballechin was an elderly, somewhat eccentric bachelor, Major Robert Steuart, late of the East India Company and the descendant of an old and respected Perthshire family. He is said to have preferred his dogs to his neighbours, in particular, a large black spaniel. When his young housekeeper died in July 1873, Ballechin acquired the sinister glamour popularly associated with the scene of any sudden death.

Three years later the major died, but not before he had frequently expressed his wish to return to earth in the body of his favourite black dog. In an act of brutal cruelty, the major's heirs shot all the dogs on the estate – a deed surely motivated by superstitious panic. Servants and later tenants of the estate reputedly heard strange sounds and sights, the most detailed account being that of a Jesuit priest who was terrified by a soft, relentless thud, as though a large animal was persistently throwing itself against his bedroom door.

Years passed, but sporadic accounts of the haunting continued.

In 1897 the Marquis of Bute took a lease on Ballechin. He decided to mount a proper psychic investigation at the house and latterly enrolled a certain Miss Ada Goodrich Freer to act as his principal investigator. She was a well-known writer on psychical research with considerable practical involvement in the subject. In February 1897 she embarked on a four-month-long experiment to find out the truth about the reported hauntings at Ballechin. Along with a lady companion and a large domestic staff, Miss Freer entertained a constant stream of house guests, all keen to encounter the supernatural.

At least 29 people, apart from Miss Freer, reported experiencing supernatural phenomena; amongst the spirits they saw were a weeping nun, a shuffling old man, a priest, and a woman carrying a crucifix. Miss Freer allegedly saw a black dog in daylight, and it was also heard and touched by others in the house. A service of exorcism was later carried out and the hauntings ceased.

The above information is from an article by A E Graham which appeared in *The Scots Magazine* (March 1979). At the time of my visit to Ballechin I was unaware of the story. The modern wing of the house was occupied by Alasdair Steven, an antiquarian bookseller. The house was literally packed to the gunnels with books of every description. From Alasdair's study there was a splendid view over the pastoral landscape of Strathtay. Alasdair told me he had originally started out in the book trade by selling second-hand books with a bicycle as his mode of transport. Over a mug of tea and a sandwich, I listened to this thoughtful, humorous man discuss the subject of books, which he clearly loved, and later was allowed to browse around the packed shelves. The only phantom appeared to be a rogue mouse which had avoided the temptation of a nibble at some cheddar set in a trap.

From Ballechin I pedalled on by the north bank of the Tay. A little before Strathtay village, I parked the bike off the road and followed part of an ancient Pictish road, now a green way, which leads over the hills to Pitlochry. Bounded by broom bushes and drystane dykes, the route takes the form of a sunken road a short distance past Milton of Tullypowrie. About 300 yards north-west of the old steading at Tullypowrie there stands an intriguing cup-marked stone, popularly known as 'The Witchcraft Stone'.

Back in the village I bought a banana and some chocolate bars at the local shop. I asked the shopkeeper if he could tell me anything of note about Tullypowrie. He seemed to be rather embarrassed by the question and quickly changed the subject.

The houses in Strathtay had trim gardens and manicured hedges. It was a delightful place, although I was nearly gassed by the suffocating fumes from a mobile shop which chugged past me: a miracle on wheels. There followed a lovely old hump-backed bridge as the road curled down to within spitting distance of the river. Three fishing rods lay resting on the bank as the slow-moving water slid by like a liquid necklace of sun-kissed pearls, one minute silvery-white, the next, charcoal grey. Suddenly a red squirrel popped out in front of the bike and scampered up a tree.

The road looped round to Weem. At the junction with the B846 stands an early 19th-century tollhouse with a low, pitched roof and semi-octagonal bay window. I rode on by the Weem Hotel, which has an outside portrait of General Wade above a sign that correctly proclaims that he stayed here in 1733. That was the year when Wade oversaw the building of his best-known bridge, a beautiful five-arched structure designed by William Adam which spans the Tay at nearby Aberfeldy.

The B846 follows the approximate line of a section of Wade road which extended from Crieff to Dalnacardoch. A fine example of an estate dyke in dressed stone appeared on my right as I neared Castle Menzies, a large and impressive Z-plan tower house built in the 16th century and open to the public. I made a worthwhile detour to the curiously named hamlet of Dull, before embarking on the punishing climb from Coshieville to White Bridge, formerly an inn.

Just down from Tomphubil (the Knoll of the People), I forked left and cruised through woodland to Braes of Foss, the only dwelling in a scintillating five-mile stretch along the north slopes of Schiehallion, that most symmetrical of mountains which rises to over 3,500 feet. The panoramic views were superb and I felt on top of the world. The road then dropped dramatically through a beautiful stretch of deciduous trees as I pushed on to Kinloch Rannoch, a somewhat demure little place.

I drained a bottle of Lucozade. The low-lying lochside road took me through idyllic woodland; superb birches rose high above a carpet of green bracken, while a hovering mist laced the tops on the other side. Loch Rannoch itself was still and black. Directly across the loch, a cream-coloured van jinked through the appropriately named Black Wood of Rannoch. The throne belonged to Schiehallion, whose cone-like sides rose up into a dark curtain of cloud.

Upon nearing my night's destination, a gaggle of geese took off from the loch, the noise of their flapping wings sounding like polite applause from a theatre audience.

After a restless night without much sleep, I awoke at 7.30 a.m. The food and accommodation at the Talladh-A-Bheithe guesthouse had been the finest of the trip so far and I learned that they mostly catered for German visitors to Scotland. Apart from the rustle of leaves, the morning was deathly quiet; Loch Rannoch brooding in dark, shimmering folds of water. My head was down, legs pumping the pedals because I'd a train to catch at Rannoch Station.

At the west end of the loch I passed three men and a sheepdog huddled round a Land Rover. Another multi-chimneyed shooting lodge sat back from the road. As I ascended a sharp incline, a car had sneaked up on my tail, the driver loudly hooting his horn which nearly made me jump out of my skin. I was glad he found it funny.

The River Gaur looked well down on its normal level. I had only about four miles to go and was in good time for the 9.48 southbound train from Fort William. At this point the landscape resembled a barren rock basin and I couldn't figure out the line the road was going to take. The Gaur Dam suddenly came into view along with a subsidiary building which resembled a fort of the Foreign Legion. These were the lasting monuments to the large-scale hydro developments which were constructed in the 1920s and '30s. I could not help but reflect on the working conditions for the navvies – a considerable number of whom were migrant Irishmen – who toiled with pick and shovel amidst such a scene of desolation.

The end of the road was soon in sight, a few houses, a hotel with its curtains drawn, and the lime green buildings of Rannoch Station. First impressions were that I had come upon some outpost in the Klondike.

Rannoch Station was in a class of its own. Hanging baskets of flowers were a colourful and thoughtful addition to the station platform. A cheery open fire glowed in the ticket office where a buffet-car steward sat on one side of an old-fashioned range, his black bow-tie the crowning touch to what could have been a scene out of the Victorian era. I purchased my £2.10 single for the short hop across roadless Rannoch Moor to Tyndrum. An elderly couple from the Home Counties followed in turn to purchase their tickets to London. The man's expressionless face was like a slab of cement and he talked down to Donnie, who was behind the small glass window of the ticket office, in a 'frightfully' condescending manner. After a communication breakdown over the correct change, the matter was diplomatically resolved by Donnie. Both parties seemed glad to see the back of one another. It had been an interesting interlude, a real culture clash between Donnie's softly spoken Highland manner and the abrupt 'touch your cap when speaking to me' attitude of the man from Kent.

The station clock was time perfect. My train was six minutes late. Time was meaningless here in any event. Bells rang and there was a sudden flurry of activity as the train came to a juddering halt alongside the platform. It was a real train, with a real engine, not one of those awful toy sprinters with 'power units' rather than real engines. I found the guard's van at the end of the train and walked back along the narrow corridor to find a seat. The separate compartments were straight out of *The Thirty-Nine Steps*: long springy seats facing one another, net luggage racks, mirrors with the words 'British Rail' engraved on the glass, and a steam heating-system. The train was packed with a cosmopolitan blend of young backpackers. In one compartment a small, fat man in a tweed suit was seated opposite some spiky-haired, giggling girls wearing the latest way-out fashions. I sat opposite a poker-faced gent in a blue cagoule who was immune to passing the time of day. Out of the window a large group of deer were slowly moving over the moor, occasionally pausing to sniff the wind and peer nonchalantly across at the iron monster in their midst.

I left the compartment and headed for the buffet car where I bought a cup of tea. The train swung round the horse-shoe curve under Beinn Dorain, the 3,523-foot mountain immortalised in Gaelic literature by Duncan 'Ban' MacIntyre. There were spectacular views of its wild corries spliced with near vertical runs of scree and rock, which hung below wisps of slow-moving mist that heralded a change in the weather. A Cockney passenger commented 'The train's been the best part of me 'oliday,' and this was doubtless no overstatement.

Soon we arrived at Tyndrum's upper station. I battled with the guard's van door handle and eventually the heavy door swung open. On paper there was a minute between making my connection with the Oban train at Tyndrum Low.

A steep, rocky track led down to the main A82 where I flew past a large white hotel and down a side-road leading to the hut on the tiny platform. I thought that possibly the Oban train would be running late as well, but a passing hill walker shouted over that the train had departed two minutes ago.

The next train was hours away. There was nothing for it but to pedal on to the next station, Dalmally. I should have disembarked at Bridge of Orchy and ridden down Glen Orchy, a quieter route. Traffic on the Oban road was fast and furious, cars flying past in groups of four or five at a time. I had to keep my wits about me and was making good progress when suddenly a Cortina swung out to overtake from the opposite direction, forcing me to slam on the brakes and lean into the verge for safety. For one long moment I thought my cycling days were about to be prematurely ended. The maniac in the Cortina had missed me by about 18 inches: too close for comfort. Nervous energy fuelled my legs as I picked up the pace once more.

On a fast downhill stretch I could see I was heading for a drooking as heavy rain-laden clouds lumbered across the sky. Sure enough, these opened directly overhead in a torrent of wind-driven rain more like a monsoon. I had only been some two miles from Dalmally but by the time I reached the village I was thoroughly drenched.

After sheltering for a spell in a beercan-strewn bus-stop I decided that my first priority was a hot drink. A damp chill was permeating my bones. I pedalled the short distance to the local hotel and dripped my way forward to the reception desk. My request for a pot of coffee was answered by a dark-haired sardine of a fellow: 'A *pot* of coffee!' he sneered, looking me up and down. 'I'm the manager and am the only one allowed a cup of coffee in this hotel.' My face betrayed no hint of despair. I simply turned on my sodden boots and walked straight out. Figures were darting out from the public bar and sprinting towards a waiting coach where heads bobbed up from inside jackets. I rode on a short distance, and round a corner came upon the sight of marquees, cars, lorries, a television van and a disgruntled policeman who was directing traffic. He waved me on as most of the traffic was turning right into the showground.

It was 11.30 a.m. and the next train was not until 2.40 p.m. At the station I dried my head with a towel beside some other cyclists who were in a similarly moist condition, all complaining of the weather. At a small service station nearby, I was grateful to find a vending machine which sold cups of instant soup. I must have had about three before I felt half-human again. Heading round to the post-office I bought some chocolate and enquired if there were any locals who were knowledgeable about earlier times in the area.

Unannounced, I called on retired farmer Iain McVean who lived a short distance away at Stronmilichan. Iain was born in 1907. He seemed flattered that his name had been suggested and kindly invited me inside his bungalow, offering to help in any way he could. I asked him if he could recall any of the old-style tramps who used to come through this neck of the woods. 'There was an old man went round every fortnight to three weeks and they called him 'Go East' because he always went the same way to Dalmally, and you never saw him coming back. We think he went through Glencoe and back down by Appin. It took him about a fortnight and he came all year round. He stayed at various crofters' houses and would help if there was any work to be done, like putting in the hay.' Iain could recall quite a few gangrels who used to tramp the old Stronmilichan road and the short time I spent with him passed very quickly.

I headed back to the station, and along with another cyclist crossed over the track to the platform on the other side. There was that familiar shunting sound as the engine and carriages pulled to a halt. There were already a number of cycles in the guard's van but I managed to find a space. My travelling companion told me of his pleasure in forsaking the streets of London for the peace and tranquillity of the West Highlands. He was headed for Iona.

Rain streaked the windows of the carriage as we headed west. Despite the conditions, Loch Awe looked exceptionally beautiful, even mysterious in a romantic sort of way. The green isle of Lismore and the rising hills of Mull shortly came into view. At last, the train took the long sweep into Oban. I had arrived. The east-west crossing of Scotland was now behind me. Ahead lay the expectation of the Uists. It would be a different world on the edge of the Atlantic.

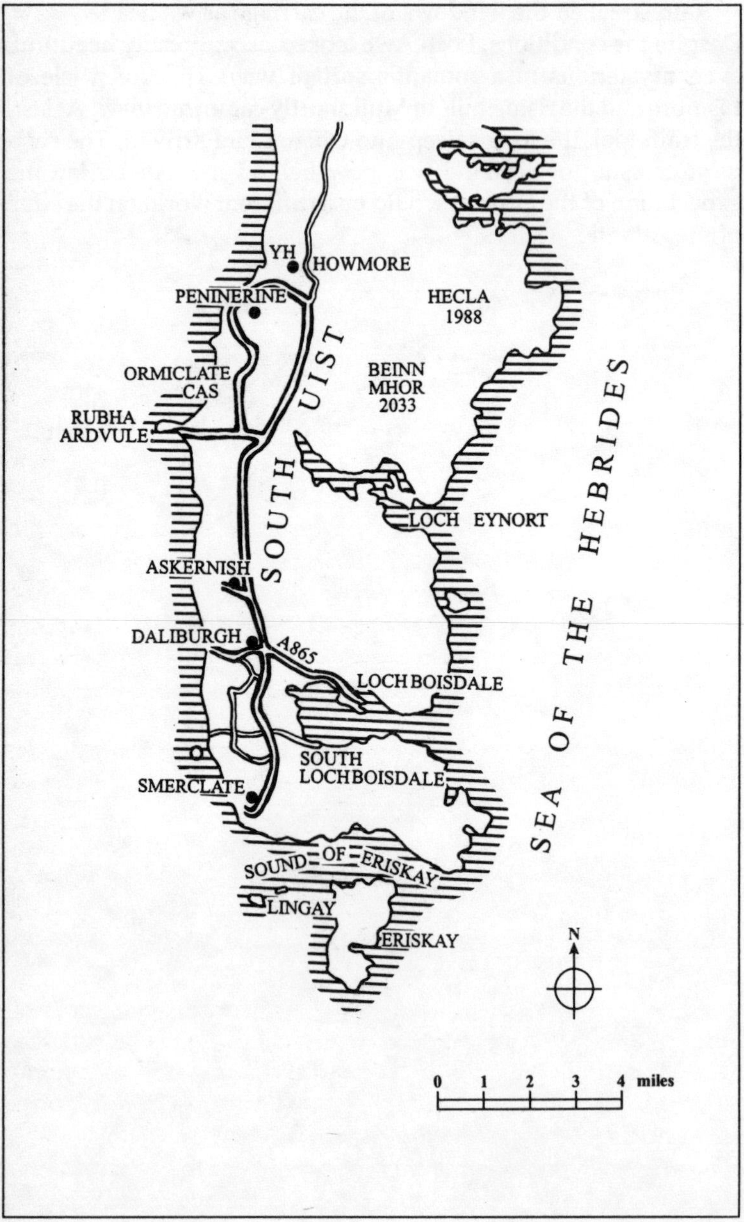
YH
HOWMORE
PENINERINE
HECLA
1988
ORMICLATE
CAS
BEINN
MHOR
2033
SOUTH UIST
RUBHA
ARDVULE
SEA OF THE HEBRIDES
LOCH EYNORT
ASKERNISH
DALIBURGH
A865
LOCHBOISDALE
SOUTH
LOCHBOISDALE
SMERCLATE
SOUND OF ERISKAY
LINGAY
ERISKAY
N
0 1 2 3 4 miles

CHAPTER 6

The Lure of South Uist

The old storytelling people
have gone home to their last
houses
under the acres of a lost
music.
These have all been sold now
to suave strangers with soft
voices.

Iain Crichton Smith, 'No Return',
The Exiles, 1984.

I HAD THOUGHT the ferry sailed for Lochboisdale, South Uist at half-past midnight on the Sunday. Instead it did not leave Oban until around 3 p.m. on the Monday, thus giving me nearly two whole days of rest, which was very welcome. I was able to telephone my friend and contact on Uist, Joe O'Donnell, who taught geography at Daliburgh School. He had the names of some informants and his local knowledge would greatly ease my path in this, a land-working and crofting community where Gaelic is still the first language.

Oban is rightly proud of its title as 'Gateway to the Western Isles'. It provides the mainland terminal for ferry sailings to Barra, Coll, Colonsay, Lismore, Mull, Tiree and South Uist. I was booked on the longest crossing; just how long was something I was about to find out.

I had previously sailed to Tiree but nothing could have prepared me for the tedium of a nine and a half hour voyage to Lochboisdale. Much of the time I spent in the lounge bar, talking to an older man who smoked heavily and drank large whiskies. I nearly fell over with astonishment when he told me what he did for a living – chest consultant! After a long haul the fairy lights of Castlebay, Barra, broke the darkness. There was great excitement at the pier as friends embraced one another and vehicles of every shape and size trundled off the Cal-Mac ferry. The arrival of the ferry is always an event in island life. Next stop was Lochboisdale.

After what seemed like an eternity we eventually arrived. It had gone half-past midnight and Joe was there to greet me as I wheeled the red machine out of the gaping mouth of the car-deck. We had a lot of news to catch up on and it was great to see a familiar face once again.

Looking back at the ferry, it seemed to be enormous in its island surroundings, whereas at Oban, the boat seemed dwarfed by the built-up sweep of the town which overlooks the bay. Here, only a few pinpricks of light came from the Lochboisdale Hotel and scattered houses, whereas the ferry was fully lit.

Once the main flow of cars had headed off into the night, Joe drove behind me, the headlights of his car helping to illuminate the lonely road to Askernish, our destination. The ride was slightly uphill all the way but this spin through the night was accomplished in only about 20 minutes or so. What I recall most was the pungent smell of peat smoke wafting up from some of the island homes. That and the stillness were my lasting impressions of South Uist on this starless night. I recalled how an islander from Scalpay, Harris, had told me that the two most memorable aspects of his first visit to the mainland were of seeing a horse and a train, and of the two, the horse made the bigger impact.

After a night spent talking and drinking into the early hours, I awoke feeling not at my best. It was strange to open the curtains of a modern kit-built 'semi' and look out on the bare and treeless wastes of South Uist, so reminiscent of Connemara, the barren coastal region of West Ireland. Joe had left for school. There was a list of provisions for me to obtain in Daliburgh, the nearest place of any size and just a short ride away on the bike.

After the unseen, unheard overnight rain, the bumpy single-track road was holding pools of water in places. I emptied my panniers and started out under an enormous Uist sky, breathing in large gulps of the fresh morning air. As I was pedalling fast down a gradual brae, the rear wheel suddenly locked and I went into a long unforced skid which left a 30-foot black line on the tarmac. My right pannier had been chewed up between the top of the wheel and the pannier rack. In the process I had written off my rear mudguard and lost a fair amount of tread from the back tyre. That apart, the damage was not of a serious nature.

As I was attempting to untangle the mangled pannier, a man wandered over from a nearby house and kindly enquired if everything was alright. Shortly another man was on the scene and enquired as to what had happened. 'You chose a good place to have an accident since you're very near the hospital,' he remarked.

After we had been chatting for a few minutes, I learned that the second man was a lobster fisherman. He had a proper screwdriver back in his shed and kindly offered to help with repairs. We wheeled the bike up to a black shed beside a house overlooking the road. Colourful lobster creels were piled up outside the shed, mostly of a modern type, although I noticed an older type of creel beside a rusty plough. 'We can't get suitable rods on the island and have to import them from Inverness,' said the fisherman in reply to my question.

Some other men shortly arrived to start work on mending the damaged creels. We passed round cigarettes while a man with a few days' growth on his face assisted my friend in tightening a nut which was out of range for my own bike spanner.

'Where will you be staying?' enquired the fisherman.

'With Joe the school teacher,' I replied.

The penny immediately dropped and the crack became more lively and spiced with jokes.

'That should be seeing you alright,' said the fisherman on completing the repair.

'I'm on my way to see John MacInnes in Daliburgh. Do you know him?'

'Ah yes, everyone knows *Iain Phedair* – he's a great one for the yarning.'

I thanked the fisherman for all his assistance. My first contact with Uist folk had been one of genuine warmth and friendship. Upon reaching Daliburgh I called at the well-stocked Co-op and purchased butcher meat, vegetables, and a number of tins. The total bill was £11, considerably more expensive than what I would have paid on the mainland.

My second port of call was the Old Schoolhouse, the home of

John MacInnes. Joe had told me that this man had an immense knowledge of family trees and the old ways connected with island life. I was excited at the prospect of meeting him but there was no answer to my knock at the door.

On my return to Askernish I passed the fishermen, one of whom waved me over to the shed where the men were still busy at the creels. A large bag of new potatoes was generously handed over to me and I was astounded when one of the younger men offered to take these and the rest of my load up to 'Spam City' as he called the new houses in Askernish.

In the early afternoon I set out once more for John MacInnes' house. Since the last of the great traditional storytellers (or *shennachies*) had long since gone to their graves, it was not so much tales I hoped to collect as information on the folklore collectors themselves. Even this type of material was in danger of being lost due to the passage of time. In particular, I wanted to gather reminiscences of Calum Maclean who died in South Uist in 1960 and was probably the greatest collector of traditional material to work in the Gaidhealtachd.

Calum was a man of the people of Raasay – *Fear a mhuinntir Ratharsaigh* – a small island off the south-west coast of Skye. One of his brothers is the great Gaelic poet, Sorley Maclean. Calum had been trained as a folklore collector under the auspices of the Irish Folklore Commission, in particular benefiting from the skill and knowledge of Seán Ó Súilleabháin. As well as collecting previously unrecorded material in the field, Calum also worked as a cataloguer in the IFC archives in Dublin. In the mid-1940s he set out to collect material on his native Raasay. The School of Scottish Studies (of which Calum and Hamish Henderson were two of the co-founders) was not set up until 1951, and the task of preserving Scottish material had been carried out by full-time collectors such as John Lorne Campbell of Canna and his wife Margaret Fay Shaw.

From Raasay Calum went to the isles of Eigg and Canna, being generously assisted by John Lorne Campbell on the latter, before arriving in South Uist and Benbecula in 1947. There he worked for almost a year and a half, concentrating his efforts on salvaging the vast fund of stories belonging to two giants of the storytelling world – Angus ('Barrach') MacMillan of Griminish, Benbecula, and

Duncan MacDonald of Peninerine, South Uist. Both these custodians of traditional Gaelic tales were to die in 1954, but not before Calum Maclean had managed to extensively record much of their repertoire.

This time there was a car in the drive of the Old Schoolhouse. The door was opened by a bear of a man with large hands, an inviting open face and kindly eyes almost hidden under large bushy eyebrows. That was my first impression of John MacInnes. In a soft, lilting voice he quietly invited me indoors having immediately twigged the purpose of my call. Big John was used to having strangers call on him from 'aa the airts' in order to tap his remarkable memory for people, songs, customs, boats, superstitions: you name it and he knew about it.

John told me that he had just returned from Birmingham with his wife Mary, who suffered back trouble and had required to consult specialists. My apologies for pouncing on them so soon after their return were brushed aside by John who seemed keen to recall Calum Maclean and his collecting.

'Calum Maclean was all things to all men,' John began. 'Nobody disliked Calum. He would turn up at ceilidhs and tell stories – he had a tremendous knowledge of the words of songs and he certainly knew a lot of the old stuff off by heart, which was a good introduction.'

'I think it was in the early '50s that he arrived at my house. It was a cold dreich day and he came with Seamus Innes. I soon realised that Calum was going to work in the style of the earlier collectors for he did not come with a tape recorder but wrote down what he heard in small neat writing. I myself did some collecting and one of the songs I got had been earlier collected by [Alexander] Carmichael, 40 years before. It was word for word perfect and the bard had never written it down.... There were some tradition-bearers that Calum missed because he didn't have time to get round everyone. He died you know, in Uist here. It was in the Bute Hospital, now the Daliburgh Hospital, which was administered by the nuns of the Sacred Heart Order, and even in his last days Calum would still be asking us the questions when we went round to visit him.'

I asked John what Calum had been interested in. 'He was interested in songs as well as stories, and the variants of songs.

Some people think that variants of songs are nuisances, but they aren't – no more than different faces are nuisances.'

When he was talking, John fixed you with his gaze, as though he could almost tell the story with his eyes. His large hands resembled shovels and he gestured with them every now and again to reinforce points of speech. Sometimes during our talk, John would stand out of his seat and literally put his back into what he was narrating or singing. Song seemed to be an important part of his being. He was entertainer and sage: a man one doesn't meet every day.

John told me that Calum Maclean was buried in Hallan cemetery which was over by the machair land and could be easily reached by bike. He also gave me the name of a surviving bard in Uist, and another on Eriskay. Before I pedalled off into the afternoon breeze I thanked John and Mary for their hospitality and said I would gladly take up their offer of another visit.

A single-track road threaded its way past croft houses, with the brooding hills of South Uist forming the backdrop to the north-east. On the way to Hallan a clearer picture of the island revealed itself, but the dominating factor was the unending stretch of sky. It was altogether a different world from the mainland; the language of the people was as different as the language of the land; there was space, acres of light, and a certain timelessness about each day.

The sloping burial-ground of Hallan was hidden from the sea by large dunes. It took me quite a bit of searching before I came upon Calum's gravestone, roughly in the middle of the cemetery, located near the brow of a slope. The stone was in the form of a Celtic cross on a granite base and bore the words:

CALUM IAIN MACLEAN M.A.; LL.D
CELTIC SCHOLAR AND FOLKLORIST
BORN IN RAASAY 6–9–1915
DIED IN DALIBURGH 16–8–1960

Below this were two lines in Gaelic: *'Bidh sinne 'n ad dheidh, Gad mholadh 's tu fein 's an uir'* (We will be left behind praising you and yourself in the dust).

On leaving the grave and walking down to the cemetery gate, I met a white-haired man in the company of a girl. He stopped to smile and say, 'I see you've been visiting Calum's grave – are you a relative or a friend?' I told him I was a postgraduate student at the School of Scottish Studies and briefly mentioned the type of work I was doing in Uist. We chatted for several minutes and I discovered that the man was a brother of Calum's, now a doctor in Bridge-of-Weir.

Back in Askernish I spent a quiet evening with Joe, writing up my notes in between reading Patrick Kavanagh's *The Green Fool*, a collection of beautifully written and amusing autobiographical sketches which capture the essence of former Irish rural life.

Earlier that evening, Joe and I had driven down to the pub at Pollachar in the southern part of the island. The bar was empty when we got there but several male patrons, all on their own, arrived at intervals and departed after consuming their drinks at lightning speed.

The proprietor was a cheery, fresh-complexioned man called Donnie MacNeil. He recalled the first time he'd met Calum Maclean was at the house of Calum Johnston [the Barra piper and singer, 1891–1972]. Donnie's first impression of Calum Maclean was that he was somewhat dour, until he suddenly burst into song.

It was Donnie who suggested I contact Alan and Jane Gillies, two elderly stalwarts who lived in a thatched house at nearby Smerclate. We left the bar and duly arrived at the elderly couple's door. 84-year-old Jane invited us to take a seat inside and mentioned that she was not a South Uist woman, but was originally from Earsary on Barra. After a short chat it was agreed that I should return to see the couple the following day, when they would try and answer my questions.

The following morning resembled night rather than day. I delayed my start but still had to contend with wind-driven rain which turned the five-mile journey into a real slog. At the top of the Garrynamonie hill I halted for a brief rest opposite a strikingly modern Roman Catholic church with a strangely angular roof. Successive winter gales had battered the external mosaics; the entire concept of this building was imaginative but its architecture was hardly suited to Hebridean climes.

Rain was literally bouncing off the road as I continued on a long descent to Smerclate. Thoroughly soaked by this time, I turned in off the road and ploutered my way through a muddy path past sodden bog-irises which led from a red telephone kiosk to the Gillies' house.

I knocked at the open blue door, then Jane's voice came ringing out – 'Come in!' As I stepped by their sullen-looking collie stretched out on the floor, it gave a low-pitched growl as if to say 'I'm the boss here, mate'. Fresh peats had not yet taken hold on the fire as I passed into the living room with its low ceiling, linoleum-covered floor and single deep-set window in the front wall. It was such a dark morning that the electric light had to be switched on. Mrs Gillies took my soaked jersey and hung it on a rail over the fire, commenting on 'this terrible weather' as she did so. Husband Alan kindly got out of his favourite seat to let me nearer the fire which now had a welcoming glow starting to appear. Pulling out his pipe with its briar bowl, the old man sent a thick cloud of smoke out of the corner of his mouth and turned to face the window. The two-roomed thatched house had no toilet and was furnished in a basic, unpretentious manner; besides, it was the people that mattered more than what their home seemed to represent to an outsider.

I gave Alan back his seat and sat by the window with my notebook on my knee. Alan told me he was born in Glasgow in 1896 but had moved to Uist when he was two years of age. He told me he'd been a merchant-seaman, a popular job with Hebrideans, and had been on the Donaldson line when the people had emigrated from the Uists to Canada during the early 1920s. Alan's watery-soft eyes were tinged with an air of quiet dignity, if not distance, as he recalled former times in Uist: the old lobster boats with their lug-sails, horse fairs at Ormiclate, gathering tangle off the shore and burning it for kelp, scavenging for driftwood, and the plundering of the famous cargo on board the SS *Politician* which sank in the Sound of Eriskay during 1941.

By this time Jane had produced a small cassette-recorder with an external microphone. I was able to stop writing and record instead. As a young woman Jane had followed the herring to various far-flung parts of the British Isles. She worked as a gutter and her terrier-like eyebrows straightened as she told me: 'At Yarmouth we used to be out at six o'clock in the morning. There was ice in the tubs and we had to break the ice with our hands before we could start to gut. It was awful hard work. After the season finished we used to search for domestic jobs until the next season would start.'

In Lerwick the girls stayed in wooden huts at the fishing, three of them sharing one bed. The season in Shetland lasted six to eight weeks, and during slack periods the girls used to entertain themselves with the communal singing of Gaelic songs. They also sang while they worked, and a marvellous spirit of togetherness prevailed. The fisher girls would try and save a few pounds to take back home, and they also bought presents for their families: 'Wee gifts, especially dishes. And they were nice shops in Lowestoft but they had the habit of putting up the prices when the herring girls went down. I remember that fine.'

'Did you ever ask the curers for a rise in pay?' I asked.

'Yes, we did complain. We had threepence an hour and were wanting another penny, but they wouldn't give it to us. The foreman put the bloody hose on us: drenched us with cold water. I remember that right enough. That was the penny we got!'

'Did your mother ever work at the gutting in Barra?'

'Oh my, she was at the gutting every time it was on. The Education Authority was giving the privilege of holidays from the tenth of May, so that the mothers could go to the fishing. Those children of a reasonable age would watch the household. I remember it fine – the boats starting on the tenth of May and the women, they walked miles and miles, starting first thing in the morning. They had to be up at the stations at maybe six o'clock. We were complaining about the hard work but they had a damn sight worse.'

Earlier I had peeped out the window and spotted the hunched figure of a man making his way through the almost horizontal rain, leading a fawn-coloured heifer by a rope. Jane told me he was a crofter from Eriskay on his way to try and sell his beast at the cattle sale which was being held today at Boisdale. Late in the afternoon the same man and his beast returned; he had obviously failed to strike a bargain.

All day the weather remained dismal. Occasionally I would peer out of the tiny window to inspect the weather, but the rain persisted. It was cosy and warm in the small room and just before lunch, Jane announced 'We are not going to treat you as a stranger'. She allowed me to fetch in peats for the fire but insisted on hobbling back and forward in preparing the table for our meal. It was a splendid spread: bacon and eggs, pancakes, bread and butter, washed down by lashings of sweet tea. Jane in her spirited way made light of such hospitality and kept up a periodic banter with 'the old man by the fire', while Alan sat, pipe in mouth, with a congenial expression on his face.

Later in the afternoon an elderly visitor hirpled into the house along with her nurse. Jane started ranting about the new doctor, sentiments about his lack of a bedside manner being echoed by the visitor. The other main item of conversation was the cattle sale. Alan seemed slightly miffed that his own cattle were to be sold on the mainland rather than the island.

Jane was keen to hear her voice played back on the tape-recorder, calling out to Alan 'Hear this!' – but Alan had left his seat and wandered outside to attend to the call of nature. I decided to leave the couple to their visitors and warmly thanked them for their kindness and patience. It had been a memorable few hours.

Next morning was bright, with scattered showers and a blustery wind. Nothing is more lovely than the islands in a shifting dapple of sun and rain when every colour seems alive. I set out on the 20-mile round trip to Peninerine, in Gaelic, *Peighinn-nan-Aoreann*, the Pennyland of the Herdsman or Shepherds or those who write satires. According to Big John MacInnes, the place-name has a number of interpretations, but the last seemed more appropriate because I was on my way to meet Donald John MacDonald, son of the great storyteller Duncan MacDonald, and the last in line of a hereditary family of bards.

The main north-south island road overlooked places such as Frobost, Milton, and Kildonan with its deserted glen; at first sight the lack of townships gives South Uist a somewhat deserted look, but this is soon lost after some exploring is undertaken on the west side. It was an easy climb up the shoulder of Ben Corary where I paused to view the serene beauty of the landscape, stark and treeless, a contrast of low-lying lochans and rising hills, the great open expanse of space on the western side being broken by scattered houses and the static army of telephone poles.

I struck off the main route and headed down by Bornish, past the ruined Ormiclate Castle, and round by Stoneybridge where the road loops round by the Atlantic shore. The waters of the great ocean were rumbling over the shingle at Croic a Peninerine, close to the remains of about half a dozen turf bothies formerly used on a seasonal basis by visiting lobster fishermen.

Donald John's two-storeyed house was set back from the road, a blue Mini standing outside. The door was open. With the bike on my shoulder, I walked up the grassy track which led to the house. It was Mrs MacDonald who answered my knock, a small bespectacled lady with a quiet demeanour; the bard had not yet surfaced, but after a short interval he emerged through the open door, tugging on a jersey over his ruffled hair. I stood up from the sofa and said 'I believe you know John MacInnes from the School of Scottish Studies in Edinburgh. I'm a student there.' His face broke into a large smile and I detected an impish twinkle in his eyes at the mention of John's name.

Donald John had a certain relaxed modesty about him. He had a considerable reputation as a local bard and had won the bardic crown at the National Mod in 1948. He had three Gaelic books to his name, one of them being an account of his experiences in a German POW camp. During the 1950s he had worked as a collector for the School, producing a large manuscript collection of South Uist tradition, much of it noted from his father and other relatives.

Once more I was fortunate in that Donald John had a small cassette-recorder which he produced for our interview. One of his uncles had been a joiner in Uist and Donald John explained the uses and value attached to driftwood in the old days. Large planks washed ashore were used in the joists of houses, or sawn into suitable lengths for wooden ploughs, carts, and wheelbarrows. 'They used to get the wood for coffins from the shop, but before my uncle's time they used to make the coffins out of the wood that was being washed ashore.'

On a different tack, I asked Donald John if he could tell me something of the early collectors of old stories who used to come and visit his father.

'Well I think the earliest one I can remember was KC Craig. That was just after the war. He used to come here during the war but I wasn't at home at the time. He released a book about my father's tales – *Sgialachdan Dhunnchaidh* it was called. And he published a book about an old lady from Snishival, about all the old waulking songs. He wrote all those long tales from my father by longhand.'

'Did you have a chance to watch this process?'

'Oh yes, I saw him sitting at the end of the table with the pen. He used to get writer's cramp in his hand and stretch his hand like that [extending the fingers back and forward]. My father's tales would take a couple of hours. If he couldn't finish one tale in the one night he had to carry on the next night. He would be writing for about, say, three or four hours at a time. My father used to tell Craig and everybody that his tales were tales that his father used to recite at home when they were young and he just memorised them.'

'Do you recall the type of stories he related?'

'The type of stories he had were the old, old ones. You see they sometimes pertained to Greece, the King of Greece and the King of Ireland. There were lots and lots about the King of Norway. I suppose that was pretty natural because of the Vikings and the Norsemen being out in the Hebrides here. I believe that's where the tales started.'

'Moving on, who followed the collector Craig?'

'I think the next one was Calum – Calum Maclean. John Lorne Campbell of Canna used to come round. I just saw him once or twice, but Calum was really the next one that came along. The first time I saw him was round about '49. I think the School of Scottish Studies wasn't even formed when he came round here. I think he was working for the Irish Folklore Commission at the time and my father was giving him the tales.'

'I could see he was completely different from Craig. His method of talking to people was different from Craig. Craig was more-or-less abrupt; his manner was more-or-less abrupt. But Calum had a certain flair, you see, for talking to people and putting them at their ease. Whenever Calum went into a house, even if you never saw him in your life before that – just about three or four minutes and he would just be like a neighbour. He would talk to you just like somebody who drops in every day. That's the kind of man he was as far as I can remember.'

'You mentioned something earlier, to do with the old type of recording machines?'

'Oh yes. That was in the late 1940s some time. It was Derick

Thomson along with Campbell of Canna. They came and recorded my father here. As far as I can remember they were working the machine from a car battery. The car was so many yards from the house and the cable was drawn from there to the machine inside the house because there was no electricity at that time. It was a wire recorder as far as I remember.'

'Donald, regarding the old traditions – the songs, the stories, the poems – do you feel there should be an opening in the education syllabus of local schools in the Hebrides for reintroducing some of these stories and songs?'

'It would really be a good thing, right enough, but I don't think there's any chance at all of it ever happening in the Western Isles anyway. I don't think Comhairle Nan Eilean would ever think of doing such a thing. But it would be one way of preserving something of the old culture of the place and of the Highlands.'

'And would bolster the language?'

'Oh, it would bolster the language. Yes it would.'

It is impossible to say exactly how old Duncan MacDonald's hero-tales are, but they are very old indeed, the remnants of a once great oral tradition. The Hebrides were in fact under Norse rule from AD 880 to 1266, when as a result of the Battle of Largs they were ceded to the Crown of Scotland.

Duncan MacDonald maintained that the disappearance of the blackhouse, with its central open fire on the floor, was one of the very important factors leading to the demise of storytelling and ceilidhing in his district. Traditional storytelling sessions did not suddenly die out but gradually decayed from about the 1860s. According to Donald Archie MacDonald, Deputy Director of the School of Scottish Studies: 'The crucial dividing line was World War One – for a number of reasons. Firstly the number of young men killed in action cast a general gloom over the communities. Those who returned from the trenches started going to the cities for work and one can really say that ceilidhing never recovered from the War.'

Born in 1917, Donald John was taken prisoner at St Valery in 1940 and never fully recovered from his five years in Nazi labour camps. In his book *Fo Sgàil a Swastika* [Under the Shadow of the Swastika] he wrote: 'A man's life had no more value at that time than that of a fly that you would squash when it landed on your nose.' Before I left Peninerine, Donald John recited in Gaelic his poem about the deserted township of Snishival. Donald John MacDonald sadly passed away in the autumn of 1987. His was one of the many welcomes I will not forget.

The wind filled out my blue jacket as I took the magical road that twists round to Howbeg with its magnificent view of the South Uist hills: Hecla, Ben Corodale, and Beinn Mhor. Across the wind-ruffled waters of Loch Roag stood the silent ruins of Snishival where the old storytellers had lived. There is not a finer view in South Uist than the view from this road.

With the wind at my tail I passed the old market stance at Loch Ollay. Workmen were engaged in road-widening operations as I felt pellets of mud splatter on the back of my windcheater; the lack of a rear mudguard was being sorely missed. The roadworks had chewed up part of the old market stance and the land was exposed as dripping peat by the excavations of a bulldozer. Once past the crossroads I forked right and back along the narrow pot-holed road which takes one by Bornish Church and out to Rubha Ardvule. The birdlife was superb: lapwings, mallards, mute swans, oyster catchers, plovers and tufted ducks.

Here are to be found the hollowed-out ruins of about 20 turf huts which formerly served as seasonal hovels for kelp-burners, winkle-pickers and later, lobster fishermen. The promontory of Rubha Ardvule collects a tremendous amount of seaweed and the Uist people formerly paid rent to the estate by way of kelp production. Although seaweed can be collected all-year round, it can only be burnt to kelp in the summer months. The bothies were communal property, used by landless cottars from the southern parts of South Uist.

The ruins of these sunken remains all face east, the traditional direction of the old houses in South Uist. The huts were dug out of the blown sand on the machair, had internal walls and entrances faced with rounded shore boulders lined with turf; roofs were of driftwood covered with sods. Some of the structures had a chimney vent made from sawn pieces of driftwood, nailed together to form a square cube without ends. Entrance was gained through small wooden doors and the people had to stoop to enter. The earliest huts probably date from about the 1830s when Lower Bornish was cleared to make way for a sheepfarm. The kelp-burners stopped using them about the onset of the Great War, although some were in later use by lobster fishermen who carried on the tradition of occupying seasonal dwellings until their sail boats were replaced by boats with engines – about the late 1930s.

With the blustery wind tugging at my clothes and hair, I left this forlorn scene and strolled over to view the heaving surf of the Atlantic as it rushed into the beach. The roads through the machair rarely intrude on the privacy of the whiteshell sands and so offer few glimpses of the Atlantic waves. I stood and watched the sea, its rolling contours hypnotic to the eye. There was a tremendous sense of power, a raw unharnessed energy which at the same time was soothing and offered a chance of contemplation without disturbance from other people or machines.

Friday was a short day as far as cycling went. In the late morning I visited a well-known Uist piper, Angus Campbell of Frobost, the nephew of another outstanding storyteller, the late Angus MacLellan. Frobost lies immediately north of Askernish so it was a short and easy ride. Most places are well signposted in Gaelic. Angus's gate was secured by orange twine and as I was fiddling with this, I noticed an elderly man with a roundish frame hovering about a shed. Angus approached me and as he came nearer I could see he possessed an interesting weather-beaten face with traces of a white whiskery growth. He was hard of hearing and I'd to repeat myself a few times until he got the gist of what I had come to see him about. Once it clicked that I was interested in his reminiscences of Calum Maclean he said 'Yes yes' and led me into the kitchen of his home.

Angus's wife Marybelle was busy kneading dough. The smell of home-baking permeated the room. She greatly eased the communication difficulties, jocularly hinting that I would have to learn some Gaelic. I detected that Angus was not entirely at ease speaking English. Seated at the kitchen table, Angus recalled (with the help of Marybelle): 'Calum Bheag [Calum Maclean's byname] would come up to this house to listen to pipe tunes. He often wore the kilt. Very often he came on foot, but his brother Alasdair, the doctor, would drop him off on his rounds – where he wanted to go.

He was a very humorous man, but he could be a very serious man too; also a far-seeing man.'

'Calum always came on his own to see my uncle and my mother, Marianne MacLellan. He took stories from my mother but it was my uncle Angus who got all the credit. The collectors all had their own clients. Peter Terence McGauchie, an Irish professor, came over for four or five years, backwards and forwards to record Peter MacInnes and Neil Walker of Bornish. At first, about 1950, he came on a bike and then later returned with a van and the recording machine. Peter had every island's Gaelic and really was a smart person. None of them were that interested in piping – it was all stories.'

The principal tool of the early collectors of the Irish Folklore Commission was the Ediphone recording machine. It was bulky, weighing over 50 lb., and recorded sound on fragile wax cylinders. At the time it was a great advance in recording long folktales. In the early days, cylinders were recycled after the material had been transcribed. It might take two or three hours, sometimes longer, to record an average length story.

Collectors were also instructed by the Commission to write verbatim the material they had recorded in octavo notebooks which were later bound. In addition, collectors were required to keep a diary, noting their movements and information about the informants themselves. For the period Calum Maclean worked in Scotland for the Irish Folklore Commission, his diaries alone fill five bound volumes (over 2,000 pages), and the lore which he collected is bound in 19 volumes, comprising over 9,000 manuscript pages. Originally he was supplied with an Ediphone machine, similar to those used by collectors in Ireland, as well as wax cylinders, which he regularly sent to Dublin together with the transcriptions.

It is a sad, if not tragic, indictment of the attitude of those running Scotland's universities that they neglected the task of preserving what remained of Scotland's traditional oral culture until the School of Scottish Studies was founded on paper in 1951 as part of Edinburgh University. This was years after countries such as Sweden and Ireland had taken the lead. In its earliest days the school erased some of Calum's tapes after transcription, but it was Hamish Henderson who made a stand against the erasing of any field materials.

In 1948 Calum Maclean had acted as native guide to the distinguished Swedish ethnologist Åke Campbell, on the second of his fieldwork trips to the Hebrides. He accompanied Campbell for the duration of his visit and kept detailed notes, being of invaluable assistance in recording Gaelic terminology.

The Hebrides had become the Gaelic heartland, an area where virtually everyone was a Gaelic speaker, some of the older people knowing only a few words of English. Despite the lack of so-called formal education, the Gaelic world was a functioning whole, though being nibbled away by the gradual intrusion of mainstream popular culture which was emerging in the 1950s. There were still many priceless oral treasures to be salvaged.

The highpoint of Calum Maclean's collecting was probably the mid-1950s when he was working as a full-time collector for the school. Francis Collinson, writing in *Tocher* 39 (1985), recalled:

> 'In those days we used Ferrographs for recording. These were great, clumsy, heavy brutes of machines weighing half a hundredweight. One of my abiding memories of Calum, who was a small man, was to see him staggering under the weight of a recording machine that looked nearly half as big as himself, as he set off on foot across the heather-clad moorland to record some informants he had in line.'

But as Hamish Henderson has often stated, the power of the tape recorder does not lie solely in preserving the spoken word, but in the dissemination of the culture preserved. At the time of writing (1992), there are over 7,000 original tapes housed in the sound archive of the School of Scottish Studies at 27 George Square, Edinburgh. How much reaches the ears of the Scottish people? The school is insufficiently staffed and funded to take on such an enormous job of outreach. The educational and political powers that be must now act, and the media do something more than inconsistent lip-service.

Angus Campbell was keen to show me a number of implements in his shed, including a salvaged piece of iron that had come off a shipwrecked sailing vessel and now served as an anvil. There were a number of old tools in the shed, with Angus acting as a patient demonstrator of their uses. Even when I said it was time for me to be off he was still pottering about the shed.

On signposts Daliburgh appears as 'Dalabrog'. I wanted to explore this straggly village, which can claim to be the capital of South Uist, with its mini-market, (former) school, hotel, garage, small hospital and churches.

The day was blustery and overcast. Away to my right the sky was clearing over the smoke-grey hills of Barra. The boglands were drowning in silence. Reeds fluttered in the wind, that seemingly constant wind, which buffeted the telephone poles – the only form of upright wood – and made the wires sing. A large grey boulder in amongst the reeds made a convenient seat for having lunch. I ate and listened. The silence was broken only by a handful of clucking hens and the distant revs of a tractor, moving in a puff of smoke across the machair below Hallan. Down from the burial-ground was a rubbish tip of rusting scrap and piles of tyres; an iron tower was perilously perched above the white face of a sand dune. Behind me was St Peter's Church, a grey slate-roofed building with a Celtic cross at one end.

A district nurse suddenly emerged from a house and ran to her car. On the other side of the road stood a squat low-roofed building that resembled *The Ballroom of Romance* in the dramatised version of William Trevor's short story of the same name. Give this austere-looking building a neon sign and the picture would have been complete.

At times it was hard to believe that this was Scotland rather than the west coast of Ireland. A canvas-backed seat lay outside on the grass, slowly rusting away. Next to it was a large bath with two pairs of taps.

I finished my snack and rode back to the crossroads, turning right for the Old Schoolhouse which sat gable-end to the road. Big John's car was parked in the drive and a stack of peats lay outside in the garden. I knocked. 'Ah, you've decided to return to the "Central Dispensary",' John said with a laugh.

Seated by the fire, John began to dispense more material from his finely tuned memory. Somehow the session turned to the subject of death warnings and I noted the following from him.

'My grand-aunt,' began John, 'was one called Anne Morrison. She was born in 1836 and married a man called Ronald Morrison. They had a croft at Boisdale. One night she heard a woman crying and weeping; it was coming from the machair and she likened this weeping to her own voice and said that it was a sign that one of her own children would be drowned off Orosay, an island that you can walk out to at low tide [west of South Boisdale].'

'She never gave her husband peace until they moved out to Saskatchewan in 1884. Now this grand-aunt of mine lived to 102. The strange thing was that her sister's son was drowned there after she went to Canada. The people of Boisdale said that there was someone weeping on the machair – the sister of the one who went to Canada and who heard this strange otherworldly voice the first time. It was a death warning.

'I got that from a man called Ronald MacIntyre of North Boisdale. Actually, at the time, Lady Cathcart was giving £100 to each family who went to Canada. In general she had a spite against the people at the south end of this island. South of Askernish was where the ordinary peasantry were living and these were the people Lady Cathcart hadn't much to do with.'

Lady Gordon Cathcart (1844–1932) was one of the richest and largest landowners in Scotland at that time. She was a woman of two sides – renowned for her generosity and kindness to people living on her estates in the North-East, but loathed by the people of the Hebrides – Barra and Uist in particular – as an oppressive absentee landowner.

She married Mr John Gordon of Cluny in 1865. He was an Aberdeenshire laird, famous in his day as a cattle-breeder and owner of land inherited from his father, the ruthless Colonel John Gordon of Cluny. From 1830 onwards, Colonel Gordon had purchased South Uist, Benbecula, Barra and several of the smaller isles where he later evicted and forcibly shipped more than 2,000 islanders to Canada. His son John passed the management of his Hebridean estates over to his wife, and Lady Cathcart inhumanely coerced the people to pay their rents by working at her kelp industry.

In the 1880s Lady Cathcart decided to promote emigration and is credited with the arrangements for 60 people from South Uist and Benbecula to go and settle in the Wapella area of Saskatchewan. The following year a further 40 families joined the settlers, but with that her sponsorship of the Cathcart Settlement ended. John's oral material is thus backed up by documented fact.

I mentioned to the big man that I was going over to Eriskay the following day, and wondered if he could tell me anything of the island's history.

'Well, prior to the first Poor Law Act in 1845, there weren't many people there. People poured in after that due to the Clearances at Loch Eynort, Ben More, etc. They were cleared to make way for the big farms. Half of the Eriskay people came from the Barra islands, especially those with the name of MacKinnon. These MacKinnons are really from the Strath area of Skye, near Broadford.'

John had acquired a deep knowledge of patronymic names and genealogies. He told me of one family who just made it to Loch Skipport in a small boat from the tiny island of Isay, off the north coast of Skye, near Dunvegan. They found the shell of a house and put a roof on it. According to John, Isay was cleared about 1852 by the landowner MacLeod. A lot of MacAskills lived on Isay and John heard from an old lady that when the first people went to Isay it was covered in heather. After clearing and cultivating the land, the familiar outcome was that the people were evicted. Apparently, one can still see the remains of their houses on Isay to this day.

I asked John if he could recall anything about the old cattle fairs that were held in South Uist.

'I was at the last of the fairs done by private bargain rather than auctioneers. This would have been about 1920 [John was born in 1907] and it took place at the Bogach Ollaidh, seven miles north of Daliburgh Cross. The drovers used to come from the north, across the fords with hundreds of heads of black cattle mostly. There were two types of drover – the big dealers, and their employees who drove the cattle and had no stake in buying the beasts. The buyers at that time expected to get a luckpenny. These drovers wore three coats: a fine coat, a strong coat with pockets for holding money, and oilskins.'

'A man called Archie Lamont lived on the main road, geographically at Snishival. He was one of these important individuals with a key job as a roads gaffer for the whole of South Uist. His house was the last one on the way south and was a good big house. Well, the drovers all poured into this house and nobody slept in there all night. John Lamont, the son, described to me the condition of the house as like a man-of-war in the course of battle, with all this crowd of men and their dogs. An old man called Angus MacIntyre stood in a position by the fire and could name every one of these drovers and who their people were: from Sutherland, Ross-shire, Perthshire and Stirlingshire.'

'They used to start the buying of cattle at four o'clock in the morning because they had so many to get rid of. Horses were sold as well, but not sheep. And Eriskay men would come across with what cattle they had. There wasn't so much grass over there and they reckoned that Eriskay cattle were poorer.'

After a fascinating afternoon spent listening to John, I took my leave and pedalled back to Askernish. I was excited as the following day would see me make my first trip to Eriskay in the hope of meeting Donald MacDonald, a bard and former collector of oral tradition for the Irish Folklore Commission back in the 1930s.

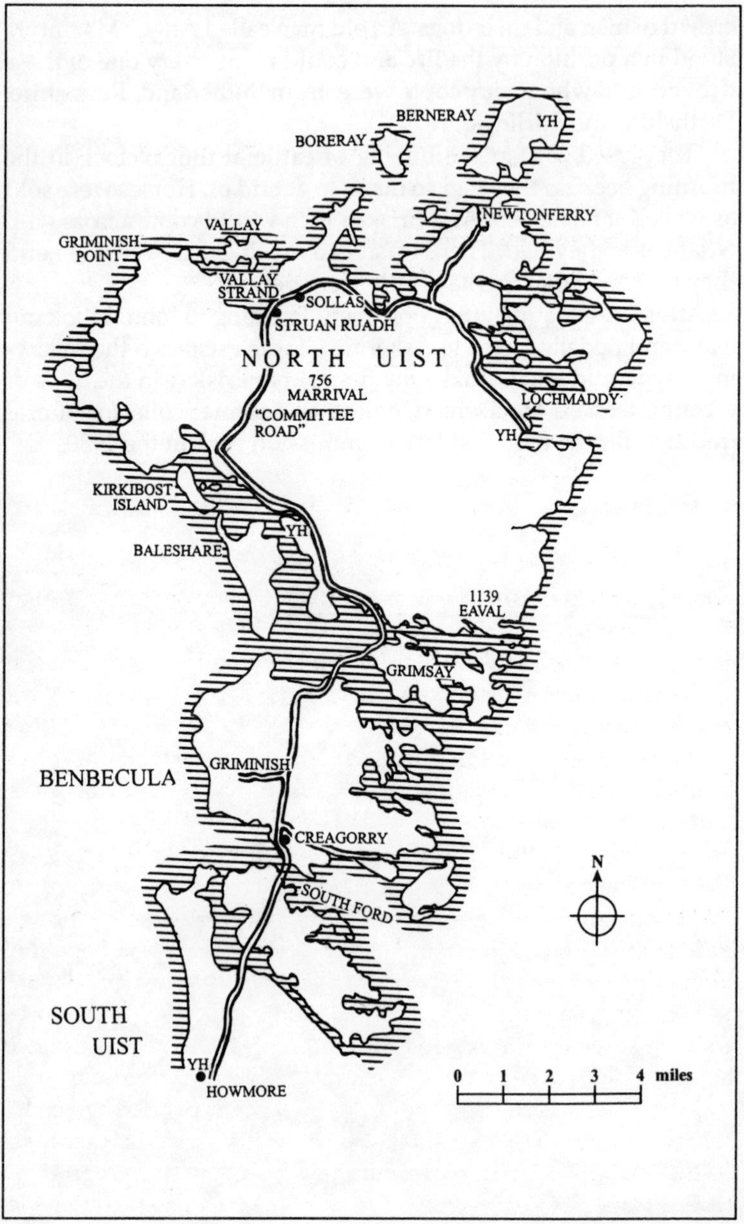
BERNERAY
YH
BOREAY
NEWTONFERRY
VALLAY
GRIMINISH POINT
VALLAY STRAND
SOLLAS
STRUAN RUADH
NORTH UIST
756 MARRIVAL
"COMMITTEE ROAD"
LOCHMADDY
YH
KIRKIBOST ISLAND
YH
BALESHARE
1139 EAVAL
GRIMSAY
GRIMINISH
BENBECULA
CREAGORRY
N
SOUTH FORD
SOUTH UIST
YH
HOWMORE
0 1 2 3 4 miles

CHAPTER 7

Eriskay, Benbecula and North Uist

The Hebrides enter the general consciousness by way of a glamourous myth which has little or no relation to reality.

Hugh MacDiarmid, 'The Sea', *Scottish Scene* (with Lewis Grassic Gibbon), 1934.

One cannot mourn the ending of a way of life that, especially in winter, was very bleak indeed; one cannot but mourn the ending of a culture that was rooted in the far distant past.

Tim Enright, Introduction to Micheál O'Guiheen's *A Pity Youth Does Not Last*, 1982.

After an excited discussion on the phone, Joe rushed into the living room and blurted out, 'We're leaving for Eriskay on the noon ferry in one hour's time'. We hastily assembled our things – a curious mixture of odds and sods ranging from football boots to a couple of enormous onions, potatoes and a bottle of an orange liqueur – and stuffed them in a holdall.

By the time we reached the jetty at Ludag my thoughts were bouncing with expectation: at last Eriskay. The Sound was glass-calm with a pristine blue sky overhead that was broken only by a trailing wisp of white cloud, high above Ben Scrien, the taller of Eriskay's two knobbly hills at just over 600 feet. Looking across to the island I could pick out some of the brightly coloured dwellings, and Eriskay looked every inch the magical place I had been told about. There was little in the way of other traffic waiting to make the crossing, so Joe and I kicked a football about the road. He was playing in goal for a South Uist football team that had a match arranged with a side from Eriskay on the Sunday afternoon.

John Harrison the 28-year-old head teacher of Eriskay School was to be our host this weekend and he shortly arrived at the wheel of the island's light blue community minibus with a cargo of 15 cases of lager and eight cases of milk. We were introduced by Joe, and John explained how on the first day of taking up his appointment he had missed the ferry connection and the priest on Eriskay came over in a speedboat to collect him. 'You know there wasn't a house for me when I arrived on Eriskay,' John said. 'I had to stay with the priest for three months before a local authority home became vacant. Accommodation here is critical, yet the Western Isles Council lack the human touch.'

It was a complaint over housing which I had heard before in the Southern Isles. John told me that from a population of about 250, the school roll on Eriskay was 43, essentially staffed by itinerant teachers.

By this time the sky-blue ferry had neared the Uist shore and we prepared to board. The ferry, *Eilean na h-Oige*, Island of Youth, was named after one of Father Allan MacDonald's poems in praise of Eriskay. The novelist Neil Munro knew and admired Father Allan, portraying him as Father Ludovic in his book, *Children of the Tempest*.

Apart from being a priest and poet, Father Allan was also a collector of folklore. He was born at Fort William in 1859, entered Blair's College, Aberdeenshire in 1871, then went on to the venerable Scots College at Valladolid in Spain, where he completed his studies before returning to take up a mission post at Oban. In 1884 Father Allan came to Daliburgh in South Uist, which was then the most populous as well as the poorest of the islands in the Diocese of Argyll and the Isles. Father Allan's interest in folklore is thought to have been hatched by Father Alexander Campbell, a native of Uist, then living in retirement at Daliburgh. Father Campbell was a mine of information on local tradition.

From 1887 onwards, Father Allan preserved items of local interest in a series of notebooks, collecting aspects of custom and belief as he went about his rounds. After 10 years in Uist his health had suffered to such an extent that he was transferred to the small island community of Eriskay as its first resident priest. Father Allan was to spend 12 years on the island until his death in 1905. He was the impetus behind the building of St Michael's at Rhuban, the church on the hill which has a distinctly Spanish influence. On Eriskay he had considerably greater scope for collecting tradition and filled six notebooks with tales of second sight alone.

Father Allan's manuscript material was later plundered by Ada

Goodrich Freer, who published *The Outer Isles* in 1902 under her name alone, when in fact it should have been jointly credited with Father Allan. This was the lady who carried out psychic investigations at Ballechin House in Perthshire and arranged for Father Allan to conduct an exorcism there.

The Outer Isles provided Goodrich Freer with the undeserved reputation as a folklorist, and while she received a highly flattering obituary on her death in 1931, Father Allan MacDonald's death passed entirely unnoticed in the wider world.

Joe and I jumped aboard the minibus, which John expertly reversed down the curving jetty to the ferry ramp, narrowly avoiding an obstacle course of assembled fish-boxes. Five passengers in all made the lunchtime crossing. Graham the ferryman, originally from Lewis, was the only Protestant living on Catholic Eriskay, and he told me the roll-on, roll-off ferry was in its first year of operation and was a far larger vessel than the previous ferry. Doubts had been raised about the size of the new boat, namely its ability to manoeuvre in the shallow waters of the Sound of Eriskay. He steered a wide arc to the modern utilitarian pier on the opposite side. The bulk of Ben Scrien dominates the view from this approach and as we neared Eriskay the island homes and church mushroomed in size.

I left the ferryman's electronic eyrie just in time to see the minibus trundle across the ramp with its rear number plate slipping down to rattle the iron ramp. I picked the plate up and got into the back of the vehicle beside Joe and an Eriskay girl who was returning home for the weekend after working in Lochboisdale Hotel.

John blootered the minibus up the twisting road of sorts as we motored past attractive homes with tiny gardens, unsightly wrecked cars, old drystane walls, and a clutch of hens who darted from the middle of the road to the safety of the verge. It was impossible to take everything in at first sight – the brightly coloured roofs radiant in the sunlight, the church on the hill, the machair lands, the toothpaste white sand of the beach and the immensity of sea and sky.

Eriskay was Ireland in miniature: a world apart. One of the cottages near the shore was named 'Celtic View' and everything about it was green and white. Eriskay is only three and a half miles long by one and a half miles wide, an islander's island if ever there was one. At the time I visited Eriskay, the island's fragile economy still hinged on fishing; accommodation for visitors was in short supply and there was no pub. Since then the Politician Lounge Bar has opened in a modern bungalow and the traditional local economy, although somewhat boosted by tourism, now looks increasingly precarious.

The centres of Eriskay life were the church and the community centre, the latter containing a small tearoom and communally run store. We arrived there and began unloading the liquid supplies. Next, it was down to John's house for a quick spot of lunch washed down with a couple of glasses of chilled French wine. John had kindly telephoned Donald MacDonald to see if it was convenient for me to visit the former head teacher, bard and folklore collector.

Donald's bungalow was the first house up from the pier. On the way down I passed a group of blond-haired children who were playing outside a caravan that served as a permanent home due to the housing shortage. I passed a house painted a Hawaiian blue with coloured stones and the proverbial scuttling hens at the door. Some of the older houses, now reduced to shells, sat on the rock-strewn ground higher up.

I came to the last house, where a brown labrador barked loudly as though it had been waiting for someone to open the stubborn gate and allow it freedom to roam. The door of the house was ajar. I knocked once and Donald's wife came to answer, showing me into a warm sun-lounge where Donald was sitting in his armchair below a shelf of books. Donald looked younger than I'd expected – a mere seventy-two. Below his thinning white hair was a slightly flushed Hebridean face which matched the colour of his polished boots with their contrasting yellow laces. Donald rose from his chair to shake my hand and after the preliminaries were dispensed with, I opened my notebook.

Donald told me he had begun collecting tradition in Uist for the Irish Folklore Commission while he was a student at Glasgow University. Initially it was all in manuscript and in 1932 he had been the first person to note folktales from the great storyteller Duncan MacDonald of Peninerine. Four years later Duncan was visited by two other collectors, William Mathieson and Peggy McClements. The former has written of Duncan that there was '... an old world courtesy about him that set one immediately at ease in his company'.

I asked Donald when he first started recording the voices of his informants and what these early collecting experiences had been like.

'*An Comunn Gaidhealach* woke up to what was happening and asked me to do some collecting for them. They gave me a recording machine in 1933/4 which worked on cylinders. It was strenuous work having to carry this machine around – an American machine called a Dictaphone which had just been invented. The stories faded from the cylinders after a while and they lost a lot of my early work because they didn't transcribe it in time. They also lost the cylinders when they changed headquarters and also because the crowd working there weren't familiar with this type of work. That would be about 1936/7.'

'What was the reaction of the storytellers to being recorded?' I enquired.

'The storytellers were fascinated with the machine because they had never heard their own voice before. Duncan in particular was, and he was probably the best storyteller ever. He had the Fenian tales – long, long tales that would take a whole night to tell. Most of them were to be found in the Southern Isles, not Lewis and Harris. Going back to the machine, it had a heavy battery because there was no electricity in any of the houses. I also got a lot of stories from a man called Duncan MacInnes – stories of a similar type to those heard on Uist, although there were variations.'

When Donald was collecting for the IFC he sent his manuscripts off to Dublin for roughly three years. Unlike Calum Maclean who was collecting in the depth of winter, Donald worked only during the summer months when he was on holiday from university.

'At that time there was a mail ferry with sail – no engines – and I might set off about 10 o'clock. It just had three sailings in those days and on the other side I depended on getting a lift, for with the heavy machine I couldn't have done it otherwise The people preferred you to come in the evenings because during the day they were always out on the land: it was a different world then. You know, [Professor James H] Delargy once told me that he used to sleep in vermin-infested houses because he loved the work.'

'What problems did you have to overcome when you were recording the shennachies?'

'Some of them could be a bit difficult through shyness. I might be there for two or three hours and would have to come back another night to record the end of the story. They knew the stories so well, they could pick up from where they left off; they'd a sort of photographic memory.'

The great international tales were like the Homeric poems in that they contain many repetitions to aid the memory, some of them being archaic phrases, often strings of adjectives in the old bardic style. 'At first the shennachies thought the recording machine was very strange,' Donald continued. 'On playing it back they always made remarks, or others did it for them. The quality of the voice recording was very good, but as I said, it faded after a while. When recording, it picked up cats and dogs and the sound of children. The storytellers didn't like being interrupted and normally wouldn't start until the kids were in bed, or if they were up, they were told to be quiet. The children were very receptive, and of course that's how stories came to be handed down from one generation to the next. Quite a lot had short stories, but only a few had the long Fenian tales. Others again, they specialised in ghost stories which would frighten the life out of you.'

'The old stories were recited as the people had learned them and these tales were accessible to the audience. But today, the children wouldn't know what you were talking about. Everything has been left too late. A better job was done of song collecting than story collecting, which should have been done fifty or sixty years ago.'

Donald contributed over 400 manuscript pages to the Irish Folklore Commission, mostly of material collected from his home island. He was paid enough to cover his expenses and Donald told me that it was Professor Delargy of the IFC who persuaded him to begin collecting tradition. He met Delargy through a mutual friend on Barra, Annie Johnston, sister of Calum. Delargy undertook fieldwork in the Arran Isles, Connemara and Galway, and advised on the making of the classic 1930s film *Man of Arran*.

I asked Donald about other collectors working in Scotland, particularly Barra.

'Campbell of Islay [John Francis Campbell, 1821–85] made a collection on Barra, but nothing was done after that for a long time. When I went to Barra first in 1937, Campbell of Canna [John Lorne

Campbell, 1906–] was just starting to collect, mostly songs. He lived in Northbay with his wife Margaret Fay Shaw and he told me he suffered from claustrophobia: he didn't like valleys even. But he was more or less full-time as a collector and seemed to have private means which enabled him to do this.'

'I used to have great nights with Calum Maclean in Barra. I knew more about the people there than Calum did, and could always tell him where to collect. The Barra people took to him. You would find one or two storytellers who were difficult to get at: you'd to soften them up. I discovered the same as Calum that there was plenty of stuff around. Calum got an awful lot of stuff after me. The bulk of my own work was between 1930 and '37.'

'I think people were more contented in those days; families were bigger and they were quite satisfied with what they could get out the sea. You could just walk into any house: nowadays they would ask what you wanted. I think it's down to mainland values and the influence of that box [television]. The thing was – hardly anyone went in for education. Actually, I was the first person on this island to graduate from a university.'

I left Donald, arranging to return the following afternoon. Later that evening we were joined back at John's house by Michael MacKinnon, an Eriskay fisherman. Michael kindly offered to give us a tour of his boat on the Sunday and said I should speak to his mother who had worked at the herring gutting in former years. We all welcomed in the Sunday with a few drams.

It was an incredibly close night and I awoke at an ungodly hour to the crowing of a cockerel. My lasting impression of Eriskay was the joyful tranquillity of that Sunday morning, with St Michael's bell pealing out over the island to summon the congregation to morning Mass. I caught up with some reading – Margaret Fay Shaw's beautifully illustrated work on *The Folklore and Folksongs of South Uist*.

Later, the three of us made our way over to Michael MacKinnon's house. He had not long arrived back from Mass and changed into a pair of blue overalls. Along with his son, we all packed into his car and set off for the harbour at the other side of the island. We bumbled along through Ballo, passing the island football pitch and a couple of houses perched on the edge of some rocks overlooking the magnificent *Coilleag a' Phrionnsa* (The Prince's Strand). It was here on the 24 July 1745 that Prince Charles Edward Stuart first set foot on Scottish soil and, according to tradition, planted a flower to mark the historic occasion – a sea convolvulus which is pink in colour and still flourishes on Eriskay to this day.

On this short journey across the island it was obvious why fishing played such a predominant role in the economy. The land was strewn with outcrops of grey bedrock amidst intermittent patches of bogland, rough grazing, irises and sedge grass.

Shortly we arrived at Acairseid. The small jetty was a jumble of lobster creels, orange nets, pallets and oil drums. Two 60-footers lay moored side by side, the first being Michael's *Regina Maris*, a converted trawler now serving as a ring-net vessel powered by a Kelvin engine. In the bowels of the boat was a small galley with cramped sleeping quarters at one end. There was enough room for seven bunk-style box-beds but not a lot else. Michael told us he normally fished for prawns and whitefish, the running costs of the boat amounting to about £1,000 per week, and while at sea the four-man crew worked an average 15-hour day in some of the most treacherous waters off the British coast. Catches were mainly landed at Mallaig, where maintenance work on the boat was undertaken. Some of the iron tackle on deck was visibly rusted, such was the corrosive power of salt water. The wheelhouse was stacked with an array of electronic gadgetry for communications, navigation, and tracing the fish. There also seemed to be an endless pile of bumph from various quangos and government bodies.

In 1984 Eriskay had four 60-footers compared with the 17 herring boats which sailed from the island in 1901 and gave employment to 120 men and boys. Today, there were a further five boats which fished for velvet crabs, but the number of fishermen was a fifth of what it had been 80 years ago.

Michael recalled some of the old superstitions which the fishermen practised, such as ensuring that you left your house by the right-hand side and that nobody shouted after you; nor were fishermen supposed to talk to women when walking to work.

After a beautifully cooked gourmet lunch back at John's house, I called once more on Donald MacDonald. The greeting was more informal this time and Donald was keen to show me a book of his poems along with a number of 1930s press cuttings all paying tribute to his work as bard and collector. Our conversation was more relaxed this second meeting, largely because my notebook and pen were laid aside.

I enquired as to Donald's island descent and he told me that his grandfather had come from Corrodale on the east side of South Uist; it had been his third eviction but Donald knew of one Eriskay family who had experienced seven evictions before they settled on the island.

The physical geography of Eriskay made them turn to the sea for a living. Eriskay was regarded by the landowners as unproductive and that was where the poor people of Barra and Uist were allowed to settle: not through choice but by virtue of being cleared from their former homes. It says a great deal for the people that they were able to turn their hand to fishing and before they could afford to buy their own boats, the Eriskay fishermen worked as seasonal hands on East Coast boats.

Once again Donald expressed his regret that the old, old stories were no longer alive on the people's lips. After a short discussion over tea I left. Donald came to the door to wave me off. My one regret was not having a tape-recorder to preserve our talk. Several years later Donald passed away but his manuscript collection of stories and lore lives on in Dublin.

In shirt-sleeves I slowly walked back up the road to Michael's house. There he introduced me to his 81-year-old mother, who was sitting in the kitchen, dressed in raven black from head to toe. Alexina MacKinnon first went to the gutting when she was 15 or 16 years old, approximately 1919. Apart from the East Coast of Scotland and Shetland, she worked in three Irish ports: Kinsale, Ardglass and Bunchrana. Along with five other girls she found lodgings in the wintertime, the Irish houses all being thatched at that time.

'At Yarmouth we worked outside, wintertime and all. Our hands would be frozen and sometimes you could hardly handle fish for the cold. We had cuts despite the cloth bandages we wrapped round our fingers for to protect them. Heavy work it was when you had to carry baskets of herring over to the one who was at the packing. But we all sang at our work for to pass the time: happy songs, all in the Gaelic.'

'When we were up at Shetland we used to go over to Lerwick

and Bressie for a dance or for shopping: just for an outing when we weren't working. You were at the gutting by six in the morning and sometimes didn't get finished till eleven at night.... I think these days are best forgotten about. We had a good time too, right enough, but is was hard, hard work for young girls.'

In 1902 as many as 60 of Eriskay's womenfolk went to the gutting in Lerwick. In the 1890s the pattern was for the fisher girls to work at the Barra fishing and then follow the herring to the East Coast fishing ports. When the Barra fishing dropped away about the turn of the century, the herring lasses started going as far afield as Shetland and English ports such as Yarmouth and Lowestoft.

In the Southern Isles most of the fisher girls came from South Uist rather than North Uist. The highest number of gutters from North Uist was 36 in 1888, while South Uist that same year supplied nearly three times as many. Gutting fresh herring was certainly no job for the faint-hearted, although there was in the girls' favour the optimism of youth and the excitement of leaving their island homes for possibly the first time in their lives. Both Alexina MacKinnon and Jane Gillies have since died. Behind their self-effacement was a quiet contentment and a resolute spirit and desire to look ahead, not back.

I drained my glass of whisky and thanked Michael and his family for their hospitality and kindness. My time with Alexina had been all too short, English not being her first language and I not having any Gaelic. Despite these problems over language, I felt that Eriskay had afforded me a rare welcome, this the island of youth where the sound of children's voices is still very much alive.

Joe's Uist football team had lost their Sunday match. It was time to say goodbye to John Harrison, who'd been invaluable as a contact. A weekend is never enough time to explore any island, no matter how small. Now it was time to leave Eriskay as the early evening light washed across its homes and hills in what was almost a surreal picture of peace and tranquillity.

This time we crossed the shallow Sound in a small green fishing boat, the defeated Uist football team maintaining a deathly silence all the way across. As I gazed over to the shadows falling on South Glendale, I reflected on the kindness I had been afforded by the people. I would not forget the island in a long, long time.

By next morning the weather had broken. I felt slightly down after the weekend heights. It was a damp but by this time a familiar ride to the Old Schoolhouse at Daliburgh Crossroads. I had postponed my visit till the afternoon, hoping for the weather to clear. It kept on raining.

The friendly face of Mary answered my knock at the door. She was hirpling with the aid of a walking-stick and complained of pain in her back. Big John was drying the lunchtime dishes in the kitchenette and five minutes elapsed before a large hand swept the orange curtains aside and in he stepped. It was surprising for such a big man, how gentle he was on his feet. Facing the fire at the other end of the cosy living room was a piano on which there were a number of framed photographs, one of them showing John standing beside and dwarfing Duncan MacDonald the storyteller, and next to him, Professor McKinnon. The year was 1953. I asked John about the photo. 'Yes,' he said, 'it was taken by a photographer for *The Scotsman* newspaper on one of the days when the Celtic Congress was being held in Oban.' John recalled that Duncan was to render one of his long tales that afternoon and he couldn't find a barber's which was open. He was on his way to the cattle market for a haircut because someone he'd met had told him that a man there clipped horses and would attend to his hair.

That afternoon session with John was as varied as could be imagined. He talked of how they obtained Russian black earth as ballast for the old sailing ships, explained the Skye navy, enlarged on how rocks were split using fires of peat and heather roots, and mused about an old folk-cure derived from the salted fat of conger eel. I was fascinated by the facial expressions he pulled when he spoke. Sometimes he would raise his jowls to narrow his eyes; he would furrow his brow to express amazement or contemplation, and all these expressions were usually accompanied by animated gestures with his hands such as punching them into the air to give weight to what he was saying. Storytellers like John were born, not made, and I found my time in this company to be an uplifting, enriching experience.

Come the evening, Joe and I made a trip to Hallan, where I showed him Calum Maclean's grave. A colleague of Joe's had lent him a copy of Calum's book, *The Highlands*, an evocative people's history of the region, rather than a stodgy historical heavyweight that repeats the same old ground. Since my last visit, a bunch of red flowers had been laid beside Calum's grave. In a beautiful elegy for his brother, Sorley Maclean has written:

Tha iomadh duine bochd an Albainn
dh'an tug thu togail agus cliù;
's ann a thog thu 'n t-iriosal
a chuir ar linn air chùl.
['There is many a poor man in Scotland
whose spirit and name you raised;
you lifted the humble
whom our age put aside.']

The following day was one of sadness. I learned that the lobster fisherman who had helped sort my bike and given me the potatoes, suddenly died after returning from a morning's fishing. Such are the inexplicable ways of life.

After a day of reading, Joe took me to visit his school in the evening. He told me that because of the education cuts there wasn't enough money to provide proper blackouts when screening slides. Nor were there updated textbooks for the pupils, and the lack of cupboard space meant that books were stored on top of desks.

Back at Askernish our foodstocks were running low – a tin of sardines was all that we could muster from the larder, so we decided on a bar supper at the Lochboisdale Hotel. We took shelter from the storm to watch the arrival of the Oban ferry, always an exciting event. Upon walking down to the pier I happened to recognise the face of Michael MacKinnon peering into the rain from under his orange oilskins as he momentarily looked up from the deck of his boat. A shouted exchange of greetings took place through the wind. It had been a poor trip and his catch was small due to the weather – mostly dogfish, some herring and an enormous squid. 'Would you like some fish?' Michael yelled. 'If that's okay with you,' I replied. Michael nodded and his son handed up a plastic carrier containing four 'dogs' with gaping mouths and lifeless black eyes. I returned the favour by later buying Michael a dram in the smoke-filled bar of the hotel.

Next morning the grill packed up on the electric cooker. I'd to collect some groceries and the wind was still blasting over Uist.

It was atrocious weather for cycling and I left for Daliburgh without even a slice of toast inside me. It seemed as though the seasons had changed from autumn to winter overnight. Rain started to pour, stinging my cheeks, as I stood up on the pedals in order to push the red machine forward. At Daliburgh the wind blew me into the post-office, which was rather bare in a functional sort of way. I thought it also sold wool but I was too busy fumbling for change to pay for some stamps to take much notice.

I moved round to Big John's house and tapped on the front window since it was pointless knocking at the door due to the raging wind. John's face appeared at the door with an amusing look of recognition in his eyes.

'We thought you were away yesterday,' he said.

'Benbecula tomorrow,' I replied.

'Come on in out of this awful weather,' John said firmly. Once inside, the two-foot-thick walls of the house reduced the noise of the storm to a murmur. I handed over a bottle of sherry to John, while Mary went upstairs to rest. After a short session I popped out to the shop for John's papers. On my return I found that another visitor had arrived: a small man wearing a dumpy hat. This was James Rafferty, a man who had herded sheep in the hills of Glen Lyon and who was knowledgeable about horses, dynamite and salmon poaching amongst a good many other things.

After James left, I continued noting down anecdotal material from John. Sometimes he would speak in a hushed whisper, or with his glasses resting on his forehead, render a few verses of some relevant Gaelic song, his eyes focused far away through the window. John's depth of feeling for the past was unmistakable and he would have made a patient and wise teacher.

I left John and Mary for the last time that afternoon. They said to look in on them if ever I were in Uist again, and I promised to drop them a line when I returned home. My four visits to the Old Schoolhouse had been amongst the happiest and most memorable occasions of the entire trip.

Later that evening I recall opening the front door of the house at Askernish to gaze across to Hallan cemetery. The wind whistled into the hall as I watched shafts of grey light chink through a battery of enormous evening clouds high above the machair. The stones in the distance soon became engulfed in a uniform grey as the light failed. Only the wind remained, cold and wild, alive to all the senses.

The morning weather forecast was uncompromising: 'Another cool day with the wind reaching gale force in exposed parts of the north.' It would be a punishing ride to Creagorry where I had a room reserved at the hotel. There was a short, sharp delivery from the heavens about 10 a.m., followed by a lull, then another cloudburst. I thanked Joe for all his kindness and help, before taking leave of the house which had served as such a fruitful base. The alternative would have been the Gatliff Trust's basic but delightful hostel at Howmore, which accommodates a maximum of 10 people.

The main north–south road through South Uist offers a different perspective of the island from the narrow roads which thread their way through the various crofting settlements. The promised gale materialised as a fierce crosswind which took all the pleasure out of the ride north.

My destination for a snack lunch was Howmore, the sister community of Howbeg. Here are the timeless echoes of an ancient spiritual past. *Hogh* is the earliest place on record in South Uist, being Old Norse for a 'burial ground' or 'place of council'. Facing the small thatched hostel are the overgrown ruins of chapels and buildings of a pre-Reformation monastery and college. At one time this would have been the hub of spiritual life in Uist. I sheltered from the wind beside the crumbling, lichen-encrusted walls and ate my sandwiches. These ancient stones exuded an atmosphere of piety which was far from dour and stubborn but rather light and airy. Amidst this hallowed ground was a place to linger, to savour, to feel: a place of sanctity that was aloof from the modern world.

I left Howmore feeling invigorated. Since leaving Penicuik I had covered nearly 450 miles and the trip was turning into an odyssey.

The main road became flatter, straighter and more windswept. If the wind was a constant bugbear, the quality of light more than made up for it: every vein and dimple on Hecla could be seen. The road took me under the gradual slopes of Heaval, where a tall grey granite statue of the Virgin and Child is flanked by a sinister rocket-tracking station serving the rocket-range near Ardivachar. With the wind gusting through my spokes, I spun across the Loch

Bee causeway and out of South Uist.

The South Ford causeway was only completed the previous year, replacing a 1943 bridge. The tidal waves licked the huge boulders of the causeway as I made slow progress in the buffeting wind.

Creagorry Hotel is strategically situated on the north side of the South Ford. Some of the old Uist stories tell of travellers and horses perishing in quicksands when they lost their way on the pre-war tidal route. The present Creagorry Hotel opened in 1885, replacing the former Creagorry Inn which stood on the site now occupied by the Co-op. The author Neil Gunn stayed at Creagorry in the early 1920s and encountered an eccentric sporting guest who was ex-military and later was developed into one of the characters in Gunn's novel, *The Other Landscape*.

I had arrived in Benbecula, the flattest island in the Outer Hebrides, which although lacking the verdant appeal of Tiree, has its own intrinsic character, dominated by the immensity of its skies and ever-present wind. From the air Benbecula appears to be immersed in water, such is the multitude of lochs and lochans which bespeckle the land, making it a haven for anglers seeking the elusive brown trout which inhabits many of the lochs.

The noted folklorist and excise officer, Alexander Carmichael (1832–1912), was posted to Benbecula during the first half of the 1870s. He and his wife stayed at Redbank House, Creagorry, although the building no longer stands. Carmichael's excise duties afforded him the opportunity of collecting old Gaelic lore, especially the private prayers, invocations and blessings which the people regularly recited as they went about their daily tasks. He also collaborated with the distinguished folktale pioneer, Campbell of Islay, the pair undertaking fieldwork in the area during September 1871.

John Francis Campbell was educated at Eton and studied law at Edinburgh University. His remarkable career included periods as private secretary to the Duke of Argyll and Groom-in-Waiting to Queen Victoria. Campbell's interest in Gaelic folktales was largely spawned by Sir George Webb Dasent who spent much of his life studying the Old Norse tales and sagas. With the help of others, Campbell amassed a collection of 800 tales from the West Highlands and Islands, although only a tenth eventually saw the light of day in the four volumes of *The Popular Tales of the West Highlands* (1860–62).

After dinner I paid a short visit to the barn-like public bar of the hotel. It was busy with locals, while the lounge bar held a contingent of off-duty military personnel connected with the rocket-range. The two cultures did not mix. Feeling slightly saddle-sore I turned in for an early night.

A new day dawned. I had a large cooked breakfast to fuel my cycling legs. About 10 a.m. I set off for Griminish hoping to track down someone who could recall the remarkable storyteller Angus 'Barrach' MacMillan, who died in 1954. In a fascinating article by Calum Maclean about his work in the Hebrides, he writes:

> 'In Barra I got information about a remarkable storyteller in the island of Benbecula. His name was Angus MacMillan, and he told tales which required not hours but several nights to narrate. He was ageing and his memory was said to be failing. No time was to be wasted, and I went to Benbecula immediately.'

From research undertaken by Donald Archie MacDonald it seems highly probable that such feats of memory are enhanced by a strong vein of visual imagery, whereby the storyteller is able to recall the tale like a continuous picture as in a film.

John MacInnes had told me that Angus Barrach's forebears were Barra people, and recited to me a few anecdotal stories about Angus, one telling of how he had to be rescued from the encroaching tide while out on the rocks fishing for cuddies.

The straggling linear township of Griminish was not all that far from the hotel and as I set out that morning I was confident of finding someone who would be able to recall Angus MacMillan. As it happened, the first person I saw was a middle-aged man walking along the road with his sheepdog. I stopped to have a chat and he was able to show me Angus's former home, before the shennachie and his sister had moved to Moss Cottage.

'That was around 1939,' the man said thoughtfully.

'Did you hear of the tale collector, Calum Maclean?' I enquired.

'Yes indeed. Calum used to come round here and he was forever with Angus, getting his stories and his yarns. 1948 was the first time I think I met Calum here – himself, and another man, an Irish professor I think. Calum used to stay in lodgings in the next house to where old Angus Barrach stayed. There's only ruins of it there now; a Mrs Wilson had it. In fact, when he was having a session with Angus he used to leave the recording machine and tapes at Angus's for the time it took. It was heavy work lumping that case around and cars weren't all that plentiful here at that time.'

I was given directions to the house of an elderly man who might be able to help further. I knocked at the door of Donald John Wilson and after a slight delay it was partly opened by a man advanced in years with thinning grey-white hair, a dirt-stained faced and clear blue eyes. He wore denim dungarees, a grey pullover and a navy cardigan that was badly frayed and covered in grime. I noticed his hands were podgy and stained brown. He led me through to a room which was poorly furnished, had a linoleum floor and a cream ceiling that was streaked with soot. A damp, musty smell prevailed throughout, and at the fireplace sat a 'modern mistress' stove which was unlit.

Light filtered through a side window but not enough to dispel the all-prevailing gloom. This was the house of The Scholar, Donald John's byname, and he told how it had been built about 1920 on the croft where he was born in December 1901. The former house had been of the blackhouse type, and the ruins could be seen opposite this present building. Donald John mentioned that he had been on the mainland only once for any length of time and that was for seven months when he worked on a farm in Argyll. In slow, broken English he told me that he had known Angus MacMillan when the storyteller was in his middle years and was 'a big, big man, over six feet in height'. Angus had died in May 1954, Donald John recalled, 'when he wasn't fully eighty years of age'. In a starker tone of voice he said loudly: 'There's no storytelling now, it's all television!'

I obtained the impression that Donald John thought I was wasting my time asking about stories, but he seemed to perk up when the subject of our conversation turned to milling, kelping, and the old houses. Religious prints of Our Lady were hung on some of the walls, while in the foreground between our chairs was a formica table on which sat a thermos flask, a tin of biscuits and a carton of long-life milk. Instinct told me to cut our conversation as I felt an overwhelming sense of loneliness which was unsettling. I returned to Creagorry feeling depressed by the old man's situation and guilty at not being in a position to help him. Maybe he was content? He seemed too trusting to be a miser, and anyway who was I to interfere, unannounced, uncalled for?

These thoughts were still with me as I pedalled out to Hacklett. It had started to rain and the sky visibly darkened. What was I hoping to find here? In the earlier half of last century only six people lived at Hacklett, but by 1883 it had become a poor, overcrowded community of 27 families, many of them squatters who had been cleared from other areas. Yet Hacklett was to emerge as one of the most noted places in Benbecula for the strength and vigour of its traditional oral culture, being home to two celebrated female singers – Penny MacLellan and Catriona MacCormick – amongst others. Moreover, the husbands of both women, Angus John MacLellan and Patrick MacCormick, were noted shennachies.

Following in the footsteps of earlier collectors, Donald Archie MacDonald recalled that visiting the MacCormick home was an experience in itself. In the early 1960s there was no proper road. As Donald recalled: 'Ian Crawford and I made these expeditions about 1962/63. Penny MacLellan was still alive and I was concerned with making good field recordings at that stage. Instead of taking one of the smaller portables, or indeed the clockwork portables which I'd used in 1954, we took out the full-size Vortexion, which weighed about as much as a sack of coal. Ian and I carried it in sacks on our backs over the moorland in the dark using torches. That wasn't an everyday experience, but it certainly stands out in my mind.' So much for the popular cartoon image of the folklore collector sitting agog in a crowded pub with notebook and pen at the ready.

I had been given the name of a contact who stayed further round at Kilerivagh in a thatched house that lay off the Uiskevagh road, about half-way between the school and a telephone box. Donald John MacKay had stayed many a time with Angus Barrach while he told his long yarns; they were relatives. He told me that sometimes Angus' storytelling would send his wife and sister to sleep, and that Angus would just leave them snoozing in their chairs by the fire rather than summon them to bed. 'Oh, he was a great character,' said Donald John. 'Even as an old man coming up for eighty he would still go on the pillion of a motor bike that belonged to Donald Maclean. And you know, Angus was a man that couldn't read or write, but if you read a book to him he could practically repeat every word.' In 18 months, Calum Maclean recorded from Angus

MacMillan such a large collection of tales that they occupy almost 5,000 large manuscript pages, bound in volumes in the IFC archives in Dublin.

I stayed about an hour with Donald John in his thatched house which was positioned above a narrow finger-like loch that penetrated the sodden boglands. Ahead, the road climbed up a brae and I decided that it was not a day for further exploration. I returned to the comforts of the hotel and had a nap before dinner.

Next day I pedalled over the hump of Benbecula, past the ridge of Reuval, and down to the North Ford causeway, constructed in 1960, and linking with the eastern shores of Grimsay, North Uist. Another little causeway completed the link to the main island of Protestant North Uist. The superb hill of Eaval dominated the view and down at ground level I formed the impression that the houses seemed more self-consciously groomed than their Catholic neighbours in the south.

The quarter-moon-shaped Kirkibost Island held my interest purely because it was so bare and flat; then suddenly there emerged a truly spectacular double rainbow. As I watched its ends filter away, I neared my turning for the narrow road which climbs between Ben Ernakater and Ben Aulsary. Known as the 'Committee Road', it was constructed by North Uist men as part of the relief scheme during the potato famine.

For almost a decade between 1846 and 1855 the potato, the main subsistence crop of the Western Highlands and Islands, failed in whole or in part and threatened a large number of the area's inhabitants with malnutrition, severe destitution and the associated killer diseases of cholera, dysentery and typhus. That said, the Highland potato famine was not on such a scale as in Ireland, where millions died. But there were similarities in that the class of people most affected were the impoverished cottars. The majority of Highland cottars were either squatters, kinsfolk of the small tenants, or families who held land in return for labour services on bigger farms but who were settled permanently in the neighbourhood. Road-building was just one of the schemes designed to afford relief to an impoverished people. Like the 'Committee Road', the 'Destitution Roads' of Wester Ross and Sutherland stand as a lasting testament to the famine relief programme of the 1840s.

At the summit of the pass I was afforded a stunning view down towards the tidal island of Vallay. Constantly changing light splintered through a mass of cloud, dancing and weaving geometric patterns on the water which had flooded the Vallay Strand, thereby cutting off the island. I stood astride the bike and tried to take in the scene, bewitched by the ever-changing dance of light between sea and sky. The descent was a thrilling spin as I flew past peat hags which were still worked and had provided the Sollas people with fuel for generations.

The view from the bedroom window of my boarding house at Struan Ruadh faced across the magical strand to Vallay. Later, in conversation with my landlady, I found out that she possessed two traditional handtools connected with potatoes – a 100-year-old potato lifter which had belonged to her grand-uncle and was known in Gaelic as a *cnochan*, and a potato dibber called a *slibheag* in Gaelic. The lifter had a five-inch wooden handle and a hooked head, while the dibber or planting tool resembled the shaft of a spade with a projecting foot rest. This latter tool had come from the Loch Eport district in the south of North Uist where the nature of the land meant a reliance on lazybeds worked with the spade and manured by seaweed. The art of making lazybeds was in terminal decline on the islands.

A snoring ginger tom, itchy nylon sheets and a tight throat all combined to disturb my sleep, but I awoke to find an idyllic September morning. Vallay was bathed in a sea of green light and the tide had ebbed to reveal the whitest of white sands. After a hearty breakfast I asked my landlady about the nature of the tides and decided I would walk over the strand to Vallay.

It took half an hour to walk across the sands in my bare feet. Underfoot it was ridged and brick hard, with numerous circular holes made by lugworms. On arrival my feet were numb with the cold. Vallay holds three deserted buildings, the most prominent being a roofless baronial-type residence erected by Sir Erskine Beveridge in 1903. A second house, nearby, formerly belonged to the farm manager and its slate roof seemed about to collapse. The last building was a low-lying cottage which was partly denuded of slates.

I dried my feet with a towel and put on my socks and boots, the rush of warmth being almost immediate. Upon walking to the back of the cottage, a mottled brown pair of wings suddenly flapped into life and rose skywards. It was a buzzard. I watched it land some yards away down by the shore; the bird started to almost tiptoe across the sand, hunching its wings as it moved, then making comical bounds forward with both its talons outstretched. I stood motionless, watching the buzzard's curious antics before it took off with a mewing cry that was almost gull-like.

Over to my left a small group of cattle were slowly moving across the strand. I wandered round by the shore and came upon a perfectly preserved sheep's skull. Time belonged to a different world; this was the proverbial place apart. In the distance rose the majestic hills of Harris, while I explored the square-shaped ruin marked on my map as Teampull Mhuir. Further along and closer to the shore were two standing stones where I rested and ate a pear. I continued to the eastern point of the island where there were large dunes and a secret bay covered with masses of marvellously rounded grey pebbles, each with a pinkish grain running through them.

At this extremity the silence was broken by the sound of the Atlantic's rushing waves. Not wishing to be caught out by the swiftly encroaching tide I doubled back and paddled over the one and a half mile strand. Puffs of blue smoke were rising from some of the chimneys of Struan Ruadh, part of Malaclete township. It was nearly noon and the water felt warmer than before.

A slight breeze had got up but the sky had the same pristine clarity. After lunch I cycled round to the Sollas Co-op and bought some cigarettes, although they only sold packets of pens when all I needed was one. From a point on the B893 directly overlooking Hornish cemetery there unfolded a splendid view off Berneray, uninhabited Pabbay and nearby Boreray. The last-mentioned island had a population of 150 in 1883. Rents were paid by draining Loch Mor and securing sandbanks, but at the time of the Napier Commission's report in the 1880s, rent was being paid in cash and by kelp. Peat for the fires had to be brought nine miles by sea and the land that was cultivated suffered badly from drifting sand. Berneray is also an island which has no internal supplies of peat, although in former years it was ferried back from some of the smaller satellite islets off Uist such as Stromay and Hermetray. There the islanders lived in turf huts while it took them several days to cut enough fuel.

The road to Newtonferry was extremely bumpy and on the return journey I halted under the slopes of Laiaval to allow a small convoy of cars to pass. There was a sharp descent followed by the magnificent prospect of a vista that stretched as far as the Skye Cuillins, the serrated edge of the hill ridge appearing under an indigo sky. A mad sheepdog gave chase on the brae down to Struan, where the sea had once more covered the strand.

That evening I was constantly diverted from my book by the contrasting shades of a glorious sunset, twilight and velvety evening sky. The buildings on Vallay for long remained as a dark silhouette before finally disappearing into the clutches of the night.

There was severe wind-driven rain for much of the following day. I madly ventured out to Lochmaddy where I lunched at the hotel: pie, beans and chips for £1.30. There were only a few visitors in the bar, one group complaining vociferously that their fish dish was cold, much to the amusement of the barman, who seemed pleased that the chef was rattled.

In the evening I called at an arranged time to see Donald and Christina Ann MacDougall. Donald was born in 1912 and was a blacksmith, crofter, former gamekeeper and shot-firer at a quarry. He spoke quietly about his time as a smith.

'A lot of iron was washed ashore at that time. It was attached to wood, you see. People would keep an eye out for this and if they wanted things made they would bring it to the smiddie. I used to make tether pins and tynes for wooden harrows from this stuff. There was a use for everything: they had to in those days.'

We moved on to discuss other topics, including the use of *muran* or marram grass as a thatching material in this part of North Uist. Over Loch Eport way, heather was used for the roofs and lasted longer than marram which required patching every second year.

When the marram ripened in the autumn it was cut by scythe on the likes of Vallay, raked into heaps then loaded onto a horse-drawn cart, the individual families collecting enough for their own needs. The marram was at its strongest when cut green, but the sand on the dunes where it grew tended to blunt the scythe blades very quickly. The grass was arranged so that the strands all faced the same way. It was then tied in bundles placed on top of one another in rows, and compressed by a plank of wood. The grass would be left until it had turned slightly yellow in colour; then on a suitably calm dry day, usually two men working as a team would start the job of thatching the roof. Apart from local houses, byres and other outbuildings were also thatched with marram. Moreover, it was formerly used in the making of horse collars and as bedding.

The night became wilder by the hour. As I lay in bed reading I could hear the blatter of rain on the window. In the morning the strong north-easterly wind was unrelenting in its ferocity. The white dunes of Vallay were steeped in a radiant light, but the fickle, changing sky soon darkened to blot out the island in a blanket of grey. The strand looked bare and inhospitable, partly submerged with a strong current driving the choppy water forward in clouds of spray. No one moved on this Hebridean Sunday.

An hour later, the scene had undergone a miraculous transformation – a blue sky had appeared with an enormous ball of white cloud hanging over the island. Light struck the faces of the dunes and I could distinguish the tumbledown dykes between the houses. The strand was constantly changing colour as though under the spell of a magic wand; wind thumped against the glass in the house and roared down the lum, making the peats glow with orange life. I meditated on how a coal fire flamed and crackled but peat had its own slow and silent way of imparting heat. I was more than grateful to have the comfort of a fire on a day such as this. I had my book. I had food. And I had the Vallay Strand – a veritable theatre of light and shade with the sky the principal actor.

It was a day of rest and prayer in the Protestant north. Much has been written about the Hebridean Sabbath and the stranglehold of religion over this particular day. I did not find it dour and forbidding. I did not go out of my way to worship but accepted that it was the normal pattern of life in these parts and that I was privileged to be a guest here experiencing such a splendid landscape.

I turned from the window and picked up a back number of *The Reader's Digest*. There was an intriguing article on 'Steam Train' Maury Graham, King of America's freight train hobos and self-described as the 'last free man'. I wondered what he would have made of North Uist on a Sunday. No trains, no towns, no fellow tramps.

Peggie came into the front room with a pot of freshly brewed tea and some scones and jam. I asked her if she had any particular memories of her time in Struan.

'I recall mostly men fishing for flounders on the banks of the *faodhail* [a river through a strand]. They stretched out a long, straight line anchored by stones at either side. Attached to this line were strips of gut that had hooks baited with sandworms. It was usually when the tide was coming in. Once the tide retreated they would walk out to see what they'd caught. I've seen them get a bucketful of flounders many a time.'

By mid-afternoon the tide was at full ebb. In the space of minutes the scene dramatically changed from something resembling a desert windstorm to a bleak curtain of impermeable grey. The outline forms of the Vallay buildings appeared then disappeared. In the foreground the shore grasses were contorted into different shapes by the wind; rain lightly pattered the window as I slowly turned the pages of Neil Gunn's *Morning Tide*.

The only event of any note was the departure of the other guest, a landscape artist from Hampshire. He was obsessed with capturing true perspectives and told me he was dreading the return to the south and so-called 'civilization'. The clock ticked on an on, as evening fell gently on the strand, the houses and the island.

The following morning I settled my bill and said goodbye to Peggie and her docile cat. The sky was thick with rain and my wheels generated a lot of spray as I set out on the 11-mile journey to Lochmaddy. I passed a large brown bull who bellowed loudly into the rain. At one stage the sombre brown moorland and innumerable lochans were lost in a sea of driving rain, as though the ocean had turned upside down. I was grateful that the wind was at my tail and picked up a fast pace as I swished along the tarmac which stretched out in the distance like a chrome line. Laser beams of light sliced through the clouds, landing on a myriad of lochans which sparkled like pearls. Shortly I was looping my way round Blashaval and had reached Lochmaddy.

At the offices of Caledonian MacBrayne I purchased a single ticket to Uig for £4.40 with the bike travelling free. The *Hebrides* was due in at 11.30. I waited in the ticket office, glad to be out of the rain and have the chance to dry off.

Pedalling the short distance back up to the hotel from the pier, I sunk a large whisky as my windcheater steamed over a radiator. The barman was a tall, fair-haired Australian who was on a working vacation. It was his fourth week behind the bar of the Lochmaddy Hotel and he told me he'd come north from the Yorkshire Dales. 'The locals here are a fucking queer lot,' he blurted out with a shake of his head. 'They don't have much humour about them and drink Grouse whisky like it's going out of fashion.' Pointing to a large whisky bottle on an optic, he continued: 'See them – we go through two per day on average'. At this juncture, a man with a hooked nose strolled into the bar and ordered a carry-out consisting of a bottle and two half bottles of whisky. As he left, the barman commented: 'That's the runner. He buys drink for some others who don't like coming in here. I've never seen spirit drinkers like them: fucking incredible they are.' I left the barman to his expletives and generalisations, as out through the small window of the bar I could see the ferry approaching.

It was a grim, cold wait for the boat to disgorge its cargo of cars, Land Rovers, a bread van, caravanette, builders' lorries, British Telecom van, haulage trucks from Skye and further afield, as well as some army vehicles. A number of backpackers walked down the gangway, one weird-looking character dressed in yellow trousers with a David Bellamy beard and a red pixie hat on his head.

In the bar lounge of the upper deck I took a seat at a varnished ship's table which was anchored to the floor and had projecting metal rings on the underside for holding glasses during heavy seas when the ship could roll and spill drinks. At the far end of the lounge a Presbyterian minister sat under a porthole wearing a trilby and long black coat, demurely clutching his leather briefcase. At the opposite end a middle-aged Catholic priest with a pock-marked face nurtured a stiff brandy and took long draws on his cigarette in between joking with two young women and their male companion.

This Scottish odyssey was almost over. My thoughts wandered back to Big John in Daliburgh, Calum Maclean's grave at Hallan, Eriskay and Howmore and the magical interplay of light on the Vallay Strand: all places and faces that were behind me now, but would live on in my memory forever more, come what might.

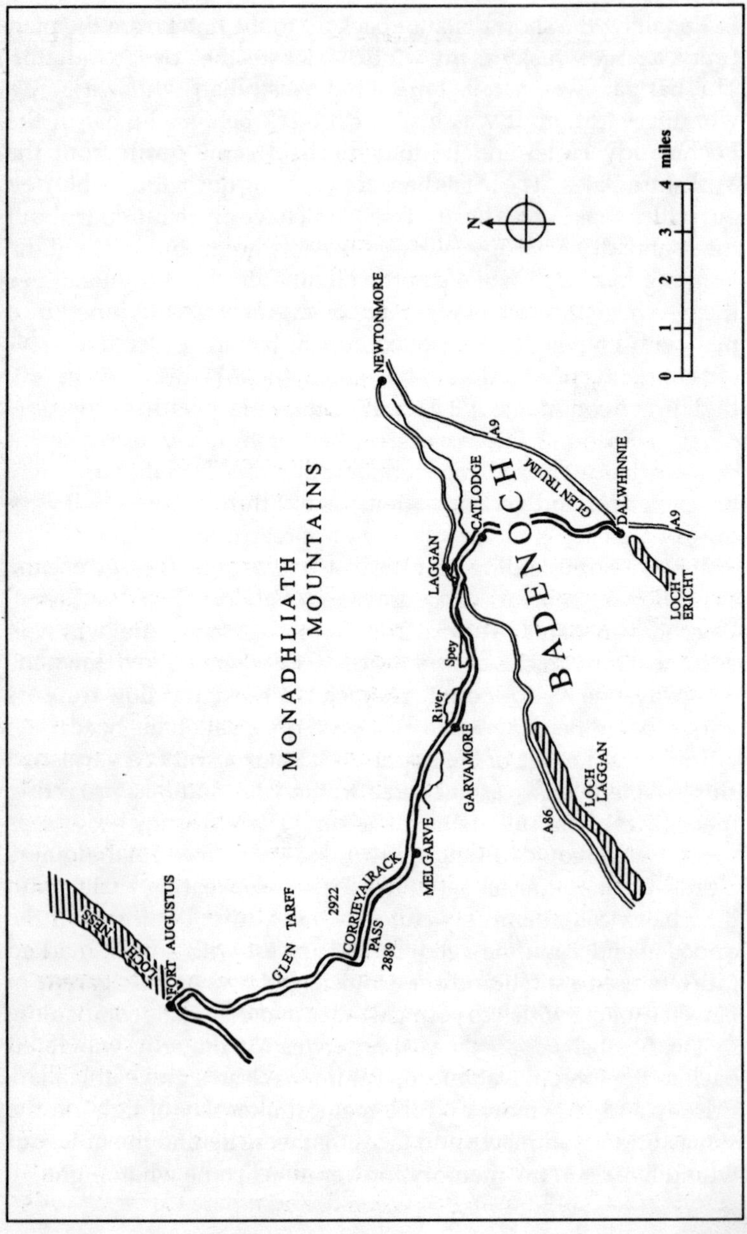
MONADHLIATH
MOUNTAINS
BADENOCH
LOCH NESS
FORT AUGUSTUS
GLEN TARFF
2922
CORRIEYAIRACK
PASS
2889
MELGARVE
GARVAMORE
River Spey
LAGGAN
CATLODGE
NEWTONMORE
A9
GLEN TRUIM
DALWHINNIE
A9
LOCH ERICHT
LOCH LAGGAN
A86
N
0 1 2 3 4 miles

CHAPTER 8

West Highland Journey

Rain, midnight rain, nothing but the wild rain
On this bleak hut, and solitude, and me.

Edward Thomas, 'Rain', *Selected Poems*, 1964.

There is no sound within the cottage now
But my pen and the sound of long rain
Heavy and musical, I must think again
To find so sweet a noise, and cannot anywhere.

Ivor Gurney, Unpublished poems.

RAIN BEGAN TO STREAK the windows of the carriage in rhythmical lines as the Inverness bound train rattled between the white gates of a level crossing at Murthly. My destination was Dalwhinnie. I had left Edinburgh at 9.20 a.m. and with a student railcard the fare had come to £5, which seems remarkable value nowadays.

I had deliberately waited until autumn when the midge season would have passed. My intention was to make a leisurely crossing of the Corrieyairack Pass on Wade's last military road to Fort Augustus, push on for Glenelg and Skye, before spending a few days exploring the former crofting settlement at Smirisary in Moidart, then back to Newtonmore by the Laggan road. On paper it looked a fascinating circuit with plenty of historical interest and some gruelling ascents – but for every hill you go up...

Strathtay looked lush and sodden in the mid-morning downpour as the next carriage played host to some loud Country and Western music courtesy of some oil-rig construction workers heading back to work. It was not a day for a bike. The bare highland hills were capped with mist and began to close in after Struan. Dalnacardoch with a handful of buildings crouched below the A9 looked a forbidding outpost. It was here that the old military roads from Dunkeld and Stirling converged, and where General Wade had established one of his many 'hutts' in 1729, later to become an inn at which James Hogg, the Ettrick Shepherd would stay during the early summer of 1803.

It seems highly likely that Hogg's account of the notorious Gaick catastrophe, published in *The Spy* seven years later, was based upon what he heard while staying at Dalnacardoch.

On New Year's Day 1800, Major John Macpherson of Lorick and four others were engulfed by an avalanche while they sheltered in a substantial forest hut at Gaick, a reputedly evil spot located deep within the hills to the north of Dalnacardoch. The episode was destined to excite the popular imagination of the day since Macpherson was much disliked on account of his recruiting activities in the area. The hut at Gaick was reduced to its foundations by the ferocity of the avalanche: stone walls ripped to pieces and carried up to 400 yards away, thatch for nearly a mile, and the shooting party's guns contorted into every possible shape.

A search party came upon one of the victims in a sitting posture as though in the act of taking off his shoes. Amongst the dead were three hunting dogs. According to Hogg, in the week prior to the tragedy Macpherson had made an exploratory visit to Gaick and encountered a mysterious stranger or spectre who seemed to threaten him before making a sudden exit from the scene. The incident is said to have greatly unsettled Macpherson and altered the entire mood of his party. Unlike a version of the same events given by Sir Walter Scott in 1827, Hogg's account is much closer to the definitive version of the tragedy, published by Alexander Macpherson much later in 1893.

I was the only passenger to disembark at Dalwhinnie. The place comprises a distillery, a hotel, some houses, a petrol station and a transport café. It still provides a convenient stopping-place for motorists and lorry drivers on the A9, which nowadays bypasses it to the east.

Rain was lashing down as I made a beeline for the café. A colour TV blinked in one corner of the room as truckers sat together eating, smoking and drinking tea from large mugs. I ordered the works: bacon, sausages, egg and fried bread. The fry-up could have graced a four-star hotel and was better than many of the breakfasts in lesser establishments.

Suitably fuelled, I made my way out of the potholed car park to take up my route along the A889 to Drumgask, more or less following the line of the old military road. Such roads were built with the primary objective of easing the movement of government troops and their supplies at a time when political unrest in the Highlands posed a serious disruptive threat.

Military roads were the first important stage in the development of Highland communications, and their extent and role has been discussed in a fascinating book on the subject by Dr William Taylor – *The Military Roads in Scotland* (David & Charles, 1976).

Wade's task was to link the military bases in the Highlands by his road system and join the network of Lowland roads. The bases were the three forts (Fort William, Fort Augustus and Fort George) along the Great Glen, and the barracks at Ruthven near Kingussie. The General was working in an unmapped country, the first systematic mapping of Scotland being William Roy's Military Survey of 1747–55.

By 1730 there was still no road linking the Central Highlands with the Great Glen. Wade's programme for the following year was to drive a road from Dalwhinnie over the 2,500-foot Corrieyairack Pass to Fort Augustus. The distance was only some 28 miles, but work on the project was impossible during winter: Wade's men were unskilled and their tools simple – shovels, pickaxes, spades, iron crows, screw jacks and sledgehammers. They also had gunpowder and fuses if there was rock to be blasted.

Wheeling the red machine up a couple of punishing braes in the pouring rain, I had nothing but admiration for the early road builders as the route dipped through uncompromisingly bleak and heavily fenced moorland with little in the way of habitation. The A889 reaches a height of nearly 1,300 feet, drops, then climbs once more before the gradual descent to Catlodge. Here were the ruins of a cottage that was formerly a veritable college of Scottish piping, being the one-time home of Malcolm Macpherson, piper to Cluny and styled 'King of Pipers'. In his beautifully written book, *The Highlands*, Calum Maclean writes:

> 'Old Malcolm Macpherson used no books, no musical scores; his method of teaching was entirely oral and he used a system of vocables called in Gaelic *canntaireachd*. That was the very system

employed by the MacCrimmons [of Skye] and other piping schools. In that little cottage at Catlag old Malcolm enforced a rigorous discipline. Pupils sent to him started at ten in the morning and continued until ten in the evening with only short intervals for meals and a break of about half an hour at four in the afternoon, when they were sent out for a walk. Sometimes young boys living in the Badenoch district walked distances of ten to fourteen miles in sleet and snow during the depth of winter for their nightly tuition and walked back home again.'

The legendary Macpherson had often walked the route I was to follow, over the Corrieyairack on his way to visit fellow pipers in Skye.

I was well and truly drenched by the time I reached Drumgask, where there are the ruins of an interesting church with a high needle-like spire. Here the A889 descends steeply to join the A86 Newtonmore to Fort William road. As the descent begins, the old Wade road branches off and runs below the Drumgask cottages to join the A86 a few yards further on. At the junction I forked left and rejoined the Wade road about half a mile further on, where electricity pylons cross the road at GR 605936. At this stage the Wade road is a heathery track, but it shortly joins the drive leading to Dalchully House. From the turn-off to this house, I had to wheel my bike along a rocky, puddle-strewn track before reaching the minor road from Laggan to Garva Bridge.

Ahead, mist groped down the wooded slopes of Black Craig, blotting out most of the steep north-east buttress known as the Dun because the remains of an ancient fort are on its summit. It felt strange to be on tarmac once more as I rode up a twisting section of road to a small, unobtrusive reservoir built by the British Aluminium Company at the turn of the century. Near its western end was a cup-marked boulder by the side of the road (563930) which curiously sounded hollow when I tapped it with a stone.

For a mile or so beyond Sherrabeg the road continued by a series of long corners, at one stage being built on an embankment and bypassing a small single-arch bridge which lay stranded on dry ground but must have been the line of the Wade road at one time. I continued over a bridge and passed a sawmill close to where another road continued up to Sherramore.

It was near here, or at a small clump of trees known locally as Cope's Turn further down near Dalchully House, that an event took place which otherwise might have altered the events of the second Jacobite rebellion. The Hanoverian General Sir John Cope had marched up from Stirling at the head of 1,400 infantrymen in order to meet the Jacobite forces which were then on the other side of the Corrieyairack, one of a number of times when they were to avail themselves of the Wade roads. Besides having a vast quantity of baggage, Cope's troops were followed by a train of black cattle, with butchers to kill them as required. It was reported to Cope that the Highlanders planned to surprise him in a pincer movement at 'Snugborough Bridge' on the Culachy side of the Pass. Estimates of the Jacobite strength place it at about 1,500 men. Once more according to local tradition, Cope is said to have tested the mettle of his men by pointing to a distant wood and exclaiming, 'Yonder are the Highlanders!'. On hearing this the Hanoverians are said to have trembled in fear, and after a huddled confab with his officers, Cope decided to turn foot and head for Inverness. The General's decision that August morning in 1745 featured among a number of charges brought against him at his court-martial one year later. This was in fact presided over by Wade but Sir John Cope was acquitted on all counts.

In the unending rain I soon came to Garvamore [Garbhamòr]. Here, as in other places, a hutted or tented camp used by the troops who constructed the military road was replaced by a building for housing both military and civilian travellers. Such buildings were known as 'kingshouses' because they stood on the king's highway. Later Garvamore became a drovers' inn and more recently a keeper's house.

Built in 1739, Garvamore still stands, although it was in a somewhat dilapidated state when I inspected it. In appearance it is a long two-storey structure, the west end having stables below and a loft with fireplace above, probably for housing troops. The walls are of coursed rubble with longish split field boulders that have been harled with a quality Scots harl. The bell-cast on the roof indicated it had been thatched at one time, with porches and a kitchen at the east end added at a later date. The 16-pane windows with shutters were partly to be seen, as was an old wooden staircase with turned bannisters and carved posts. Upstairs in the former inn were three rooms with low, sagging ceilings and flooring that had considerable movement when walked upon. Wide lathing on plaster was exposed in parts and indicated the age of the building: if walls could talk what stories they could tell.

Garvamore had also been one of the stations for the 'Moving Patrol', set up by the government after Culloden in an attempt to curb cattle-raiding by the Highlanders. It worked like a mobile cordon of 200 to 300 Redcoats, each patrol consisting of sometimes only four soldiers, at other times, six or more. There is nothing to be seen of the actual Patrol Huts, and but for Robert Louis Stevenson's *Kidnapped*, few of us would have known about the Patrol's existence.

Another intrepid tramper of this route was the eccentric Victorian author George Borrow, who came over the Corrieyairack from Fort Augustus in deep snow up to his waist on the first of his marathon Scottish treks in 1858. Nowadays Borrow's books, such as *Lavengro*, are little read, although in some quarters he has become a minor cult figure. He was born in 1813 and grew up to be a wild, rebellious youth, over six feet tall; a formidable fighter, excellent horseman, intolerant of authority, at home in the company of gypsies and astounding as it seems, possessing a working knowledge of at least 30 languages, including such unusual tongues as Old Norse, Manchu, and Romany.

From early in life Borrow suffered from recurrent attacks of severe depression which he referred to as 'the horrors'. He was an enigmatic character who probably liked it that way. Here was a man who would doff his hat to a passing stallion, who believed in the curative properties of ale for horses; a man whose CV included spells as a Bible seller, trainee lawyer, itinerant hedge-smith and snake-catcher. Add to this his dodgy temper, cantankerous moods, and a neurotic roadside ritual – shared by the famous Dr Samuel Johnson – of having to touch objects such as posts, trees and stones in order to avert evil spirits: all in all, a man out of the ordinary.

Borrow set out to walk from Fort Augustus to Dalwhinnie on 11 October 1858, hardly dressed for the venture in a pair of ordinary shoes beneath his black surtout, and carrying a small knapsack and a green umbrella, the latter his favoured piece of protective 'clothing'. From his quirky but perceptive tour diaries, it transpires that his crossing of the Corrieyairack amounted to something of an epic. At first he secured the services of a junior guide, but Borrow of the mighty strides soon loses his way and becomes engulfed by the drifts of snow. Fortunately, he waded out of this predicament to find the right course, celebrating with a slug of whisky from his flask.

Garvamore is described by Borrow as a 'large desolate stone house with broken windows'; there were to be no black ale and capital dinners for Borrow here, simply an oatcake washed down with milk that was kindly supplied by a shepherd's wife. Borrow rewards her with a shilling and receives a curtsey. In darkness he completes the last few miles across the moors to the inn at Dalwhinnie: a considerable day's outing by any standards.

Continuing on my journey, I arrived at Garva Bridge across the Spey, a fine example of a double-arched Wade bridge, the first of its type that Wade built. The tarred road continued on the other side, being maintained by the Hydroelectric Board. There was flooding in places as I rode up a long, gently-rising stretch past a plantation where a solitary stag loitered below the trees, ever watchful of my progress. The tarmac road is simply laid on top of the Wade route at this stage, and the last stretch before Melgarve was in poor condition, being more suited for walkers or cross-country vehicles.

The area around Melgarve, marked on modern maps as Drummin, used to be the summer shieling ground of the Laggan, where cattle were taken every season for the hill grazing. Checking the map, I noticed a number of old shielings were marked further up near the watershed of the Spey.

The uninhabited cottage at Melgarve makes a convenient bothy for travellers on the Corrieyairack route. In former days Melgarve had served as a stance for cattle droves, which were taken over the Pass from as far afield as Skye, Muir of Ord and Strath Halladale in Sutherland. Even when the military road was abandoned about 1827, the bridges on the route were still in relatively good repair until the middle of last century and contemporary records show the Corrieyairack was still used by drovers after that time.

Since leaving Garva Bridge the storm had increased in its ferocity and I was grateful to find the shelter of this lonely outpost.

The bothy door was secured by tightly knotted twine which took me a few minutes to undo, before I opened the creaky door and peered into a downstairs room which had a stone floor and walls covered with graffiti. There was a bed with mattress but it looked an uninviting hole: it would do for the bike.

Taking out my torch I ventured upstairs to a room which had been denuded of its pine panelling in mindless attempts to obtain firewood for the downstairs fire. However, a second room was in perfect order, free from litter and vandalism and would make a perfect howff for the night.

Discarding my sodden anorak, boots and over-trousers, I unzipped the flea-bag and tried to rub some warmth back into my bones. I lit some candles and morale was boosted by the reassuring purr of the stove as I brewed up some tea and later a tin of stew mixed in with spaghetti Bolognese. Apple pie and a few drams brought me back to life as I relaxed in the bag with a copy of Alastair Borthwick's classic account of his gangrel days in the 1930s – *Always A Little Further*. No other book could have been more fitting for my present situation. Occasionally as I looked up from the pages, the candles slowly dripped their grease and shortened as the wild rain drummed the skylight and slates. The spartan simplicity of my surroundings did not matter; it was enough to be warm and dry, content with one's lot. At five to midnight I snuffed out the candles and retired to my dreams, full of expectation that the weather might change for the better.

Next morning there was no such luck. The day was blustery and raw with intermittent heavy showers; light mist swirled around the tops and seemed to cling like glue to the summit of the Pass.

Leaving the bothy as I had found it, I wheeled the red machine along an increasingly rutted track which was more like a stream than a road. On the lengthy uphill climb I crossed a footbridge that had been repaired with railway sleepers, but most of the fords called for more desperate manoeuvres and sometimes not inconsiderable detours to get the loaded bike across the swollen streams. In Wade's time, most of the Corrieyairack burns were bridged.

All thoughts of keeping my feet dry vanished with every plunge into the ice-cold water, the bike minus load being carried on my shoulder as I made a return dash back to collect the rest of my gear.

This was the only way to make progress.

The most testing part of the climb are the 13 traverses which zigzag their way up to the summit. Wade originally built 18 traverses, each one supported by retaining walls, although five were taken out in a later construction. Their steepness seemed unrelenting and I stopped for an impromptu brew after negotiating the second traverse. Stuffing some chocolate into my mouth I set off, back bent into pushing the bike up the punishing inclines. The combination of the grey of the mist and the unsightly electricity pylons resembled a vision of Hell.

Near the top of the Pass I left the bike by the track and scrambled up to the site of the General's Well. It was a disappointing huddle of stones. I did not linger but set about the final push to the top with renewed energy. Upon reaching the summit I let out a yell of delight. There was no view, just heather and dripping rock.

The descent was relatively easy as I tried to remain in the saddle with my boots poised on the pedals, not risking the possibly dangerous confinement imposed by the toe-clips. The present day route bypasses 'Snugburrow Bridge' as it is shown on Roy's map, taking a lower path of descent by a Bailey bridge erected in 1961 by the Royal Engineers. I rattled over the wooden slats, then dismounted for another pushing section before reaching Blackburn. Here I had some difficulty in fording the burn as the water was quite high. A Land Rover with a stalker and two toffs was crawling up the track towards me and I noticed they had shot a stag. There followed a rocky uneventful slog down to Culachy, the view livened by the deep green gash of Glen Tarff and patches of rust-coloured bracken on the hillsides.

Crossing the Corrieyairack with a bike had been an experience I would not like to repeat under similar conditions. Fort Augustus and tarmac roads could not come quickly enough. Rain was bucketing down as I entered a shop to buy more candles and headed for the nearest café to enjoy a reasonably priced hot meal. It was six and a half hours since I had left Melgarve and ahead lay a nightmare joust with the busy A82 to Invergarry. Apart from the buffeting wind, I had to contend with spray thrown up by speeding vehicles which gave me precious little room for safety as they raced past in an impatient stream. I reached Invergarry in near darkness, eternally grateful to be off that awful road.

My contact man was 76-year-old John MacAskill, who looked every inch a retired head stalker. Although my visit was unexpected this Friday evening, he showed me true Highland hospitality and welcomed me into his living room, where there was a roaring coal fire. John said I could sleep in his barn for the night and I brought out my flask to pour him a dram, only to discover embarrassingly that it yielded nothing but the dregs. With a hearty laugh, John reached for his sideboard, where there was full bottle and poured me a glass. His plan was for us to adjourn to the local hotel after we had dispensed with the interview, which I recorded on a small Sony tape machine.

I was keen to find out if John had memories of the old-style travelling packmen who were still coming round to remoter areas of the Highlands up until the 1950s.

'I remember one old boy called McQueen,' John said as his mind ticked back over the years. 'He used to come round here when I was just a small boy at school, and I believe he was coming here before the Great War. He would be going as far as Kinloch Hourn by the road, then over the hill to the like of Arnisdale.'

'What was he like in terms of appearance?' I asked.

'Oh, he'd a beard that was almost white, very closely clipped you know, and you could buy a good open razor from him, a shaving brush, collar studs and things like that.'

Later John mentioned an old coffin route that funeral parties used to take from Glen Garry to Kilfinan burial ground on the north-east shore of Loch Lochy. He told me the route went over the western shoulder of Ben Tee and people erected cairns at resting places along the way. This was an age-old custom and it was said to be unlucky for any member of the party not to add a stone to such cairns, which also served as waymarkers.

Our discussion was short and we soon left for the pub. I do not recall much about the rest of the evening, except that I enjoyed myself and John's company thoroughly. Straw served to pad the floor of Jock's barn and water dripped onto my sleeping bag through an unseen hole in the corrugated-iron roof, although that night I would have been oblivious to anything.

By the time I rose next morning, John had left for Inverness. The rain was as unrelenting as ever and the prospect of a damp, hungover day in the saddle had as much appeal as strychnine-sweetened tea. I had another informant to track down over by Glenelg, a retired crofter-shepherd with exactly the same name as last night's host.

In driving rain it was a sobering climb up the A87 from Invergarry. Morale was at its nadir. On a good day, this road rewards with a splendid panoramic view over the Glen Kingie and Knoydart mountains. Today there was cloud and rain and more rain. I stopped for a hair of the dog at the Cluanie Inn, a former military and coaching inn which is one of the oldest in Scotland and known to many hill walkers, who arrive with tongues dripping at its door. Inside it had lost its old character and I did not stay long.

Hemmed in on both sides by the flanks of high mountains, Glen Shiel was a forbidding spot, with convoys of cars bound for the Skye ferry at Kyle of Lochalsh. In places the modern road follows the line of Caulfeild's military road from Fort Augustus and it was the route taken by Dr Johnson and James Boswell in 1773 on their way to the Isles.

At Shiel Bridge I bought soup, rolls, yoghurt and other provisions at the petrol station shop. Nearby is Ratagan youth hostel and I have happy memories of staying there 20 years ago when the warden went out lobster fishing in a small boat on Loch Duich.

I was following Boswell and Johnson's route up the switchback single track road which twists its way through Ratagan Forest to Glenelg. When the hefty Dr Johnson made the journey he rode on two horses alternately, such was the exertion that his weight placed on the poor beasts. The forest climb was a killer, and once more I was denied any view, this time of the magnificent Five Sisters of Kintail.

Scallasaig up from Glenelg village was the home of my informant, the other John MacAskill, who was born in 1900 and whose father and grandfather had shepherded a short distance away at Beolary. John was a fund of knowledge about Glenelg's history and traditions over the last 130 years, and while I was drying off by his fire, a splendid meal of tea, scones and home-made oatcakes and cheese was being prepared by John's wife. After demolishing the spread I got cracking to John about the old days, asking him if he could recall the packman McQueen.

'Yes, I remember that fellow when I was going to school and long after it,' John replied. 'He belonged to a well-known family in Beccles down in Suffolk. He was what you would call a very respectable pedlar – well brought up and that – but he took to the drink I think, and had to leave home. He was such a respectable-looking fellow that he used to get employment in Lord Burton's shooting lodge at Glen Quoich when he had guests and they needed a bigger staff. Old McQueen was there doing the washing-up at the end of the shooting season. And when they held their Ghillies' Ball... every time there was a ladies' choice, Lady Burton went and took McQueen, and all the other fellows were annoyed you know – them with their tweeds, plus-fours and stockings. I think the old pedlar got a suit from the butler. He was a lovely dancer.

'I remember when I was a boy at Beolary, where I was born, my sisters who are all dead now, they were terribly interested in dancing, and I remember McQueen taking half a night putting them through a dance called Petronella. It used to be danced regular here, and my brother would play an old melodeon. That was old McQueen; he was a decent old fellow.'

A fair proportion of the pedlars who had regular beats in the West Highlands were of Irish extraction, or at least assumed to be Irishmen by the local population. These men came from large families whose small hill farms could not support all the members of the family and thus they took to selling their wares about the countryside.

'Were there any other characters you recall?' I asked John.

'There was this gentleman, Joe Wilson. I don't exactly know where he belonged to originally but that wasn't his actual name. In one time of his life he was attending to horses as a jockey. Something happened and he went on the tramp. He used to come round here collecting rabbit-skins, sold onions and things like that. His wife was called Jean, a big heavy woman who sold children's clothes, laces and all these things to the women. Joe used to live in a cave right down near the shore at a place called the Market Stance, where they used to hold the old cattle sales or fairs away back in the early 1900s. It didn't please them so they shifted to a cave further along the coast, quite close to this place called Camusfearna [Sandaig] in Gavin Maxwell's book, *Ring of Bright Water*. They lived there for years and used to gather whelks when the tide was suitable.

'This day they got in contact with an old worthy called The Pelican who used to play the fiddle very well in the old style. He had a little cottage but the parochial board took him over and he was in a house down at Galltair. They tell me he originally belonged to Dundee. So this night they had a good drop to drink and they went back to the cave. It was a calm night. Well, Old Jean appears to have taken too much, and when they came to the shore at the cave, they left the boat – it was ebb tide – but didn't tie it up. They went to the cave and started making food or drinking: I don't know. But anyway the tide and north wind got up and Jean by that time was sleeping, lying drunk in the boat. It floated off down the Sound of Sleat and landed in Knoydart.

'The boat was found in the morning and Old Jean was dead. The Pelican reported it and called at a keeper's house. The keeper asked: "Is Jean dead?" "Ah dae ken," says The Pelican, "but she's baith killt an droont". That was what he answered . She died of exposure you know. They didn't assault her or kill her, by any means.'

Gavin Maxwell writes about this incident in *Ring of Bright Water*, and it is interesting to compare the slant he gives to the story with the version I tape-recorded from John MacAskill.

Darkness was closing in at Scallasaig and I wanted to get quickly settled in the bothy further up Glen More before the spate made the river dangerous to cross. Taking a single pannier loaded with provisions, as well as the sleeping-bag, I asked John if he would look after my bike. He told me Suardalan was last inhabited as a cottage in 1922 and now served as a bothy for estate workers and hill-walkers. The rough track near the river was so badly water-logged that I had to gain height to find dry ground, and in the mounting gloom nearly overshot the bothy and got lost.

A sign indicated that Suardalan was one of the howffs maintained by the Mountain Bothies' Association. Inside it was like a palace as far as bothies are concerned. There were signs of recent repair work and I found a berth in a small wood-panelled room upstairs which had a leaky skylight. Downstairs there was a supply of emergency rations, a stack of dry firewood and a shelf of books and copies of *The Scots Magazine*. According to the tattered bothy logbook, Suardalan was the responsibility of the Braes of Fife Mountaineering Club. I had the place to myself and felt like a guest at the Hilton, even if I only had two Irish ten pence coins and tuppence to my name. Tomorrow was a Sunday, and Monday a Bank Holiday. However, I had enough food to see me through until I could cash a cheque.

The following morning the rain eased, then eventually stopped. After collecting my bike I rode down to Glenelg village and on to neighbouring Glen Beag, where I inspected the famous brochs which stand there. Returning to the bothy I read for most of the day in front of a rather smoky fire. I did not see John until Monday, when he was in fine form and gave me a lot of information about funeral customs, local place-names, whisky distilling, more on the pedlars and lastly, a short anecdotal yarn about a dwarf who frightened herring fishermen in Loch Hourn with his terrible voice. John also told me about his childhood recollections regarding the last of the cattle droves which came over from Skye.

'I remember two droves,' he said. 'I would have been about five I think. But I can still remember watching them and I think my sister and brother were there with me. This drove was stretched over the best part of three quarters of a mile and there must have been about three hundred-and-four animals there, for I remember the drovers counting them. The beasts were a wee bit stottery on the gravel roads. The roads at that time were not made up and the cattle took badly to them. They had come across the Narrows [of Kyle Rhea] in a *gabbart* – a rowing boat with four oars that took eight animals at a time. Before, they used to swim them across at dead tide; one animal tied to the other's tail, and this was how they did it. But not during full Spring tides. The Narrows have a current of eleven knots at full Spring tides and it would be too dangerous. And they had what they called the "Stances of the MacLeods". This was where they rested the animals on their journey. Near that cave down beside the sea was one of them, and another was on top of the Mam Ratagan. The next one was over at Shiel Bridge in the hollow near the petrol station.'

On Tuesday I said farewell to John, having managed to cash a cheque at the local hotel. The old inn which Boswell and Johnson stayed in, much to their disgust, was down near the pier for the Skye ferry. Boswell had this to say about their lodgings: 'Out of one of the beds, on which we were to repose, started up, at our entrance, a man black as a Cyclops from the forge. Other circumstances of no elegant recital concurred to disgust us.'

With the sun beating down I crossed over to Kylerhea by what is the shortest ferry crossing to the island of Skye. There followed a punishing climb up to the Bealach Udal, followed by a glorious spin down Glen Attoch. Skye was bathed in sunshine and looked magnificent. After a brief flirtation with the Kylakin–Broadford road I forked left at Skulamus. Once more I was on a quiet road whose ribbon of tarmac cut through deserted moorlands which were a uniform brown splashed with patches of purple. Near to Kinloch there unfolded a dramatic view across the Sound of Sleat to the Rough Bounds of Knoydart.

I halted to take in this majestically wild scene which no camera could have captured. Further along I dipped between an avenue of birches and other wonderful trees, before there unfolded a second magnificent view of Loch Hourn, serene and land-locked, being reminiscent of a Norwegian fjord. The purple-grey clouds of early evening capped the knuckled fist of mountains which makes this one of the grandest stretches of coastline in Britain.

Pressing hard on the pedals, I cruised along the remaining seven miles to Armadale, passing the ruins of Knock Castle, some architecturally interesting free kirks, Ostaig House and the Clan Donald Centre. The amber lights of Mallaig appeared as tiny specks in the distance and I was able to make out the Morar coast before the view was gradually swallowed by the dusk. At one point on the ride I caught a flashing glimpse of the setting sun, before it dropped out of sight like a molten ball of fire.

My destination was the Grade 2 youth hostel at Armadale. Once there, I made a telephone call to Glenfinnan House Hotel, the home of Charlie MacFarlane, my contact man for Moidart.

The hostel was not far from the pier. Since the Armadale–Mallaig ferry was not until 11.30 next morning, there was time to visit the Gaelic college, *Sabhal Mor Ostaig*. Founded in 1973, the college is housed in an attractively converted farm steading, with the aim of 'educating people for a career in the West Highlands, rather than training them for the professions of the cities', a feature of the existing education system which in the past has drained the crofting areas of their best leadership and talent.

The Cal–Mac ferry *Pioneer* had a completely different atmosphere from the *Hebrides* on the Uig to Lochmaddy crossing. Instead of quaint varnished tables and seats, the lounge was colourfully decked out in tangerine bucket chairs; the voyage was much shorter, offering magnificent views of the cliffs of Eigg and the impressive serrated ridge of the Rhum hills. With the mainland coast in sight all the way, this was a mere hop rather than a true sea journey as experienced on the crossing to Uist. Two other cyclists were on the ferry and we all managed to squeeze in beside the first three cars to be unloaded.

The A830 Mallaig–Fort William road is partly single-track, the last trunk road of its kind in Britain. The 20-mile section between Mallaig and Lochailort breaks steering racks, suspensions and sensitive motorists' hearts with its blind summits, hairpin bends and the mixing of heavy summer tourist traffic with fish-laden juggernauts. I decided to give this road a miss and take the train to Glenfinnan.

After experiencing what must be the most scenically beautiful train journey in Britain, I shortly reached Glenfinnan and pedalled down from the attractive station to Glenfinnan House Hotel, which is situated in beautiful grounds on the west bank of Loch Shiel. I was kindly ushered into the lounge, and after several minutes, in strode the kilted figure of Charlie MacFarlane, an inimitable character and much-valued friend of the School of Scottish Studies. Charlie immediately took great interest in the work I was doing, waxing lyrical from below his handlebar moustache about local history, place-names and traditional music. He is a keen piper and a charmingly hospitable man, modest in manner and still retaining the old form of Highland dignity, which is not so prevalent these days. Over a beer and sandwiches he provided me with a list of possible contacts for the Moidart area, giving an informative brief about each person. He went on to suggest that I should return to his hotel after my excursions, when he would put me up in one of the staff rooms free of charge.

With morale high, I warmly thanked Charlie for his generous

OS 33, 32, 40

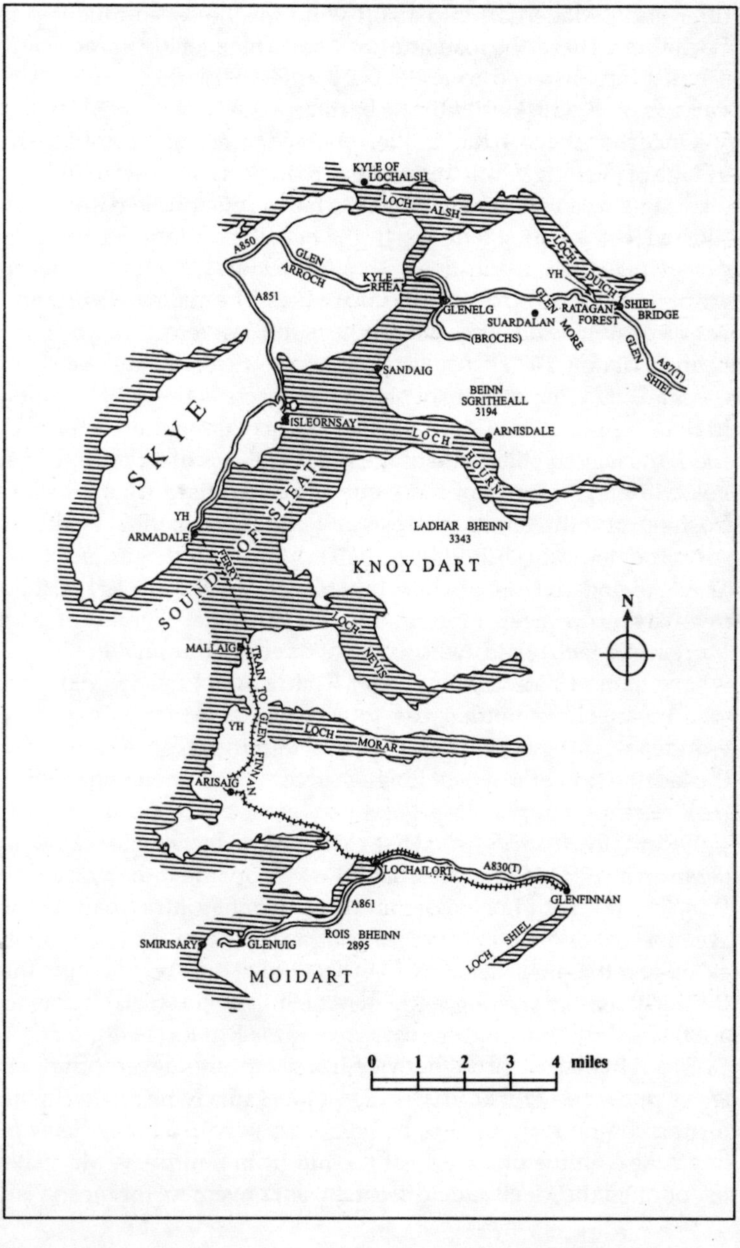
KYLE OF LOCHALSH
LOCH ALSH
A850
GLEN ARROCH
KYLE RHEA
A851
LOCH DUICH
YH
GLENELG
GLEN MORE
SUARDALAN
RATAGAN FOREST
SHIEL BRIDGE
(BROCHS)
GLEN SHIEL
A87(T)
SANDAIG
BEINN SGRITHEALL 3194
SKYE
ISLEORNSAY
LOCH HOURN
ARNISDALE
SOUND OF SLEAT
YH
ARMADALE
FERRY
LADHAR BHEINN 3343
KNOY DART
N
LOCH NEVIS
MALLAIG
TRAIN TO GLEN FINNAN
YH
LOCH MORAR
ARISAIG
LOCHAILORT
A830(T)
GLENFINNAN
A861
ROIS BHEINN 2895
SMIRISARY
GLENUIG
LOCH SHIEL
MOIDART
0 1 2 3 4 miles

offer and pedalled off into a stiff wind for the seven-mile trip to Lochailort. There, the roadside hotel had a blazing log fire and over a half-pint I listened to a Cockney angler discuss the merits of various malt whiskies with the barman.

Once more back in the saddle, I pressed on along the A861 to the village of Glenuig. Until this modern road was constructed in 1967, Glenuig's sole access by land was a hazardous bridle path which twisted its way along the coast from Lochailort, nine miles away. In places the path was only one and a half feet wide, sloping at a sharp angle to a sheer drop over cliffs into the sea. The mails were brought in by a postman and pony, while other supplies were ferried by boat.

In his book *The Highlands* (1959; repr. 1990), Calum Maclean gives an engaging account of his time spent collecting oral tradition in the Glenuig area. At one stage of the ride along the Loch Ailort road, the jagged silhouette of the Black Cuillins of Skye appeared below a narrow band of red cloud. I pushed hard up a hill near Roshven and three miles later swung into Glenuig village with its scattered homes, a church on a small hill, and a whitewashed hotel. The blue-and-red hull of a boat lay stranded by the tide as I pushed my way up a steep brae, bound for 'Seannlac', home of Mrs Margaret MacDonald, who is mentioned in Calum's book and whose name I had been given by Charlie MacFarlane. Margaret was busy selling bottled gas to a customer when I arrived. 'I wonder why they don't put regulators on these containers,' said the lady customer in a posh English accent. 'You soon know when they're empty,' replied Margaret.

Originally from South Uist, Margaret MacDonald came to Glenuig in 1950. Her late husband Ronnie operated the passenger ferry to and from Lochailort until the coming of the road. I was given a seat and a cup of tea in Margaret's warm kitchen while I explained the purpose of my visit and how I was keen to visit the formerly remote crofting settlement of Smirisary which I had read about in Margaret Leigh's *Spade Among the Rushes* (1948).

Sunlight blazed through the bedroom curtains next morning; it was a perfect day for Smirisary. The oldest surviving link with the former community was Angus MacIsaac, who lived with his wife in a house on the other side of the hill from Smirisary. Margaret telephoned the MacIsaacs to see if it was convenient for me to visit them. In shirt-sleeves I sped downhill to the Glenuig Inn, trundled over a cattle-grid and took the narrow road which creeps by Samalaman House to be replaced by a rough stony track which ended at a bungalow situated in a hollow. The MacIsaacs' house lay up a slope, a short distance from the track and was reached by a footpath. Some Jacob's sheep were munching grass outside the porch door as my knock on the door was answered by an elderly thickset man with a full, weather-beaten face. Angus invited me inside to the front room, which was tightly packed with furniture, including a Scots dresser and an old spinning wheel.

In a slow but purposeful manner, Angus explained how the MacIsaacs had originally been bailies to Clanranald and were an old, old Moidart name. He believed his people had settled in Smirisary after being evicted from Kinlochmoidart, and mentioned that, sadly, the old community at Smirisary had been replaced by those with holiday homes. He went on to tell me that hippies had moved into some of the Glenuig cottages and how the place was nothing like what it had been in his young days. 'There used to be nine families living down at Smirisary in the 1920s. The old houses had heather thatch until it became scarce when they started to burn the hill ground for grazing. I heard my father say the heather lasted 25 years on the house. In the end, rushes were used for thatch but they rot quicker and had hayseed in them which tended to sprout.'

Angus kindly agreed to lead me over to Smirisary. At the crest of a secret-looking overgrown path we looked down on the ruins of the MacNeill brothers' one-time home, mentioned by Margaret Leigh in her book. Arriving at Smirisary was like entering a lost world in miniature, as enchanting and rocky a location as any on the west coast of Scotland. Out to sea the view was dominated by the Sguir of Eigg, rising sheer from the island like a blade of an axe, dominating the neighbouring Isle of Muck and set against the backdrop of the spectacular hills on Rhum which rose high into a cloudless, serene sky of indigo blue. Through binoculars it was possible to pick out the distant island of Coll, which lay far out over the Ardnamurchan peninsula, the most westerly point on the Scottish mainland.

'I remember when you couldn't see a rush or any bracken,' said Angus, looking down at the scene below us. 'It was all corn and potatoes in those strips. The MacNeill's croft and my father's croft were running together in the old runrig system, and we had to mark out the hay strips with hazel sticks. Stones which were permanent had been left in the corners of the strips for marking purposes when we cut the hay, but once the grass got up it was difficult to see them, so that's why the tall rods were used. Now it's just been allowed to go back to nature: sad in a way.

'Smirisary as I remember was a real community, with old and young about: cutting the peats, bringing in the hay, fishing for saithe off the rocks in Autumn. And people helped one another then. Money wasn't so important; any arguments didn't last long – the place was too small for there to be arguing. And no-one bothered locking their doors. Angus MacNeill's was a great ceilidh house in the old days and I remember going there to play Catch the Ten and The Bachelor. There would be stories, or talking about the day's work; everyone sitting round the fire and the older men smoking their black twist.'

Old Charlie MacPherson who lived in a blackhouse (now in ruins) at the Goirtean had a fund of stories which were passed on to Angus Ruairidh MacPherson, from whom Calum Maclean recorded a version of a complex wonder-tale, *Cath nan Eun* or 'The Battle of the Birds'.

Smirisary in its heyday was virtually a self-sufficient little world. The crofters had their crops of oats and potatoes, gathered brambles and wild mushrooms, collected scallops and whelks off the seashore, and went out in small boats for lobsters. When the weather was unsuitable for their small boats to reach the pier at Glenuig, oatmeal and flour had to be carried in sacks on their backs a not inconsiderable distance over a footpath which the crofters themselves built up in places with stone steps. In later years a puffer called at Samalaman with supplies of coal, but peat was the main fuel until 1939. Angus MacIsaac told me the coming of the telephone was the first thing to open the place up to the outside world, a public kiosk arriving at Glenuig in 1937.

The authoress Margaret Leigh first saw Smirisary in March 1940. In her book she describes life in this remote township between 1942 and 1947:

'The township of five households was sheltered from the east by high braes, always steep, in places sheer, with tracks leading to more arable above and the great world beyond.... Thus I found Smirisary, and even on that raw March day of wind and hill showers, I fell in love with it.'

The Scottish patriot Wendy Wood also came to live at Smirisary for a time. I asked Angus what he had made of Margaret Leigh: 'She was a bit of an odd character, a rebel of a woman but she had the education and spoke French. Mrs Croall [the former lady laird at Samalaman House] was very good to her and used to feed her on occasions. She called Leigh, her "atheist friend". I remember that she had a pony and made the men in the township do all sorts of jobs for her.'

Angus took me down to Margaret Leigh's former house, now a holiday home, a short distance up from the shingle beach where the waves heaved against the shore. His normal deadpan expression became animated when he talked of all the changes which had occurred, how the hippies had tried to take over Glenuig, and the feudal airs of a certain Major Clegg. Angus's son had found marijuana plants growing on a hill, and Angus explained how the hippies had invited him and his wife to one of their parties but he had gently declined saying he was too old for any hullabaloo.

Major Clegg, a retired South African army officer, had managed the estate for a time, but according to Angus he was 'a bit touched' and had the habit of speaking down to people. On one occasion in Angus's house he had gone beetroot with rage and thumped his fists on the table after a disagreement with Angus over who owned the foundations of one of the Smirisary houses which Clegg wished to turn into a holiday home. Angus and Samalaman Estate share the grazing rights at Smirisary, and as the tenant, Angus has certain legal rights over some of the ruins.

On a perfect autumnal day such as this it was easy to fall in love with Smirisary and to understand Angus's attachment to the place of his birth. Now, he and his family were the last of the local people to live in the area and he felt under severe pressure from all the incomers who had adopted the place, some only for a short time before they moved on elsewhere and were replaced by others. It was a pattern all-too familiar in the Highlands of recent years.

Next morning the rain was coming down in sheets. This was no day for cycling. I decided to follow up a couple of contacts I had for the Mingarry area to the south of Moidart. By the time the daily mail-bus arrived I was soaked to the skin. My destination was simply Hughie the Gamie's, which was immediately accepted by the driver, who enquired: 'Friend of his?' 'Just visiting,' I replied. Apart from one other lady, I was the only other passenger. Tom the driver was a jovial character who chain-smoked Piccadilly plain cigarettes but had a Woodbine voice. All the way down to Kinlochmoidart he barked out descriptions of local interest; 'There's the trees marking the Seven Men of Moidart,' he exclaimed above the drone of the engine. Rain was streaming down the windows of the small bus, but the view up Glen Moidart was nonetheless a haunting one.

Hugh the Gamie was not at home that day. Instead, I made for the shelter of a nearby motel. The weather and appearance of the place reminded me of the Bates' Motel in Alfred Hitchcock's classic thriller *Psycho*. It was the sort of place you might run into Kenneth Roy, formerly of *Scotland on Sunday* fame. I sat in the lounge, which was decorated with tartan kitsch, and ordered a beer. Rather than having a passion for stuffed birds, the proprietor was a danceband musician who had one album to his name, the cover of which decorated some of the walls. We got chatting and he suggested I should speak to his father, John 'Ton' MacDonald, a former Gallipoli veteran born in 1893.

In a quiet back room, 'Ton' explained how his grandfather had been a gamekeeper, forester, factor and butler. During the winters, 'Ton' had worked as a stonemason's labourer and did some woodcutting to make ends meet. The main form of seasonal employment at that time was with the gentry who came up from England to hunt and fish. During the season, 'Ton' worked as a stalker and ghillie. In 1910 he joined the Lovat Scouts as a sharpshooter, seeing active service at Suvla Bay, Gallipoli. Turkey had entered the Great War on the side of Germany in October 1914. Gallipoli was the long finger of land thrusting into the Aegean from the Turks' foothold in Europe. A planned invasion of the peninsula in April 1915 by 75,000 men was stunningly mismanaged and the Turks, who knew of the approaching invasion, had massively strengthened their defences. With measured pride, 'Ton' told me: 'It looked as though

Sir Ian Hamilton was going to lose every man on the peninsula, so General Munro went over and surveyed the situation. I was ten days in front of the last man to leave, who was an officer as I recall. I was beside Alasdair Lovat [Lord Lovat's brother] when he was wounded at Suvla Bay. He was second in charge of the 29th Brigade. Alasdair Lovat was speaking to me one moment, when a shell suddenly came in and landed four or five yards away. He was struck in the groin and fell like a stone. I shouted for the medical that there was a man wounded. They gave him a jab in the arm, cut his clothes away, dressed him and took him off in a stretcher. He lived a good while after that, but eventually died. When General Munro took us off the peninsula, we went to Alexandria and then to Cairo, keeping the Arabs back because they were after guns and ammunition. I finished up with the cavalry in Cairo. I came home, then joined up again in 1917, this time with the artillery of the Cameron Highlanders – the county regiment.'

The rain continued through until Friday lunchtime, when I left Glenuig for the seven-mile ride back to Lochailort. I halted at one point to observe the slow and graceful flight of a grey heron which was flitting to another stance on the shoreline of the loch. The bird's wide flapping wings were mirrored in the waters of the loch, a truly magnificent sight. Further along, a solitary whelk-gatherer was stooping amongst rocks near the jetty. At the Lochailort Hotel I met a man called Dick Gillies, who kindly gave me a lift in his battered car to Glenfinnan, the rear wheel of my cycle poking out from the boot.

In the evening I had a short discussion with Farquhar MacRae, who had been part of a remarkable band which used to tramp over the hills in order to play at local dances in Glenuig and Kinlochmoidart. Calum Maclean had recorded the band one night at Inverailort Farm when he was collecting material for his book in the early 1950s. 'It was possibly 1954,' suggested Farquhar. 'Calum stayed at Glenshian Lodge Hotel. At first we thought he was one of the geologists that were going about the area, but by the time we had met him, we knew that he was knowledgable about everything connected with music. He got us to organise a night at the farm on the Cameron-Head estate and came along with his recorder and a bottle of whisky. Calum set up his machine on a table in the middle of the room and we were all round it.

'There was the stationmaster Walter Begg on fiddle, Angus MacNaughton on fiddle, a brother of mine – Dougie – also on fiddle. I played fiddle and accordion. Our drummer was my sister Margaret. Calum fairly kept us going that evening and encouraged us to play more and more. It was a great night.'

Next morning , the view from my bedroom window was out of this world. Over the crystal water of Glen Shiel, a thick band of mist obscured the base of Sgurr Ghiubhsachain, but its conical summit pierced the mist and stood out magnificently against the bluest of skies imaginable. In full Highland dress, Charlie MacFarlane piped the hotel guests in for breakfast, then gave a short recital, the volume of which was too overpowering for a pair of American ladies who didn't know quite how to react and with heads bowed, nervously raked through their handbags.

Later in the day I spoke to 66-year-old Angus MacDonald, known locally as Angus the Gate. He warmly recalled the days of the *Clanranald*, a steamboat owned by local landowners which used to ply up and down Loch Shiel between Glenfinnan and Acharacle with mails, passengers and other supplies. The service stopped when the Lochailort–Kinlochmoidart road was built. I asked Angus if he could recall Calum Maclean's visit to Glenfinnan. 'He stands out in my mind, very much so. I was the barman in the Stagecoach Inn at the time he came round with his recording machine. The last time I saw him here was in 1955 and I think he was staying at Lochailort. One of the maids, Jessie MacDonald, sang for him in the bar. Calum was an interesting character. I remember he had lost the power in his left arm, for he was working the machine all the time with his right hand. He played back the song he recorded and was conversing away in Gaelic with some of the regulars in the back bar.'

After lunch back at the hotel, Charlie offered to take me down Loch Shiel in his small blue sailing boat. Millions must have gazed down this beautiful and romantic waterway from the graceful sweep of the Glenfinnan railway viaduct that overlooks the monument to the raising of the Prince's standard on 19 August 1745 as a rallying-point to the clans.

On both sides of Loch Shiel the hills rise to over 2,000 feet and

Charlie would frequently halt rowing in order to point out various topographical features, translating their Gaelic names into English, and expanding on their derivation. Jacobite history seemed to be his great passion. He told me that the constant shifting of the local population in this area had broken the strands of oral tradition. Beyond Guesachan we hoisted the sail and cruised home without recourse to the oars. It had been a magical sail.

That evening I sat with a book and a drink in the splendid lounge of the hotel, which contained atmospheric oil paintings and mounted stags' heads on the walls. The silence was broken by the ticking of a pendulum clock, the shuffling of cards from a game of bridge at the next table, and the periodic calls from the players of 'two spades, three hearts – double – no bid'. My finances were nearly exhausted and sadly this would have to be my last night in Glenfinnan.

After Mass next morning, I called on Father Calum MacNeil the local priest. Pouring me a whisky from his decanter, Father MacNeil explained he was originally from Barra and added that he was one of the priests who had officiated at Calum Maclean's funeral in South Uist. Father MacNeil was also something of a poet and self-described 'pirate publisher' in that he edited a bi-monthly news-sheet which carried a column by Charlie about place-name traditions in the area. Later some teenagers arrived to play records on Father MacNeil's stereo, so I headed back to the hotel to thank Charlie for all his hospitality and say farewell.

Thankfully, the wind was on my tail for the long easterly ride along lochs Eil and Laggan to Newtonmore. My head was down for most of the way and I recall little of what was an uneventful, quiet journey. After a light evening meal, I flopped onto the guesthouse bed, too tired to write up my notes but content and satisfied with the outcome of my West Highland journey. Despite almost persistent rain, it had been amongst the most memorable of fieldwork trips, and the warmth and kindness of the people would stoke the embers of my thoughts for many a day.

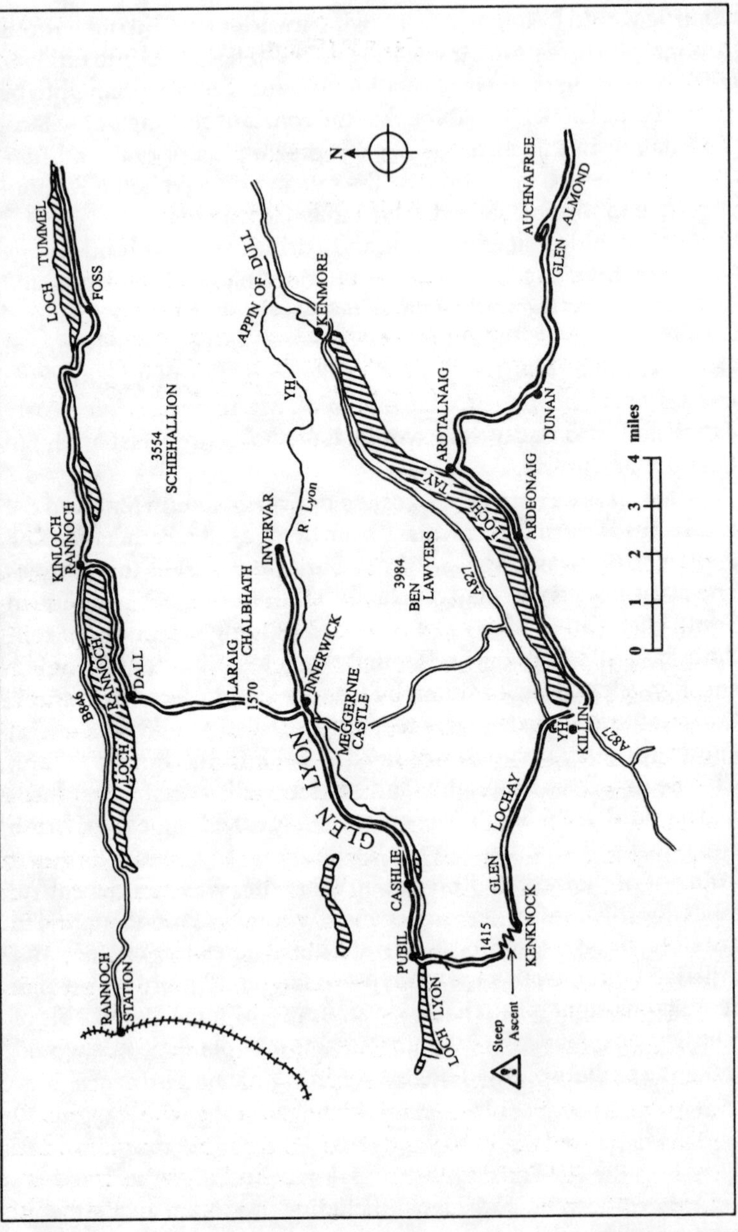
LOCH TUMMEL
FOSS
KINLOCH RANNOCH
3554 SCHIEHALLION
B846
LOCH RANNOCH
DALL
RANNOCH STATION
LARAIG CHALBHATH
1570
INNERWICK
MEGGERNIE CASTLE
GLEN LYON
INVERVAR
R. Lyon
YH
APPIN OF DULL
KENMORE
N
3984 BEN LAWYERS
A827
LOCH TAY
ARDTALNAIG
ARDEONAIG
DUNAN
GLEN ALMOND
AUCHNAFREE
CASHLIE
PUBIL
LOCH LYON
1415
KENKNOCK
GLEN LOCHAY
YH
KILLIN
A827
Steep Ascent
0 1 2 3 4 miles

CHAPTER 9

Punishing the Spokes in Highland Perthshire

> People who spent most of their natural lives riding iron bicycles over the rocky roadsteads of this parish get their personalities mixed up with the personalities of their bicycle as a result of the interchanging of the atoms of each of them and you would be surprised at the number of people in these parts who nearly are half people and half bicycles.
>
> Flann O'Brien, *The Third Policeman*, 1967.

The large former county of Perthshire lies at the very heart of Scotland, centrally placed between north and south, east and west. For the touring cyclist and mountain-biker it offers compact hill-ranges spiced with adventurously rugged tracks as well as some enticing byroads through magnificent glens, not to mention the variety of flat carseland in the south, some long and fertile straths and the opportunity to follow some beautiful rivers.

Another May arrived. In Scotland it is as well to be circumspect about the weather at this time of the year, and remember that hill weather can be notoriously fickle at any time. Nothing is guaranteed, nothing can be taken for granted despite what the calendar may say. Bearing this in mind, a friend and I decided to tackle four days of cycle-camping in the heartland of the Perthshire Highlands, an area steeped in Celtic mythology and offering a great deal of historic interest between the folds of its hills.

Along with Iain Smart, a Dundee town-planner, the two of us had been doing some serious scanning of the Ordnance Survey maps for a number of weekends during the long winter nights. Our idea was to find a suitable route that would avoid the main arteries such as the A9 Perth to Inverness road, and allow us freedom to explore the hills and glens, including that gem in Perthshire's crown – Glen Lyon, the longest and one of the finest Highland glens in Scotland.

Perthshire also boasts magnificent rivers such as the Almond, Earn and Tay – the Almond being the most secretive, the Earn the most diverse in character, and the big River Tay possessing a stronger flow than the Thames and Severn put together. The Tay's massive catchment area spans Scotland, stretching from Tyndrum – which is further west than Glasgow – to Braemar in the north and Forfar in the north-east. A route was hatched which would see us follow the Almond for much of its course; the Earn we would miss out, and the Tay we would see only now and again. Besides, there were equally enchanting water courses such as the Braan and River Lyon. It was impossible to take them all in during four days in the saddle.

We packed our gear on Mayday, deciding to share our load, which consisted of sleeping bags, stoves, pots and pans, food, a Vango Force 10 featherweight tent and the usual camping paraphernalia that ensures a measure of independence in the open. Next day's forecast was for it to be colder than of late, with sporadic showers and northerly winds strengthening later in the day. Work commitments meant that we had no other option but to leave on 2 May and take an early morning train to Perth.

Upon leaving Perth station, fate struck Iain's 'Hercules' (a modified and rather temperamental Halford's tourer) when he discovered that it wouldn't budge from low gear. 'Hercules' had cost Iain about £50 in 1976 and by cycling into work, thus saving on bus fares, he was able to pay it off in the space of three months. After 11 years and a lot of use, the green machine was feeling its age.

Undeterred, we pedalled out of the Fair City by the A85 Crieff road and found the first of our quiet byways after forking left at Huntingtower. The hamlet of Tibbermore came and went in a few seconds as we struck north by an eerie single track which skirted a moss and led into the village of Methven. With its long main street and buildings fronting the road, Methven reminded me of any number of Irish towns, except that it had fewer pubs.

Our first port of call was to visit Jim Ogg, a retired ploughman who lived with his wife in a semi-detached cottage near the western outskirts of the village. After a minute or so, Jim answered the front door, his large frame seemingly engulfing the doorway. I noticed he was holding a walking stick in his left hand and Jim later told me that his left leg had been amputated in the early 1970s. I told him we were hoping to have a chance to hear his reminiscences of farm work in the era of the horse and mentioned the name of a local farmer who had told us that Jim would be the best man to see.

The name clicked and Jim invited us into his living room, where there was a glowing coal fire. On top of the mantelpiece was an ornament of Clydesdale horses as well as other memorabilia connected with them. 'Tak a seat,' said Jim in his deep husky voice, which reflected Perthshire Scots.

After some small-talk about what we were doing, I produced the tape-recorder, which is always a prickly time when meeting an informant on the first occasion. Informants can dry up through shyness, but Jim was eager to reminisce and the microphone was soon forgotten about once he got into his stride.

'Ah left the school in 1919 and had twa years soartin cattle before Ah wis given an orra-beast tae drive. Ah wis drivin a pair [of Clydesdales] before Ah wis 17, an that's a lot o years ago now.'

'Can you recall your first wage?' I enquired.

'Aye, that!' Jim uttered, raising his voice.

'Ten bob a week an yer meal an milk an bide in the bothy. Then it rose syne tae a pound a week an it wis a pound a week for a long, long time afore ye got anither rise. Fowk desnae ken nothin aboot it nooadays wae the pey they get!'

Single ploughmen on farms in eastern Scotland lived in self-catering bothies up until the 1950s. The bothy system appears to have originated on the larger farms in Strathmore and the Carse of Gowrie, where it was in existence at least by the end of the 18th century. During his early days as a bothy chiel, Jim had to rise at 5.30 a.m., sort his pair of horses, and put in a full day's work for a further nine hours, six days a week.

With a hint of bitterness, Jim explained how the farmers expected the ploughman to put in that first hour in the morning for nothing. The horses had to be fed and groomed, and Jim was of the opinion that the working horses on a farm were of more importance to the farmer than the actual men!

Unmarried ploughmen were hired twice a year at the May and

November feeing markets, when they had to stand like cattle and wait for a prospective employer to engage them. There was no such thing as a written contract of employment. The bargain was sealed by a handshake and the exchange of arles – a small sum of money which, if accepted by the farm worker, was tantamount to a binding agreement with the farmer that he would serve with him. Married men were hired only once a year and the main feeing market for them in Perth was Little Dunning. I asked Jim what he could recall about these days.

'It wis a great way o daen at a feein market in Perth at thae days. Aa the High Street wis all laid wae stalls – sweetie stalls, an aa the batter o the day, ye ken, aa the ploomen. Ye ay kent a plooman when ye seen him – some o them jist hed their cords oan; they were nae dungarees or overalls worn in thae days by the ploomen. It wis aa corduroy breeks or moleskin trousers that were worn, tackety buits – changed days now. But the High Street in Perth wis crowdit; tram cars used tae run down the middle o the High Street an ye had tae jump oot the road for the bell wis ay ringin awaa.

'The stalls wis ay jist on the wan side o the street. The greatest place o the lot wis up at St Paul's Kirk yonder at the tap o the High Street. Then they had "Flit Friday"; that was the first Friday efter the November Term, an that wis ay anither holiday wae the ploomen. But Little Dunnin wis the main day tae engage tae the fairmers. It wis a great day, the Little Dunnin – ye could hardly get moved on the High Street on Little Dunnin day at wan time – hardly get moved for crowds.'

In the congested High Street of Perth a fair amount of haggling went on between farm worker and farmer, with usually the latter having the upper hand. According to Jim, arles amounted to about half a crown in old money, but temperatures could still rise over securing the best terms and conditions.

'Was there such a thing as a "grapevine" whereby the farm workers could get an idea of certain hard taskmasters?' I enquired of Jim.

'Oh aye, oh aye – there wis ay somebody hed a word tae say aboot some farmer: "Oh for God's sake dinnae gan tae so-an-so," ye ken. "Oh, he's awfie mean, he'll hardly pay ye, the horse is no very guid" or somethin like that. So ye stayed clear o thae lads [laughing] – ye never went near them at aa; ye ay kent no to go near them. Ye see, that wis the thing, an the like o thae fairmers jist hed tae tak ony man that wis fair stuck for a horse syne. This wis hoo they used tae work it, and they wid say tae thirsel, "Oh, he'll be desperate fir a fee, Ah'll mebbe get him fir a bob or twa less a week." An this is hoo they used tae work it, a lot o thae fairmers: they didnae bother.'

At this point in our conversation I interjected with a question about the role of the Brotherhood of the Horseman's Word – the ploughmen's secret society to which the majority of horsemen once belonged. An air of hushed reverence descended on Jim's voice and his features became elongated. For long surrounded by an air of mystique, the Brotherhood has been described by the folklorist and poet, Hamish Henderson, as 'a cross between a farm-servant freemasonry, an underground trade union and a working-class Hellfire Club'.

Jim now spoke hesitantly and much slower than before. I could sense we had ventured into a forbidden zone, so the conversation was switched back to the end of an era – when the working farm horse gave way to the early tractors. 'Fowk wisne very keen on tractors tae begin wae,' Jim said. 'They'd nae cab an in winter ye'd be sittin oot in the cauld, frozen stiff despite yer big coat, leggins, an a pair o gloves: ye wir never warm an damned glad tae see nicht, Ah'm tellin ye. It wis fine in summertime but nae use in the winter. Some said it wis the best thing that ever happened because they didnae need tae rise sae early in the mornin, an when it come tae Saturday dennertime ye wir finished till Monday mornin. That wis the benefit o tractors, but that wis aboot the only benefit o the early tractors that come on the scene. Ye wis ay tied up wae a horse but a tractor could jist be shoved in a shed an forgot aboot.'

Despite the attention they required, there was no doubting Jim's devotion to the working horses, which were at their peak between six and eight years of age. As they became older and less fit they were handed down to the next ploughman in the farm hierarchy, until the really old horses served solely as orra-beasts, fit only for lighter loads and such things as pulling the harrow.

Jim Ogg belongs to an increasingly rare breed of men – those retired ploughmen, many of whom are now in their eighties, who had to experience hard graft when there weren't machines to do the work for them; they had little option but to accept perpetually low wages for long hours, had few holidays, and their bellies were fuelled on an uncompromising diet consisting mainly of porridge.

Such men deserve our respect. The mirror of memory can distort, overlook, select and suppress. Listening to Jim educate us about his bothy days, it quickly emerged that despite the odd grumble or two, he had a rounded, fuller attitude to life. He may have uttered the occasional curse but there was nothing romantic about a five a.m. rising on a frostbound winter morning, or the task of spreading dung on the fields. For Jim it was part of his life: immediate, inseparable – like the unspoken bond between man and beast, each tethered to the other for their working lives.

Bothy life could be and was coarse. Some bothies were worse than others and the more harum-scarum cooking techniques of certain single lads did not always endear them to their fellows, each lad taking his week's turn to undertake the necessary routine of bothy chores. But bothy life also had its lighter side, replete with jokes, pranks and music-making. Every bothy seemed to have its melodeon player, or at worst, someone who could twang a few notes out of a Jew's harp. There were individuals noted for their scurrilous ballads, and who gave it their bawdiest best when it came to an impromptu performance. That was also part of the bothy scene – the camaraderie amongst fellow workers who owned few possessions and were never sure where they would end up in six months time.

When it was time to leave Jim's company, we left a man who had given us food for thought, made us count our blessings. Limping to the front door to see us off, Jim gave us a hearty 'Cheerio' and shut the door behind him.

Doubtless he returned to his fireside seat to stoke up the fire and kindle his memories. For an hour he had shared the latter with us: the privilege had been ours.

We crawled out of Methven by a steepish brae on the north-east side of the village, being overtaken by a coal lorry on its rounds. Ahead lay an open road and freedom. Soon we were riding between a beech hedgerow through open, undulating farmland interspersed with plantations. From the road northwards, we could see the gently rounded Logiealmond hills, which heralded the first flank of the Highland boundary fault line.

Just below the farm of North Ardittie we halted astride the bikes at the top of a steep hill and caught our first glimpse of the River Almond as it meandered through a flood plain, partly disappearing in woodland. The freedom of the descent was glorious as we swung round a fairly sharp corner and rode over one of two bridges lying side by side across the river. The older one was an impressive humpbacked affair which was no longer in use. After a sharp, breathless push up the punishing Millhaugh brae we shortly reached a watering hole nestling inconspicuously to the rear of the charming village of Harrietfield. The Drumtochty Tavern takes its name from a book called *Beside the Bonnie Briar Bush* (1894), stories of rural life written in the Kailyard tradition by the local Free Church minister, John Watson, under his pen-name of 'Ian Maclaren'. Such tales were popular in America and in translation on the Continent. They offer a rose-tinted view of rural life far removed from the immediacy and harsher reality experienced by many country people at that time.

The Drumtochty Tavern was a place with its own character, enhanced by a roaring log fire in the cosy snug that had nicotine yellowed walls and attractive old mirrors. We sank our ale and left because our journey was still in its infancy.

It was an easy ride out from Harrietfield, where we looked over to the impressive buildings and grounds of Glenalmond's Trinity College, an independent school which serves to boost the local economy and numbers some well-known FPs amongst its ranks, such as the actor Robbie Coltraine and the former Scottish rugby captain, David Sole. At a dog-leg descent and climb a short distance along, a road struck north for Logiealmond Lodge and the former slate quarry which bites into the face of Craig Lea. Migrant workers from the Sleat area of Skye used to journey to Craig Lea last century in an effort to find work as quarrymen.

Steady progress was made along this traffic-free byroad until we reached the start of the two-mile-long Sma' Glen, where the raw north wind was funnelled straight into our face. Few glens are as short, or as beautiful, as the Sma' Glen, which resembles a miniature Glencoe, straddling the A822 between Gilmerton and Amulree.

Bare upper rock and scree on the rugged hills gradually gave way to grass and heather in a glorious blend of colour, while through the twisting, narrow green floor of the glen rushed the River Almond, now with a truly Highland character.

The A822 had recently been resurfaced and the smooth black tarmac gradually swept under our wheels as we pushed northwards. In winter, the Sma' Glen can take on a starkly sinister appearance, as low-lying cloud blankets out the tops and dramatically shrouds and swirls round the shattered crags, bringing the rocks menacingly close.

Here, traces of the Celtic imagination linger round every corner. The area is dotted with memorials of the legendary Fingal and his third-century warrior band, the Fianna. Down in a field to our right we could see the massive boulder known as Ossian's Stone, which reputedly marks the grave of Scotland's first bard, son of Comhal by his half-deer mistress. This stone was actually moved from the line of the present road when General Wade's soldiers were undertaking the mammoth feat of constructing a road through the glen in the 18th century. They discovered a small cavity under the centre of the boulder, which allegedly contained ashes, bones and evidence of a funeral pyre.

It was through this pass that the clans passed before assembling at Amulree for the 1715 Jacobite Rising. There they were issued with weapons before marching to the Battle of Sheriffmuir. Cattle thieves and more legitimate drovers also used to drive their beasts on the hoof through the Sma' Glen. One of the oldest trysts was held at Amulree for many years. Some accounts speak of it lasting for a week, although it declined with the rise of the famous tryst at Crieff. Amulree still continued to be an important drovers' stance, a merging point for droves coming from Glen Lyon via Glen Quaich, from Lochaber by the Minigag Pass and Tummel Bridge, and for the Aberdeenshire cattle, which were herded over by Kirkmichael and Loch Skiach, or along the more easterly route by the King's Ford at Inver and up the old drove road through Stathbraan.

At Newton Bridge we left the smooth tarmac of the A822, destined for a joust with some rough stuff which OS Sheet 52 showed as a track leading through Glen Almond to Ardtalnaig on the south side of Loch Tay. From our viewpoint, the Glen Almond hills seemed to merge and we had doubts as to whether we could penetrate this lonely area, seldom visited by the casual tourist. Moreover, maps can occasionally be misleading or out-of-date as to what is actually on the ground. We would take our chance despite a bold sign which declared 'Private Road to Auchnafree and Conyachan: Authorised Vehicles Only'. We were sure this was a public right-of-way – and was a bicycle a vehicle?

Wheeling our machines through the gate and over an iron cattle grid, we set out on a good unsurfaced track which held only occasional pot-holes. Just to the north of the track, about a mile apart, are the ruins of two deserted settlements – Craignafarrar and Dalmore. Conyachan was spelt 'Conichan' on our map and not far beyond it, we came upon a tiny burial ground which held some interesting gravestones but had sadly fallen into neglect. The map also marked some curious features to the south, such as Kirk of the Grove and the Thief's Cave. There is now no sign of the latter, which was obliterated by a rockfall, although it reputedly could hold 60 men. A man named Alistair Baine is said to have had his hideout in this cave because he lived off the proceeds of sheep rustling, until he was caught and hanged at Perth. The Kirk of the Grove (also known at 'The Preaching Stones') consists of several large stones where, it is said, the men of Glen Almond took their last sacrament before heading north to the Battle of Culloden. Only a few of the Glen Almond men were to return out of a contingent estimated at 120.

The old burial ground lies close to the Conichan/Auchnafree march dyke and was a rather spooky place, with slanting tombstones and carved mortality emblems such as the Death Skull adding to the sombre atmosphere of this graveyard in the wilds. Peering skywards we could see the weather was changing for the worse. Above 1,000 feet, snow covered the tops and upper corries. More seemed to be on the way as we swung round by Auchnafree, a dour-looking L-shaped shooting lodge which boasted 12 chimneys and adjacent homesteads, one of which had a light on. Auchnafree is from the Gaelic, *achadh na frithe*, 'field of the deer-forest'. Since the late 1700s the glen has been sparsely populated, the land given over to deer, grouse and sheep.

We continued towards Dalriech, passing a shepherd who

remarked upon the approaching bad weather and gave our bikes an inquisitive look. Ahead stood a 10-foot-high memorial topped with white marble, commemorating those who fell in the Great War. The going was becoming decidedly rough, with deeper ruts and small streams to negotiate. On we scrambled by Lechrea until we reached a small dam, beside which was parked a SnowCat vehicle with a small trailer. The stony track now became a narrow sheep walk which intermittently plunged into small streams as we neared the watershed of the Almond. Sleet began to fall as Iain and I struggled to cross a deep burn with steep banks on either side. To add to the discomfort of wet feet, the sheep walk disappeared, leaving us to hump our fully loaded machines over waterlogged peat hags which saw us squelching up to our knees. So much for any track. This was Hell!

Some respite was obtained at Dunan, a dry but windowless howff which had pencil graffiti scrawled on its walls, some dating from 1941. Thankfully, we were partly able to dry off and enjoy a cup of tea from the flask along with some chocolate. The weather outside was grim but there were signs it was going to break up. As we once more picked up the track to the rear of Dunan, a brown-coloured Land Rover approached with three occupants – two males and a female. Waves were exchanged as we headed into the wind-driven sleet, at last being able to cycle on the track. There was more flooding on this track and as we were now well and truly soaked, it was a simple case of wading through the water regardless.

Upon reaching Claggan, the weather changed dramatically, with splinters of sunlight poking through the clouded sky, rewarding us with atmospheric views across Loch Tay to Meall Garbh and its outliers. Once more we met up with the Land Rover trio, who told us they had been out collecting frog spawn. The keeper, who was in his 30s, mentioned that there was not much communication between his estate (Ardtalnaig) and Auchnafree. The track had not been completed as this would have encouraged poachers, so there was our answer to the bog-hopping section before Dunan.

The track now became a surfaced single-track road as we plunged down the steep hill from Claggan to Ardtalnaig, negotiating an extremely tight hairpin bend in the process. All the time the Ben Lawyer range was clearing under a sky full of movement, and the views were truly magnificent. At one stage on the road to Ardeonaig, I watched Iain as he cycled under a perfectly formed rainbow of stunning clarity.

Bang on the stroke of 6.00 p.m. we arrived dripping wet at the Ardeonaig Hotel. It was a small, rather prim-looking establishment with little outward sign of life. We tried the front door and found it locked. We rang the bell. The door was eventually opened by a bespectacled young lady who had a highly unflattering strip of Elastoplast across her nose.

'You're a couple of drowned rats, aren't you,' she quipped, before leading us into a charming little lounge bar. I took a seat by the window as Iain went up to order our drinks. Suddenly, there was the sound of loud voices and in swaggered three anglers who were soaked to the skin and tight as coots.

'Who broke yer nose, hen?' bellowed the first of this drunken middle-aged trio upon seeing the barmaid. She continued serving Iain, delivering an icy stare in the direction of the first drunk, who by this time had slumped into a chair and was hauling off his sodden shoes and socks. He then proceeded to rest his feet on a low bar stool like Lord Muck.

To cut a long story short, the hotel proprietrix arrived on the scene, and an unsavoury wrangle ensued between the three drunken fishermen and herself over the fee she was charging them for the use of a boat and ghillie out on Loch Tay that afternoon. 'I'm not paying £35 to catch fuck all!' shouted a bald-headed character whose backside was poking above his jeans.

'That was the arrangement,' continued madam, somewhat shaken but still puffing away at her cigarette.

'You're just a snotty bitch!' retorted the drunk, 'I'm paying fuck all!'

'Step this way, if you please,' retorted madam. Slurring oaths as he lurched towards the hall door, the main protagonist was followed by madam, who bore a striking resemblance to Dame Edna Everage, as well as the hotel chef who had now intervened in the fracas. Although for a time there was a further heated exchange, the black fishers, as Iain called them, were forced to settle their account and slunk away with their tails between their legs.

The cabaret was over. We ordered a round of cheese sandwiches, then set out once more on a killer of a climb up to Tullochcan. Nearby Camusurich possibly means 'bay of the curach or coracle', and from the road just above it, we faced over to Kiltyrie, locally reckoned to be the central point of the Scottish mainland.

In the early evening light, shadows danced across the tarmac as we dipped and climbed above the southern shore of beautiful Loch Tay. The trees were lime-green in colour and heavy with foliage, at intervals forming tunnels which blocked out our shadows, but on other occasions giving way to reward with marvellous views westwards to the twin peaks of Ben More and Stob Binnein. Whereas the blind summits mean the motorist can rarely take his eyes off the road, the cyclist has freedom to look around him and listen. Without any doubt, this is one of the classic cycling roads in Scotland, most traffic preferring the A827 road to Killin on the other side of the loch. That evening only an occasional car passed, and we virtually had the road to ourselves.

After 44 miles on differing surfaces we arrived at Killin about 8.00 p.m. This attractive Highland village is closely associated with the Clan MacNab, and their burial-place is on a small island in the river just below the falls of Dochart.

A gap in a plantation on the south side of the village afforded us enough space to pitch the tent out of view. We offloaded our gear, then cycled back into the village to enjoy a fine evening meal at a small café. Beneath the swaying tops of high firs we both slept like corpses that night.

Since we were really only carrying emergency rations, we treated ourselves to a fry-up at the Coffee House Restaurant next morning. Our socks, which we'd stuffed into the bottom of our sleeping bags, were nearly dry, and with a big breakfast inside us we were ready for stage two of the journey, up Glen Lochay and across the hill to Glen Lyon by a former Hydro road which we had heard was sometimes closed by locked gates at either side of the pass.

There had not been much rain overnight and we slept under only the fly-sheet. Killin also boasts a Grade 2 youth hostel as well a plenty B&B accommodation. Before leaving the village, we set out to find the standing stone which marks the reputed grave of Fionn, the Celtic warrior king. It sits in a field near the schoolhouse and is fairly easy to locate. The hills of the Tarmachan range, which rise above Killin, were thickly coated with snow and had an alpine quality about them in the morning light. At a large, well-stocked store in the village I purchased a pair of thermal gloves and a tin plate for just over £4.

The narrow twisting road up Glen Lochay was another delight to cycle. It closely followed the River Lochay and wound its way through lush trees that were sun speckled and home to a host of singing birds. Arriving at Kenknock after midday, we found there was no gate to bar access to the road which snakes up the Laraig nan Lunn (Pass of Staves) and descends steeply into Glen Lyon. Our panniers felt as though they'd been filled with lead as we started this punishing ascent, halting at the fourth dog-leg to brew up at a convenient stream by the side of the road. Suitably refreshed, we simply wheeled the machines up the rest of the way, every so often taking a stop to admire the majestic scenery.

On the glorious descent to Pubil, a raw north-westerly bit into our faces and made us glad that we had added an extra layer of clothing. The full extent of Glen Lyon has been curtailed by the building of the Lubreoch Dam, a massive concrete wall which sits at the head of the glen and absorbs Loch Lyon. The water is piped to the power station in Glen Lochay. The name Lubreoch, is from the Gaelic, *lub riabhach*, 'the brindled loop'; *lub* being the word for land inside a river meander.

The Gaelic name for Glen Lyon is *Cromghlearn nan clach*, or the 'Crooked Glen of Stones'. There is a traditional Gaelic saying that Fionn or Fingal, one of the heroes of Celtic mythology, had twelve castles in the crooked glen of stones. In effect, the castles are a series of stone-built fortified homesteads dating from the Iron Age. The best-preserved examples are near Cashlie farm, dating back to the time before the Scots arrived from Ireland to found their kingdom of Dalriada.

To be honest, I found the little settlement of estate houses at Pubil to be slightly disappointing. But it was the hills of the upper glen which drew the eye. These have summits mercifully free of afforestation, and displace the present day by the very atmosphere they create. It can be sensed in the hanging corries which play tricks with the wind; a primeval mood of wind clawing naked rock – sighing, shrieking, whistling its eerie lament as it has done over the millennia. It is the wind that is savage, not the great lumps of stone which comprise the so-called ring-forts of the glen. The wind is unseen, untamed, otherworldly, dominating and raw, lending itself to sudden gusts, then lulls, and eventually, silence. It is the wind which buffets and torments the cyclist, not the rain. Whereas the wind is force, rain is only inconvenience.

On the drop down to Pubil it was impossible to completely ignore that great eyesore of a dam that the Hydro engineers constructed in the 1950s. Power, pipelines, pylons – these are necessities of the modern age. We cannot live in a vacuum of wilderness. However, some places must remain sacred for their wilderness quality. These places we must treasure. They are essential to man and his fellow creatures if we are to achieve a sense of balance.

The modern houses at Pubil look as though they were built for Hydro workers, when in fact they were built for Meggernie estate by the Hydro Board as part of the compensation paid for the inundation of the upper glen and also up at Lochs. The old drowned farmhouses and cottages that the houses of Pubil replaced included the historic and very isolated sheep farm of Invermearn at the western limit of Loch Lyon, which more than doubled its size when the dam was built.

We had cycled 13 miles from Killin by the time we reached Pubil at 2.45 p.m. The former settlement of Lubreoch has been swallowed up by a plantation and there was nothing to be seen of it. With the wind partly behind us we pushed off towards Cashlie, hopeful of being able to locate the legendary stone known as the Bhacain. We had a rough idea where it was – near one of the ruined homesteads on the south side of the road, not far from the bridge over the Lyon leading to Dallchiorlich farm. After 15 minutes of searching, we came upon this enigmatic two-foot-high stone, which from a certain angle resembled the profile of a large dog's head. Local legend holds that Fionn's warriors used to tether their staghounds to this stone after the chase. It was also said to have had a mysterious effect on those who crept under the protruding 'jaw' in order to ensure a safe delivery of their child. Judging by the height of the stone, this would be a fairly awkward manoeuvre for any pregnant woman.

A short distance away, near Cashlie, Iain stopped to investigate an old limekiln on the north side of the road and found a dead mole lying on its back. The glen road was blissfully free of traffic, the route holding close to the passage of the River Lyon, which was our friend and companion for much of the way. Glen Lyon seemed to have its own local climate as the wind moaned high amidst the ever-watchful hills. Beyond Stronuich, river and road curled northwards, the glen changing character and becoming more narrow. Just before Gallin, a tarmac road turns off to the left behind an old quarry and leads towards the drowned land of Lochs.

The road began to climb from opposite Moar, where a little tongue of land spreads out into a bend of the Lyon. On it there are the remains of a tiny hamlet called Ross, which fell into decline in the days of the sheep clearances. Past the estate farm of Gallin, we were soon high above Meggernie Castle, home to the Campbells of Glen Lyon, the oldest part of the castle dating from about 1588. Meggernie was built in two stages – the tower house by Colin Campbell, third of the Campbell lairds of Glen Lyon, and the remainder by his great-grandson, who became the most detested Scotsman of his generation. Another notorious family who came to buy the estate in the mid-1860s were the Bulloughs, recent millionaires from Accrington in Lancashire, who ran the place as a hunting reserve. After the Great War Meggernie was purchased by the Wills family, the great tobacco barons. They exploited the massive sporting potential of the estate, while the Bulloughs moved to purchase the Inner Hebridean island of Rhum, in the process gaining a reputation as one of the most unwelcoming of landowners in Scotland.

By late afternoon Iain and I reached Bridge of Balgay, where the post-office stocked a useful array of outdoor equipment and served teas outside on benches down by the riverside. Chaffinches flitted down to eat the crumbs from our plates as we relaxed in the late afternoon sun. From here it was only a short ride to Innerwick, where we spent a short time deciding on the best place to camp. Just up from a small car-park that boasted exceptionally clean toilets, we found the perfect spot close to a waterfall which fell into a deep pool. There was plenty of dry brushwood within easy reach of the camp and we soon had a roaring stick fire on the go.

Long before hikers and campers came to Glen Lyon, the area was a regular stamping-ground of travelling people who, on the good authority of Duncan Campbell, used to lodge in corn-drying kilns, which had thatched roofs and were warmer than any tent. Duncan Campbell was formerly the parish schoolmaster of Fortingall and later edited *The Northern Chronicle* in Inverness for 26 years. He was born at Kerrowmore near Innerwick in 1827 and lived for nearly 90 years, publishing a voluminous book about Glen Lyon in 1910, called *Reminiscences and Reflections of an Octogenarian Highlander*. In it he writes:

> 'In childhood I looked on the coming of the tinkers as a great and welcome event. They usually had a donkey or two with them, and I got liberty to ride these animals. Peter Ruadh was a good piper and set people dancing. I liked to sit on the steps leading down to the fireplace and watch them at their work, men roasting horns and shaping spoons out of them; women scraping and polishing the moulded and sliced spoons, the better sort of which were not without embellishment; other men making tin lanterns and cans, and old cunning hands mending pots, pans, rings and brooches.'

The people of the roads lived by their wits and what man and nature provided, sometimes fishing for freshwater pearls obtained in the mussel beds of the River Lyon. According to Campbell, the tinker women 'did not dare to tell fortunes in our district because they were scared of church denunciations. As herbalists they had a knowledge which was frequently useful to sick persons and beasts.'

There was still enough daylight left for us to take a load-free spin down the glen to the hamlet of Invervar. The view back from the road a little to the east of here is unsurpassable, sufficient to bring the most blasé of travellers to a standstill. Astride our bikes we could see the Lyon widening to encircle a small island against the magical backdrop of high rugged mountains extending for miles in silhouette.

Round the next bend on a wooded knoll are the remains of Carnbane Castle, the former stronghold of the MacGregors and Campbells. We pedalled back to Invervar, where there was a ruined circular lint mill, now fully restored. Lint is a Scots word for flax, the cultivation and preparation of which has gone on for many centuries. At one time almost every household had a patch of flax, from which such items as bed linen were produced. The mill at Invervar dates from the 1770s and is the last survivor in this area of a Scottish rural industry that has completely disappeared. The building of the mill is credited to Ewan Campbell of Lawyers, who built a great many such mills in the Highlands. Normally these were water-powered, rectangular and rather larger than the Invervar mill, whose circular form is unusual, perhaps unique.

As well as the old lint mill Invervar has other signs to offer of the changing times. The first house on the left, just west of Invervar Burn, was at one time a wayside inn. There was also a blacksmith's smiddie, a meal mill, a grocer's shop, schoolhouse and the workshops of a joiner, shoemaker, tailor and weaver.

About three-quarters of a mile west of Invervar, on the south side of the river, stands the farmhouse and steading of Inverinain, where in remote times sojourned the *Bodach Odhar*, one of the three goblin saints of Glen Lyon tradition. The story goes that the *Bodach* (literally 'old man') used to rest himself on a stone seat which was to be found on a little bank to the east of the house. This seat is called *Cathair-innean* (the Chair of St Ninian), and was said to repair itself whenever it was chipped – and woe to the person who raised hand or hammer against it.

In near darkness we returned to our camp, to find the embers of our fire still hot. We quickly set about rekindling it because the night air had turned chilly. A few stars appeared before the night sky clouded over the moon and we retired to the tent stinking of woodsmoke but content with our day. We soon fell sound asleep to the sound of the waterfall.

Next morning the sky was overcast and a fresh west-northwesterly wind was flapping the sides of the tent. At least it was dry and we could pack our gear in relative comfort. The spot we had chosen to camp in had been idyllic and I was sorry to be leaving. The post-office was just opening when I arrived at 9.30 a.m. There, I was able to stock up on tinned food and matches, having a pleasant chat with the owner who said he was planning to extend more into the camping line of goods.

North of Innerwick, a range of hills separates Glen Lyon from another great east–west valley, whose most significant feature is the nine and a half miles of Loch Rannoch. We were camped just off the public right-of-way which runs over the Laraig Chalbhath to Dall on the south shore of Loch Rannoch. In the Black Wood and caves of Rannoch, and among the hills and valleys between Rannoch and Glen Lyon, many Jacobite supporters were forced into hiding, having been exiled from their native lands after Culloden. Chief among them were the Stewart chieftains of Bunrannoch, Allan Mor of Inverchadden, and Stewart of Crossmount. On one occasion they were hiding near the pass that we were about to cross, their whereabouts being known to some of the local inhabitants, without whose assistance they could not long survive. One evening a party of Hanoverian soldiers arrived at the inn at Innerwick, intending to cross over to Rannoch the following day. The story goes that their bugler passed away the time by making love to the servant girl of the inn. She heard about their plans and cunningly assumed interest in the soldier's bugle, asking if she might be allowed to inspect it. No sooner was the bugle into her hands than she blew loud blasts, thus warning the two Stewart chieftains of a nearby military presence and enabling them to escape.

An inauspicious start was made to our journey over the hills by the rough, boulder-strewn track when we took a wrong turning and ended up following the aptly named 'Pass of the Swine', the Laraig a' Mhuic. In our attempt to not lose the height we had gained we decided to cut across the heather to join the correct route, only to be thwarted by a steep-sided gorge and a deer fence. There was nothing for it but to retrace our steps.

Reaching the more-or-less level top section of the pass at a height of 1,570 feet was a punishing slog since our machines weren't mountain bikes and we had to push the laden bikes most of the way. One consolation was the splendid vista which opened up behind us, stretching across to Meall Ghaordie and Beinn a' Bhuic, with the Lairig Breisleich (the Pass of Rout or Confusion) separating these two mountains.

Under a scowling, threatening sky we were back into the saddle once more, punishing the spokes on a rocky and deeply rutted track which would offer good sport to mountain-bikers. We were able to make progress in first gear until the track became prone to flooding in its latter stages, our wheel rims sinking into black, clawing, glutinous mud. That, and the occasional boulder-strewn fords we had to manoeuvre added up to some adventurous off-roading for a pair of touring machines. In all fairness, the middle section of this route had been rather drab and featureless. We now arrived at a deer fence bordering an immense green blanket of trees, tightly planted together and all of the same variety.

A sign at the fence warned walkers of the danger (presumably from rifle fire) during the stalking season. To their credit, the Forestry Commission had turned the right-of-way into an excellent, springy track which was perfect for cycling. We raced down this twisting route, brake levers regularly in action, and emerged in the grounds of Rannoch School. The school is in the Gordonstoun mould and occupies the former mansion house of Dall estate. Pupils in their green uniforms were changing classrooms when we descended through the trees; we were somewhat bewildered by the sudden sight of so many people after not seeing a soul for ages.

West of Dall is the true Black Wood of Rannoch, a lasting remnant of the ancient Caledonian Forest or Wood of Caledon which cloaked much of the Highlands until it was gradually destroyed for its timber, for farmland and fuel, or to remove the dangerous haunts of wolves which used to slink beneath the trees.

The road along the south side of Loch Rannoch creeps along within spitting distance of the water, except where it loops slightly inland at Carie. On the opposite shore is Aulich, where Allan Breck, the popular suspect of the famous Appin murder reputedly spent a night after the killing of the Red Fox. For the next two and a half miles to Kinloch Rannoch the road followed the gentle indentations of the shoreline without a gradient in sight.

A nicely cooked, reasonably priced bar lunch was obtained at the Kinloch Rannoch hotel, and at The Country Shop across the road we were able to stock up on provisions. The sun had broken through the clouds as we made a leisurely journey along the undulating road to Tummel Bridge, then along the south side of Loch Tummel by beautiful Foss, which was the highlight of day three. In woodland near the west end of the loch we found the perfect secluded spot by a lazy stream in which to erect the tent.

Soon a tin billy of tea was bubbling away on the fire as we toasted some slices of bread pronged on a fork that was tied to a long stick. Making a fire is a pleasurable diversion. Unless you are very hungry it should take time. You find the most sheltered location, fix your stones, gather the wood, fill the tea-can, make yourself at home, and only then strike the match. The true gangrel makes setting a fire a gentle art, and there is something pagan about the flames as they leap above the cracking sticks. Once there was a suitable pile of glowing embers the spuds were wrapped in tin-foil and baked in their jackets for about 40 minutes. The skins came out crisp and near black, the insides a crumbly soft delight. As we filled our bellies by the dying heat from the fire, I looked skywards to see a dark cloud scuttle past the quarter moon with its hazy corona. The night had belonged to us; a simple pleasure, but perfectly rewarding in its own way.

Iain woke me next morning with a shout of disgust. He had discovered a huge black insect in the middle of his bowl of muesli: such are the joys of camping. Sunlight illuminated the sides of the tent, and by 10 a.m. it was feeling distinctly warm. This was to be our last night under canvas. Iain had discovered that his brakes weren't working on 'Hercules' and he decided to visit a relative in Pitlochry, then catch the train home.

From Pitlochry I continued down a surprisingly quiet A9 to Ballinluig, where I crossed the River Tummel to Logierait. I was relieved to have been spared the maelstrom of traffic which usually flies along that dangerous road. From Logierait I crossed the River Tay to Balnamuir by a disused railway bridge, but please note – access is no longer permitted on this bridge. I was now in the Bishopric, formerly part of the See of Dunkeld, stretching from Grandtully to Inver, an area which was almost akin to an island in former times were it not for the ferries across the Tay at Balnamuir, Balmacneil and Inver. This part of Strathtay, a lush and fertile valley, is prone to serious flooding when the Tay bursts its banks.

Passing the toll cottage at Balnamuir I soon reached Kinnaird House, an imposing mansion two miles to the south, nowadays a prestigious hotel but formerly belonging to the Atholl family. Westwards my view was towards the Braes of Tulliemet, great cycling country with its own distinctive character. Five years earlier I had pedalled through that area on my way to record one of the last woodsmen who still cleared trees from the forests by horse-power.

Further down the Bishopric road is Dalguise House. This was

rented by Rupert Potter from 1871–81 and here his daughter Beatrix found childhood inspiration for some of the characters which became world-famous through her books for children. The lovable Mrs Tiggywinkle is based on the Potters' laundress, Katie MacDonald, who lived nearby.

Looking across to the other side of Strathtay from Dalguise, the most striking building is Rotmell farm, built as a model farm for the Dowager Duchess of Atholl. I soon came to the end of the B898 and once again had to joust with the traffic for a short distance on the A9. The widening of this road has totally destroyed the character of Inver, an old weaving village whose chief claim to fame lies as the home of the famous 18th-century Scottish fiddler Niel Gow, whose cottage can still be seen to this day.

My next change of direction involved a sharpish climb up the A822 Strathbraan road, which in its initial stages affords a good view over the cottage roofs of Inver. Strathbraan extends fully nine miles from Inver to Amulree, taking its name form the River Braan, which runs through its entire length. The main road on the south side of the Braan was originally engineered by Joseph Mitchell, who was of the opinion that it was the best specimen of Highland roadmaking which existed in his time. I flirted with this road for only about two miles before branching off and making a short but rewarding detour up the Rumbling Bridge road, which runs for a short distance along the north side of the Braan. This narrow byway was built by statute labour and the military, originally being part of the old drove road which threaded its way up to Amulree. Rumbling Bridge is an interesting humpbacked bridge built in 1773–74 at the top of the Falls of Braan, where the river thunders through a narrow gorge. This little road was a gem to cycle. I emerged at Trochry on the main Strathbraan road. Trochry is a rare example of a Pictish/Cumbric name which has miraculously survived, although its exact derivation is unclear.

Strathbraan is sparsely populated these days, but at the end of the 18th century it sustained a Gaelic-speaking population of about 1,400. Sixty years ago there were still a few Gaelic speakers left. The climate and soil of Strathbraan was very good for flax growing, its main crop in former times. As a consequence of this, there were a great many handloom weavers. As this type of weaving fell into decline, the population of the strath gradually dispersed to other parts, especially the employment offered by the bleachfields in Perth, and the cotton mill at Stanley.

A blustery crosswind hindered my progress up to Ballachraggan, where I turned sharp left and followed the signposted right-of-way which would take me out of the Highlands by Glen Shee – not to be confused with the other, larger Glenshee of ski resort fame. I crossed the swift-flowing Braan once more, and started the climb up from Aldmad – which would rise to over 1,100 feet. Dogs started barking as I passed the house, but thankfully they were in a compound.

I was now following what people in the low country used to refer to as 'The Old Highland Road'. For long it served as a cart-road and drove route, linking Highland Strathbraan with Logiealmond and the Perthshire Lowlands. In between was an area dissected by parish boundaries and the pull of two distinct cultures, both Highland and Lowland settlements revealing a similar story of depopulation. Glen Shee today is a glen of ghosts.

On the ascent there was time to pause and take in the outshot valleys of fertile Strathbraan extending to the more distant hills of Breadalbane. Out over the striking architecture of Drumour Lodge lay the faint upland remains of Parktown of Ballinloan and beyond, the hill shielings of Old Ballinlick, now swallowed up by afforestation. Nor could I see the lonely former settlement of Salachill. As the track neared Rosecraig, my eyes were drawn south to the moorland basin which unfolds onto what was formerly settled land at Loanurgun, Corrody, Marchford and Blackhall, now only names preserved on older large-scale maps.

For a short distance the track became a green way. I dumped the machine and wandered across to inspect the ghost ruins of Rosecraig farmhouse. The walls stood their full height, the old slated roof completely gone. It was like looking into someone's soul. Inside was a mangled iron bedstead, a fireplace and an old-fashioned oven. Above the gaping doorway is a date-stone with the weathered initials 'L McL' and the date '1827'. The initials stand for L. McLaren, a Strathbraan man who was the first person to occupy Rosecraig. Until the mid-1930s it was occupied for 23 years by a family called MacMartin, the father being a shepherd who belonged to the Isle of Skye. They were the last tenants bar one. It was the custom for outby places in hill areas to provide hospitality for travellers, and at Rosecraig a night's berth was afforded drovers from Glen Cochill making their way to the Perth Sales. Other flocks also halted here, but during the day, to prevent the glen being choked with sheep and the subsequent mixing-up of different flocks. The idea was to stagger each drove.

In all its moods Glen Shee is a place to be savoured by those who appreciate tranquillity. I tried to imagine what the scene must have been like when the drovers and their dogs were driving sheep through the glen. But on sunless days in winter, the place lends itself to a certain mood of pathos – the gaunt walls of the old farmhouse, the cluster of larches nearby, their tops shaken by the icy wind as the sullen cry of the curlew responds in the distance.

Between parallel stone dykes I continued down the track, first passing the tumbledown ruins of a cottage marked as Letter on larger-scale maps, then the fank of Auchmore on the other side of the charming Shochie Burn. Old stories tell that Auchmore was once an inn, as was Little Glenshee farmhouse at the foot of the glen. On the way down the glen I was stopped in my tracks by the sight of the Lomond Hills in distant Fife. Moreover, the glen had another surprise in that it becomes a more rugged defile towards the Lowland side, rather than at the Highland end where the land fans out towards the hill of Rose Craig: the geography is back to front.

Soon I was out of Glen Shee and out of the Highlands. From the farmhouse the rough track drops down to a narrow road, where I splashed through a concrete ford which could prove awkward in times of spate, although there is a wooden footbridge nearby.

And so I rolled on past moorland and scattered farms, every few hundred yards spotting another type of bird: curlews, lapwings, oystercatchers, plovers – even a barn owl which took off from a fence post, its body seeming disproportionately large for its wing span. It was a glorious run to Lochend, then into the Chapelhill Hotel for a pint of beer and a bite to eat. There would be lots to tell Iain when I next saw him. There would be other trips, other days.

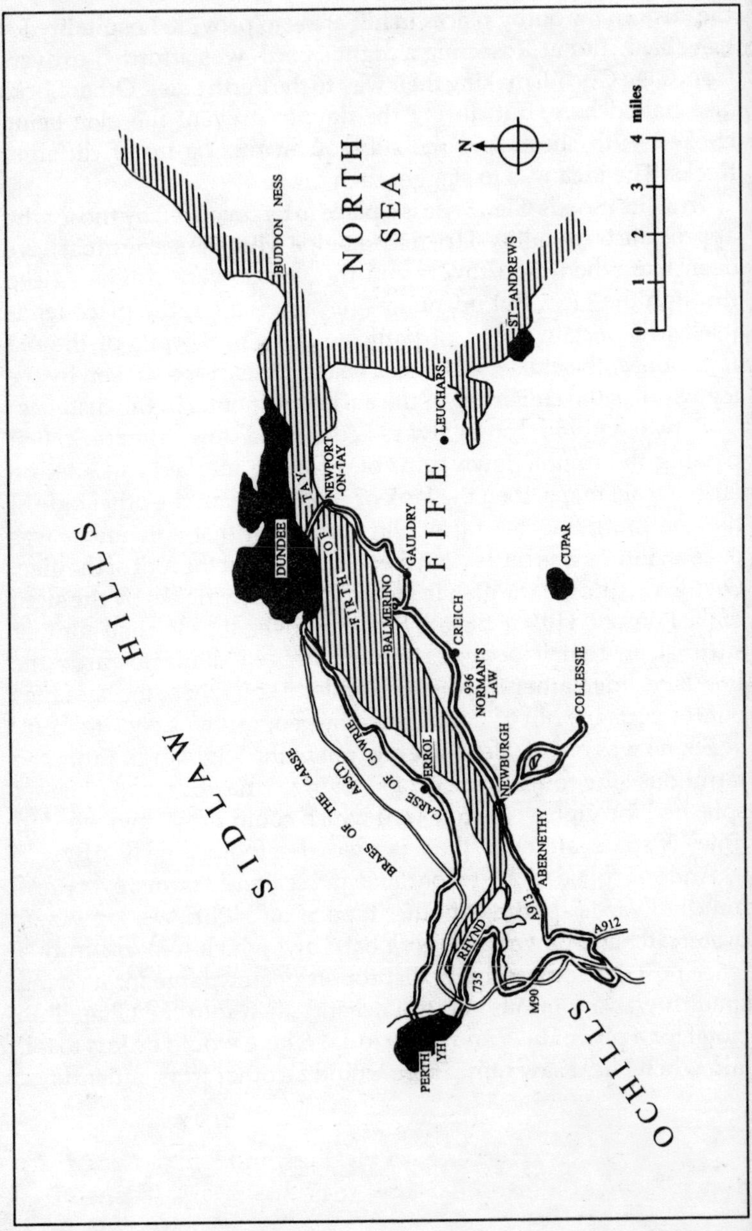
SIDLAW HILLS
NORTH SEA
FIFE
OCHILLS
BUDDON NESS
DUNDEE
FIRTH OF TAY
NEWPORT -ON-TAY
LEUCHARS
ST. ANDREWS
GAULDRY
BALMERINO
CREICH
CUPAR
936 NORMAN'S LAW
COLLESSIE
NEWBURGH
ABERNETHY
ERROL
CARSE OF GOWRIE
BRAES OF THE CARSE
A85(T)
RHYND
735
M90
A913
A912
PERTH
YH
N
0 1 2 3 4 miles

CHAPTER 10

East Coast Travels

> When one comes to the end of a journey one feels a desire to turn back and cast a glance over all the impressions one has gathered, even though they should be as casual as a collection of shells picked up on a sea-shore. Scotland itself could only be known by someone who had the power to live simultaneously in the bodies of all the men, women and children in it. I took a chance cut through it, stopping here and there, picking up this or that object, gathering shells whose meaning was often obscure or illegible to me.
>
> Edwin Muir, *Scottish Journey*, 1935.

TWO SUMMERS WENT BY. The Kalkhoff had lain dormant in the attic. It was now autumn and with the easing of the equinox gales I now felt the time was ripe to stir the red machine from its slumbers and take a gamble with the October weather. Where to? I unfolded a large routemaster map and my eye was drawn to the east coast. Fraserburgh to Portsoy looked an interesting jaunt but the logistics of getting the bike to 'the Broch' decided me against it. Other routes were ruled out due to the proximity of busy main roads which always seemed to hug the coastline. There was one possibility – the Firth of Tay and the chance to explore some forgotten roads in North Fife, before pushing on to Perth and then a spin through the flatlands of the fertile Carse of Gowrie to Dundee.

Originally my intention was to take the bike on the train to Leuchars, visit the Norman church there, then skirt Tentsmuir Forest and head on to Tayport. Instead, I made the decision to set off from Dundee.

It was overcast but reasonably calm as I pushed my way up the flyover which curls its way onto the Tay road bridge. Although this is a toll bridge, pedal cyclists can cross free of charge. The mid-morning traffic was fairly heavy and the southbound carriageway had been reduced to one lane due to bridge repairs. Thankfully, I was able to jink between the traffic cones into the inside lane and avoid being mowed down by the speeding cars and lorries.

I breathed a sigh of relief on reaching the other side without mishap. Soon I was riding through Newport-on-Tay, which is virtually joined to its near neighbour Wormit, the atmosphere being in sharp contrast to the high-rise buildings and busy streets of Dundee. On my OS map (Sheet 59) was marked the curious place-name feature of Pluck the Crow Point. The derivation of this odd-sounding name is from the expression 'I've a craw tae pluck (or pook) with ye', meaning 'I've a bone to pick with you'. It could possibly signify a place where there had been a dispute of some kind.

A good view of the two-mile-long Tay railway bridge (one of the longest bridges in Europe) can be obtained from the road above Wormit's old station. A vigorous campaign to have Wormit station reopened was unfortunately met with an unsympathetic rebuff by British Rail. It would have been of considerable advantage to not only the citizens of Wormit and Newport, but also to cyclists (amongst others) who wished to explore North Fife. This is a fascinating corner of Scotland, rich in interest and relatively ignored by tourists, who are drawn like a magnet to the ancient city of St Andrews and the string of fishing communities along the East Neuk of Fife.

By now the sun had reared its head and an easterly breeze was on my tail. I had crossed the railway line and was following a quiet backroad to Gauldry, passing newly harvested cornfields whose golden appearance was in distinctive contrast to the inky waters of the Tay. Strictly speaking, Gauldry is known as The Gauldry, an attractive village which sits on a rise and enjoys magnificent views over the Tay to Dundee and the Sidlaw hills. There is a small post-office and a pub, the Gauldry Arms, which had not yet opened by the time I arrived.

Upon leaving the village, a small van emerged from a byroad to my right, a road offering a dramatic plunge down to the sleepy hamlet of Balmerino. I stopped for a breather and gave the brakes a check because the bottom drops out of this road. The descent was the king of all free-wheels – breathtaking, exhilarating, thrilling as you descend as fast as you dare.

Balmerino is home to the time-encrusted ruins of a 13th-century

Cistercian abbey. Locally pronounced Balmernie, the place takes its name from St Merinach, who accompanied St Regulus when he brought the holy relics to St Andrews.

The abbey evokes contemplation and peace, tinged by a hint of melancholy since the chapter house and neighbouring 500-year-old Spanish chestnut tree are only just standing with the aid of iron stanchions. Surrounded by beautiful trees on two sides, the ancient walls breathe a perfect stillness. Apart from the intermittent barking of a dog in a nearby garden, I was the only living soul in attendance. Wheeling my machine into the abbey grounds, I found a wooden seat where I could bask in the sun and enjoy my lunch. It was bliss. Peace, sacred peace. No traffic, exhaust fumes, blaring stereos – just the rustling leaves and the silence of ancient walls.

Balmerino Abbey was founded in 1229 by Queen Ermengarde, wife of King William the Lion and a direct descendant of William the Conqueror. The site was chosen because of the salubrious nature of the climate, and along with Culross Abbey, Balmerino was a daughter-house of Melrose Abbey, the first of 12 Cistercian abbeys founded in Scotland.

Though a house of note in its day, Balmerino could not vie, either as to the number of its inmates, or the social importance of its Abbots, with such establishments as those of St Andrews, Dunfermline, and Arbroath. The abbey probably never contained more than from 20 to 25 monks, with a similar number of lay brethren called 'converts', who assisted in the secular business but were exempted from the monastic vows.

On Christmas night 1547, an invading English force of 300 men burned Balmerino, but little damage was done to the masonry. The Abbey was soon repaired, only to be further damaged 12 years later by the Reformers. It remains a place of solitude, as delightful in its own way as anywhere on the east coast of Scotland.

Leaving the abbey, I followed a narrow, twisty road to the Kirkton, a cluster of attractive properties, some with red pantile roofs, which are a distinctive feature of the older buildings in Fife. I completed the circuit to Byres, passing picturesque cottage gardens, before exhausting my low gears half-way up the gruelling ascent to Priorwell. Wheeling the machine at walking pace, I stopped every now and again to take in the views across the Firth of Tay to Dundee, the city belonging to a different world.

From Priorwell I crept along the undulating backbone of the North Fife hills, now out of sight of the Tay but with the added consolation of discovering a hidden upland scene that yielded surprises round every corner. At Hazelton Walls I came to a crossroads, checked the map and headed straight on before dropping down to Creich. It seemed that I was at the back of beyond. Creich comprises a crumbling castle with nearby farm, a small row of cottages and a ruined kirk. Originally three stories high, the castle is tucked away in a hollow, framed to the west by the breast-like pap of Norman's Law, the most striking hill in the district. The castle is now roofless, but the greater part of its walls are still standing. It is one of several strongholds in the north of Fife which for security were partly surrounded by a marsh, and which may be regarded as the lineal representatives of the lake-dwellings of our prehistoric ancestors.

I took some photographs, smoked a cigarette, then pedalled round to the roofless old church that was discontinued as a place of worship in 1832. Its walls were clothed in heavy masses of ivy, a refuge for the occasional owl to give its nocturnal hoot at the silent graves below. It was truly a cyclist's road which led me to Brunton, a tight huddle of homes as dead to the world as the kirkyard I had just visited. Not a soul stirred, not a curtain twitched; there was not even a sign of the village cat. In days gone by the old cottages echoed to the clatter of looms weaving osnaburgs and dowlas, the coarse linen made from locally grown blue-flowered flax. Stacked like corn, the flax piles were a common sight hereabouts, and up to the end of the First World War were harvested by women and children.

Wisps of white smoke rose from only a couple of lums as I pedalled out of the village and past an impressive stone-built manse. Shortly after Pittachope farm I reached the crest of a 1 in 10 descent. Once more the Tay came into view, and out over its sandbanks and reedbeds lay the Carse of Gowrie with the Sidlaws forming a natural barrier to the north. I paused to take in the scene, then flew down the hill to join the Newburgh road at some cottages.

A distinctive feature of the south bank of the Tay at this point are the number of abandoned salmon bothies, or lodges, which provided seasonal accommodation for the commercial salmon netsmen who fished the river. Some of these buildings have unusual names such as California, Deil-ma-Care, and Scalp.

There was more historical interest as I pedalled on by the once-proud castle of Ballinbreich. It is picturesquely situated on a bank overhanging the Tay, about two miles below the town of Newburgh. Ballinbreich Castle was a seat of the Earls of Rothes, whose main residence was at Leslie. Traces of a moat which surrounded the red sandstone walls of the castle used to be visible, but have now gone. The barony of Ballinbreich anciently formed part of the great lordshhip of Abernethy, which seems at one time to have included most of the lands stretching along the southern bank of the Tay from Abernethy to Balmerino.

At the eastern side of Newburgh I swung past a farm and halted to gaze over a gate at the few surviving ruins which make up Lindores Abbey. Founded in 1191 by Tironensian monks, Lindores is not a patch on Balmerino, but was probably a more important religious house since it possessed the revenues of 22 parish churches as well as its landed property. The abbey is built of red sandstone which came from the quarry of Hyrneside. Apart from having important fishing rights on the Tay, the monks had the privilege of being allowed 200 cartloads of brushwood from Kinloch moor, plus the exclusive right to cut peat on land that is now Ladybank, formerly 'Our Lady's Bog', then shortened to 'Ladybog' and eventually Ladybank.

I offloaded my gear at the Burnside House Hotel, then took a spin out to Grange of Lindores and the nearby 13th-century kirk of St Magridin at Abdie. From there I followed a backroad past the farm of Berryhill, eventually arriving at the old-world village of Collessie, which still has a few thatched cottages and a handsome church. Collessie must rank as the quaintest inland village in Fife. Out from the village I waited for the setting sun to fall behind West Lomond as the evening sky turned blood red. With my front lamp flooding the road with light, I found a wonderful feeling of contentment as I pushed my way back along the B937 by the flat calm waters of Lindores Loch. Back at the hotel I demolished a delicious mixed grill and later passed the time with some friends who had arrived to see me.

Over breakfast next morning I was entering some details in my field notebook. An American couple were seated at the next table, incessantly yattering away to one another about all things Scottish.

'O-ban's a nice village,' drawled the elderly man.

'Yeah,' replied his wife, 'everybody we saw was happy.'

'Say, mister, you're quiet. What are you doing?'

'I'm keeping a record of my journey,' I replied, looking up from my bacon and eggs.

'Keeping a jounal! Gee, you can put in it that you met an eccentric American couple who bamboozled you with wild ideas.'

The man was wearing a red-checked hunting jacket and went on to say he and his wife were heading to St Andrews to watch a golf tournament.

'You're a bike rider, huh?'

'A pedal cycle not a motorbike,' I explained.

'Hell, I once had a Raleigh with narrow tyres. Back home, those with fat tyres just want to be a little different, like the guys that have four-wheel drive.'

I squared up my bill and headed into the morning drizzle. A dank mist clung to the roofs of Newburgh as I wound my way up the main street, then nipped down a side-road to the waterfront. Resting the bike against a wall, I took a short walk along the front, looking over to Mugdrum Island, which divides the river into two at this point. Long ago the island was called Reedinch on account of its abundant reeds, which today covered it from tip to toe. Mugdrum supported its own farm and was inhabited until about 1926, but all trace of the buildings has gone and no one lives there anymore.

Shortly a boat came into view, chugging downriver in the deep water channel which is close to the shore. It was the sandboat *Harry Hood*. For many years now sandboats have plied their trade on the River Tay, bringing sand and gravel up to Perth and at the same time keeping the vital navigable channel clear. Originally, pontoons were poled along the river with the assistance of a sail if the wind was favourable, and the sand was brought on board by bucket. These primitive craft were superseded by steam-powered vessels, which in turn were replaced by diesel craft.

The *Harry Hood* is the last of such boats still working on the Tay.

Generally it makes about five trips per week from Perth down to Flisk Point and Balmerino, uplifing sand from the dredger, which sucks up the sand off the banks like a hoover. Approximately 30,000 tons of sand a year is dredged from the Tay, mostly going to golf courses for bunkers and green dressing, but also used by football clubs such as Manchester United and the Scottish national stadium, Hampden Park.

The gears clicked smoothly into place as I left Newburgh by a sharp brae, soon entering Perthshire as I rode the four miles to Abernethy along the A913. A fine, light drizzle known in Scots as 'smirr' had soaked my jacket by the time I reached the quiet Perthshire town, which possesses one of only two round towers of the Irish Celtic type in Scotland. The tower was an intriguing monument, rising high above the market cross in the main street. The Romanesque windows of the belfry suggest that the tower was built in the later 11th century. Long before this Abernethy was important as a principal seat of the Pictish kingdom and the seat of a Celtic bishopric. A carved Pictish sone can be seen at the base of the tower. It is also on record that Malcom Canmore met William the Conqueror at Abernethy in 1072, possibly at the tower.

In the nearby Pitblae Cottage tearoom in School Wynd I escaped from the rain. It was a homely, traditional sort of place and a coal fire was just taking hold in the grate as I sat down at a table by the window and ordered a pot of tea and scones. Suitably refuelled, I doubled back and down a narrow, pot-holed road to Ferryfield near the confluence of the Rivers Earn and Tay.

Ferryfield House, the home of Tom Jarvis, was built in 1751 and was an inn up until 1929. There were formerly two ferries – a mile-long crossing across the Earn and Tay to Cairnie, and a 300-yard hop across the Earn to the Rhynd peninsula. The former was known as 'the Ferry of the Loaf' on account of the legend that it was used by the Thane of Fife when he was fleeing from Macbeth. The story goes that the boatman was paid with a loaf of bread. At one time, ferry boys were employed to look out for customers on the far banks. Travellers wishing to cross from Cairnie to Ferryfield raised a white board to summon the ferryman. Tom Jarvis' grandfather regularly used the ferry to Rhynd when he was undertaking repairs of Elcho Castle as a stonemason.

Tom Jarvis is the last of the independent fishing proprietors who still net salmon on the Earn by the traditional sweep net and coble method. A coble is a flat-bottomed boat used in salmon fishing. The Earn is a far muddier and siltier river than the Tay because it comes off agricultural land.

Tom's father first went to the salmon fishing about 1916, working as a 'ropey' – usually a young boy who was employed to take the ropes off the winch and other lighter tasks. The season on the Tay formerly was from 5 February each year to 20 August. Some days the river would be frozen over and the men had to hack clear the ice before they could pay out their nets. I asked Tom if his father had described to him what conditions were like.

'It was a hard life they had in those days, especially in the spring of the year and in February and March when there could be frosts and blizzards. I've heard my father saying he'd come in after a shift and his jacket was frozen solid. He tried to take the buttons out but the jacket just tore – it was so hard that it just broke away. And one year he'd to break the ice in a big curve to get the net in the river. The ice was up to seven inches deep – so it was a very hard life for little money. And in the bothies, even although they had a fire on at either end, if they went to sleep through the night and somebody didn't stoke up the fire, the water in the kettle would be frozen solid come the morning. It was a different world then to what I know.'

The seven-man crews fished two eight-hour shifts on the tidal sections of the Tay. Above Perth where the river is non-tidal, Tom recalled that his father had worked 14-hour night shifts. Salmon fishers were recruited from the Western Isles as well as locally. Up to 200 at a time used to make the annual pilgrimage to the Tay fishing from the Outer Hebrides.

'They'd bring some meal with them and a barrel of salted herring and they'd live off that for most of the summer,' explained Tom.

'What were some of the bothies like in the old days?' I asked.

'Well, I've heard my wife's father talking about the Abernethy fishing station in the 1920s. Their bothy was on Mugdrum Island and there was no way they could get rid of the rats because Mugdrum was infested with rats at that time. And he's woken up in the morning and counted over 40 running about the floor in the bothy. It was riddled with holes. You see, it was just the earth floor in the bank of the river. If they blocked up one hole, ten minutes later another one was burrowed through. All their foodstuff had to be kept in glass jars. And often when they were sitting eating their food, a rat would jump up on the table to get the food.'

I left Tom sitting by the fire, smoking his untipped Gauloises Disque Bleu cigarettes and drinking a mug of coffee.

Following the A913 to Aberargie, I forked left and tackled the gradual climb up the A912 which winds through Glen Farg, a narrow tree-choked den. The mist and chill drizzle gave it a brooding atmosphere broken only by the swish of passing cars, which had their headlights on. I continued past the Bein Inn and under a disused railway bridge. Within a short while I had passed under the busy M90, turning right a mile or so from Glenfarg village and onto the famous Wicks of Baiglie road. It takes its name from the fact that in olden times the whole of the district here, east and west of Balmanno Hill was known as 'The Baiglie'. The 'Wicks of Baiglie' are the heights above Baiglie (a farm to the west of where the high road emerges into Strathearn); 'Wick' being Scots for a cleft in the face of a hill. The road appears to date from only about the middle of the 18th century and was the usual coaching road from Kinross to Perth in Sir Walter Scott's time, having become part of the turnpike from Queensferry to Perth in 1753.

Until opposite the farm road to Lochelbank, the road offers an extremely tough ascent. I dug into the toe-clips but was soon forced to dismount. Leaving the Wicks of Baiglie road at Scarhill (formerly a shepherd's cottage), a very old track crosses the Ochils over the west brow of Balmanno Hill to East Dron. Parts of the track have disappeared although the route can still be followed to this day. It was known as 'the Drove Road', though sometimes it was called 'the Loudeners' Road', owing to the fact it was frequented by travelling bands of migrant harvesters going to and from the Lothians. This track passed by the now forgotten hamlet of Lusty Law (or 'The Baiglie' as it was sometimes spoken of), which last century contained upwards of 20 families, many of whom rented small pendicles. The site is marked to this day by a couple of tall trees, some loose stones from the ruined cottages, and the remains of a well.

One of my informants, retired farmer Henry Kinnaird, was born at Lochelbank farm in 1913. He told me that most of the Lusty Law houses were made of turf and daub, rather than stone. Apart from crofters and weavers, the hamlet also had other trades such as shoemaking and joinery. Henry heard from his father that a cattle market used to be held at Lusty Law annually in May, right up to the latter part of the 18th century. It was in the style of an old-fashioned tryst, with farmers buying and selling livestock by private bargain.

The weather was too inclement to visit Lusty Law and I had been there a few years ago, having walked the Path of Dron. The way ahead snaked round the eastern shoulder of Balmanno Hill and crossed over the M90, before providing an electrifying free-wheel descent into Strathearn. Wind-assisted rain bit into my cheeks as I sped downhill to Dron, cursing the conditions which had prevented me from enjoying what is a magnificent view on a good day. Westwards through the mist loomed the turreted tower of Dron church, but I was now well and truly soaked and could not summon up the energy to make the detour.

Bridge of Earn was approached by a rather nondescript private housing scheme that comprises part of Kintillo. The route which I had planned would take me round the Rhynd peninsula, a fascinating corner of south-east Perthshire, and one that is often neglected by the casual tourist. After a stiff climb I reached Rhynd, the high walls of Elcho Castle veiled by mist which swept over the Tay from Kinfauns. Further round the Rhynd, and less well known, are the foundations of a Cistercian nunnery concealed below fields at the bottom of Grange of Elcho farm.

I rode on and reached the Fair City of Perth by way of Friarton, the busy traffic providing a shock to the system as hardly a vehicle had passed me since leaving the Bein Inn. I cut down a steep hill which led down to Perth harbour and was surprised to find two fairly large ships berthed at the port. The harbour lies 22 miles upriver from Dundee and is believed to have been established as early as the 10th century. The original port of Perth was situated on the west bank of the Tay (at the east end of the old High Street). Quays extended downriver until Lime Shore was reached in 1833. This is where the Tay sand and gravel company operate from today. The idea that Perth could rival Dundee as a shipbuilding centre barely seems feaasible today, but records show that between 1800 and 1880 nearly 500 vessels were constructed at Perth, and in the last 30 years of that period, Perth launched more ships than Dundee. The advantage in building ships at Perth lay in the fact that timber could be floated down the river in the days of wooden ships.

That afternoon I found adequate lodgings with a congenial retired music teacher, who sang in her kitchen and chased marauding squirrels off her balcony. Apart from her little eccentricities she was a genuinely warm-hearted person and provided me with a piping-hot bowl of homemade mushroom soup and a stiff whisky, later crowned by a main course of roast chicken, potatoes and vegetables.

Next morning a dense blanket of fog concealed much of the Fair City. It was a long, hard pull up from Bridgend by the Murray Royal Hospital to the top of Corsiehill. This quiet backroad is neglected by all but local traffic, and only a handful of cars passed me on the five-mile switchback road that leads to Glencarse. In fine weather this route offers breathtaking views down the River Tay across to Fife, but this morning the fog enveloped the hedgerows and trees, providing an altogether dreich atmosphere to the ride. After a hair-raising plummet down S-bends, with my brakes screeching like a banshee, I arrived at the Glencarse Hotel. Here I regained some composure and warmth, taking my time to savour a few cups of coffee and a cigarette. Suitably recharged, a bridge took me over the treacherous A85 dual-carriageway between Perth and Dundee. It was a cold, uninspiring ride as I stole through the murk and on past Hawkstone and Chapelhill. I was now on the B958 to Errol. In a short while the Grey Stone of Clashbenny was sighted through the swirling fog on a rise in a field to my right.

Port Allen is well worth a look, being reached by a narrow tarmac road which leads down to the Tay immediately after Mains of Errol farm. The westernmost farmhouse was formerly an inn, and the old weighbridge is still embedded in the roadway outside. Along with Inchyra and Powgavie, Port Allen provided a berth for cargo boats unloading coal from Newcastle and Fife, as well as lime for the surrounding fields. Freight of an earlier perod included porter, wine, sugar and foreign timber, all to the order of local lairds. Following the disastrous harvest of 1772, Port Allen was also the scene of Meal Mob riots.

The next turn-off down to the right leads to Daleally and the first large expanse of reedbeds. It was here I had recorded retired gamekeeper, Tom Logie, one of the few men still alive who had cut reeds with the 'heuk' or sickle, in between working at the salmon fishing and on estate orchards during August and September. It was about November that the blade came off the reeds and they became like canes. Errol Park Estate owned the reeds, which were bought by the railway company as bedding for the wagons, the best canes being reserved for local thatching purposes. As Tom Logie recalled:

'My first year at reed-cutting was 1918. My father was cutting reeds and I'd go and bind them, and carry them ashore to the banking. At that time you were paid six bob a hundred. It was terrible work for that. You had a short day, going away at eight in the morning and finishing about three or four o'clock in the afternoon. Sometimes my father had 200 bundles; he was a devil at the work.'

The reed bundles measured about 36 inches at their foot, between six and eight bundles being carried ashore at a time. About 15 to 20 reed-cutters were employed, all stripped to the skin and usually with an old stocking wrapped around their cutting arm to protect them from being scratched by the jagged canes. Due to the mud, the men wore discarded high leather sea-boots as protection on their feet and legs. Nowadays the reeds are harvested by machine.

Continuing my journey through the Carse, I reached the large village of Errol. At a sharp left-hand bend just down from the village, an obscure painted slogan on a wall announced: 'You are now entering Black Dog City'. The principal industry of Errol of old was handloom weaving. At one time 300 weavers were employed and the music of the looms could also be heard in Westown and Leetown and in the small crofts throughout the district.

I pedalled past the impressive market cross, which was topped by a unicorn, and stood in a triangular square that contained a few shops. A fair proportion of the houses bordering the curling main street are clay-built, the batter of their lower walls being evident as you cast your eyes along the pavement. The Carse of Gowrie contains clay deposits and was the location of innumerable small brickworks last century. This was a traditional clay building area and brick-built properties can be seen in Errol, as well as in the immediate countryside.

The word 'carse' means much the same as 'haugh' – a stretch of alluvial lands beside a river. Now the character of the land was truly Lowland: the going flat and easy, despite an oncoming easterly wind and the never-ending fog. Moving at a steady pace along the low-lying roads, I noted that the landscape was characterised by large, open fields, occasional shelter belts and the ongoing march of electricity pylons. It was a day for tucking in low behind the handlebars, riding at the limits of exertion rather than sauntering along.

Twice I had to venture over the Perth to Dundee railway line at well-signposted automatic crossings. The journey was epitomised by a ghostly silence, only occasionally interrupted by a rabble of crows or an undetected skein of geese winging their way across the flatlands. In just over two and a half hours I was passing the mudflats of Kingoodie. Invergowrie beckoned and my jouney was almost over. The traffic of Dundee was soon at hand. I was shaved by a double-decker bus approaching traffic lights on the Perth Road: a welcome back to civilisation. But had I not left that far behind at Balmerino?

The Kalkhoff was laid to rest for the next three months. Thoughts of another journey were never far from my mind. Winter closed in. Once more I scanned the maps for a new route down the east coast. My idea was simple but bold. Two days after the heaviest snowfall of the winter, I would embark on a mid-February jaunt down the backroads of the Angus coast, following the fisher trail from Montrose to Auchmithie.

Owing to the fact that cycles now have to be booked onto the totally inadequate 158 Scotrail express trains, I was forced to rely on the forecasting prowess of the Aberdeen Weather Centre. A fine dry day with long periods of sunshine and a continuing thaw was predicted for Wednesday. That would be my day.

The 9.26 from Edinburgh rattled into Dundee railway station 15 minutes late. The £3 booking fee seemed extortionate for the short journey to Montrose. I unhooked the back pannier and manoeuvred the Kalkhoff into the tiny, cramped vestibule between the First Class compartment and the rear end of the train. It was a two-coach train and a maximum of two cycles were allowed, according to the ticket inspector.

Soon we were rattling past the wealthy suburbs of Broughty Ferry, a string of deserted golf courses, Carnoustie, the long sea-front of Arbroath with its gloomy station, then open countryside and Montrose. This pleasing east-coast town is situated at the mouth of the South Esk River and surrounded by a remarkable river-basin more than two miles square. Montrose has a long history, in recent times indirectly benefitting from the oil boom.

The air was sharp and invigorating as I stepped off the train, hauling the bike behind me onto the platform. It was a calm, crisp morning under a cloudless blue sky, as if winter had stolen a day out of spring's calendar.

Hugh MacDiarmid (Christopher Murray Grieve), one of the great poets of the 20th century, spent 10 years in Montrose from 1919 to 1929. He was the guiding light of the Scottish literary renaissance in the '20s and by his poetry, mainly in the Scots language, has been a powerful influence on modern Scottish writing. He planned to be a teacher but spent 20 years in journalism, working for 10 of these as a reporter on the local paper in Montrose, as well as serving for two years on the Town Council, where he fought his corner for the low-paid and unemployed. Forever controversial and with strident political views, MacDiarmid's time in Montrose was a triumph of creativity. At 16 Links Avenue he composed and wrote his celebrated epic poem, *A Drunk Man Looks at the Thistle*, a work that is hallmarked by its extraordinary imagery. Never a poet of the ordinary people, MacDiarmid was a man of contradictions, professing to enjoy the life of a local reporter because it brought him into contact with the community. He was buried in his native Langholm in 1978. The words engraved on his tombsone – 'I'll hae nae hauf-way hoose, but aye be whaur Extremes meet' – were adapted from a book on Nietzsche.

After negotiating the bridge at the railway station, I pulled away full of expectation. The main A92 which cuts through the High Street was choked with lumbering artics and a long stream of cars. I nosed carefully forward and out into the main road, picking up speed but conscious of the heavy traffic which trundled by. In no time at all I was crossing the mock-suspension concrete bridge which spans the South Esk estuary. The tide was out and the river-basin on my right was an impressive expanse of mudflats harbouring a solitary boat.

Forking second left at the roundabout, I was soon making my way along the quiet street of Ferryden on the south side of the estuary. A quick spurt was made to the end of the village, where some of the older properties were gable-on to the street in the manner of the Moray Firth fisher touns. There was not much more to the village than its long, straggling main street, some of the houses above being built in terraces. At one time it was a great centre for smuggling. The fishing industry began falling away about 1912, the decline being hastened by the onset of the First World War. In 1928 Ferryden had 16 motor fishing boats and several mosquito boats giving work to 60 or 70 men, mostly engaged in line fishing. All the herring drifters had disappeared. There were several disadvantages to the Montrose fishing. The harbour was bad, with a sandbar across its entrance and a fast tide making it difficult for sail boats to enter and leave. There were no really good fishing grounds within easy reach, the sea-bottom being sandy and flat, whereas off Gourdon and Arbroath it was rocky and not so heavily fished by trawlers because of the risk to their nets.

But Montrose had one big advantage: bait for the lines. The estuary abounded with mussels, so that bait could be had at an exceedingly reasonable price. In the old days vessels came from as far away as Banff for bait. Baiting of the lines was done by the womenfolk. 'Sheeling' [shelling] the mussels took about two hours, and the baiting of the lines another three; it was hard and laborious work.

The mussels were gathered from the scaups by men working from salmon cobles using long-handled rakes. In the street I got cracking to one old-timer who had done this job. David Dick was born in Ferryden in 1908. I asked him about 'gaun tae the rake'.

'Aye, the river used to be full of lovely mussels, from the brig right down near to the lighthouse. We gaed to the rake in between jobs and ye made a good enough week's wages. Ye went for them at low tide, put away yer anchor an just raked them into the coble. Then ye filled them intae bags when ye landed: fit ye caad a "murlin". Ye got wan an six a murlin at that time an ye'd fill 15 tae 20 bags fer a tide. They usetae come an pick them up fae Gourdon – for the lines ye see.'

I thanked David for his time and slowly climbed out of the village by Usan Road, passing a farm and a coal lorry which was making deliveries at a nearby house. Looking back, I could see the town of Montrose unfolding, gradually becoming more distant as I gained height. Before reaching Usan House, a sharp turn to the right is made as far as the railway line. From here there is a short straight to Seaton farm. A twisting course was made through this farm, before swinging round and down into what remains of Usan, formerly Fishtown of Usan.

Trundling down the track, I parked the bike against the wall of one of the old roofless cottages which were in a small line with a curious turreted tower rising above them. I found out that this had been a coastguards' watchtower. By 1835 Usan boasted a population of 142, the bulk of whom were fisherfolk. You can still see the tiny beach that was called the harbour – merely an opening between rocky reefs where the Usan folk beached their boats.

The Cadger's Road, which can still be followed in part, ran from Usan across Montreathmont Moor to the market cross at Forfar. The King's Cadger held a strip of land along the shore called Stook Hill, on condition of supplying the royal court with fresh fish daily, when early Scottish kings were in residence at Forfar Castle. The castle was destroyed in 1308 – so that gives an idea of how ancient this route must have been.

Usan today is still home to a bag-net salmon coble and some small lobster boats. When I arrived under a gloriously sunny sky, a handful of men were busy working on boats that had been drawn up the steep incline which overlooks the natural haven. The whole place was a clutter of upturned boats, net-drying poles, nets, coils of rope, oil barrels, lobster creels and tiny sheds. Below the former salmon bothy stands a remarkable sandstone structure which was connected with the salt industry and also served as a commercial ice house in the second half of last century.

A few years ago I had spent a glorious afternoon with salmon fisherman Dave Pullar and his son, when they took me out in their coble, inspecting the nets as far round as Scurdie Ness. Today, I was content to prowl around with my camera, before heading back through the Seaton, taking a sharp left for Boddin.

Not that far along I halted at a white gate and saw a grassy track head under the railway bridge, leading to a tiny burial ground. Dedicated to an obscure Celtic Saint, St Skae or St Skeoch, this is all that remains of the medieval parish church of Dunninald. The lands of Dunninald were part of the property of Restenneth Priory. This enchanting place is perched on top of high cliffs, and earlier I had caught a glimpse of it from the train. It offered precious tranquility broken only by the lonely cries of gulls who were swooping high over a calm, silver-speckled sea. Buried high above the sea were local lairds and farmers, Boddin lime quarriers, a minister, a Montrose skipper and an Usan fisherman.

Once more into the saddle, I experienced a slight setback with the Kalkhoff's gears, which doggedly refused to take the upper five on the larger cog. Somehow it did not matter. I was perfectly content to be enjoying the ride on a blissfully quiet road. For the cyclist it is a glorious swoop down to Boddin. I braked hard at the Z-bend which crosses the main railway line, employing that cyclist's privilege which the motorist so envies – the ability to pull up almost anywhere at the roadside to take a view. And what a view it was. Immediately below me a rising grey plume of smoke was issuing upwards from the salmon foreman's cottage that lies below Boddin farm and overlooks a remarkable 18th century limekiln situated by the sea's edge at the tip of Boddin Point, while away to the south, jagged cliffs were interrupted by a magnificent three-mile sweep of sand which embraces Lunan Bay until Ethie Haven and the table-like top of Lang Craig. It was the perfect spot to take a breather and open the flask.

A taxi slowly making its way up from Boddin was the only other sign of human life. Back into the toe-clips, I experienced the short-lived sensation of speed as I raced down to the end of the road. Boddin is a fascinating spot to explore. There is an underground ice house, past and present salmon bothies, the enormous limekiln perched by the sea, and a steeply descending slipway for launching the coble. Nearby, a line of rusting bag-net anchors caught my eye, before it was time to hit the road.

I simply walked back up the brae with the red machine by my side. It was too good to hurry such a magical place. An attractive estate lodge was situated at a junction, where I turned left and resumed a leisurely pace. Looping round the tree-lined road, I passed a cottage, sheltered by trees at a bend, where a black cat was crouched asleep on a ledge at an upper window. On the way to the crossroads at Woodside, pigeons scattered in noisy bursts from the tops of the trees. I pedalled on by Nether Dysart, Buckiemill and Lunan village, before the exhilarating descent down to Lunan Home Farm. A wide road leads down to the beach car-park past the farm. 'Sleeping policemen' have been installed to regulate the speed of motorists. Although marked on relevant OS maps as a hotel, the Lunan Bay Hotel is now a nursing home. This was a pity. It would have made a convenient half-way halt for a bowl of soup. Not to worry, I still had more tea in the flask, as well as some sandwiches and a bar of chocolate.

There were only three parked cars in the vicinity. I wandered through the dunes and had my lunch on a deserted beach with only the breaking waves as company. At this time of year the salmon stake nets which stride out into the bay are not in evidence. Lunan also has an old hip-roofed salmon bothy and estate ice house with an unusual castellated turret. During the high-summer season the car park can be crammed; the spell of the sea broken by bustling day-trippers from nearby towns. Today it was all so very different. An out of season bonus which made a mockery of so-called 'winter'.

After relaxing on the sands, I got astride the bike, clicked into middle gear and made my way up past the ice house, once more reaching the road, where I crossed a narrow bridge after the kirk. The meandering course of the Lunan Water gracefully glided under the bridge before twisting round to enter the sea. I paused at the bridge, savouring the moment as the water slid by gracefully below me. An ever-so gradual ascent took me within sight of ruined sandstone walls which comprise Redcastle. Situated on a steep knoll, the castle was built for King William the Lion in the 12th century as a royal hunting seat.

Directions to the elusive settlement of Ethie Haven were not in abundance as I rode to Cotton of Inchock, forking left after a field which contained some highland cattle. To reach Ethie Haven, follow the sign to the farm of Ethie Mains, branching left after North Mains. This forgotten Angus fishing settlement and salmon station was known to local fishermen as Torn Ha'en and is hidden from view except from the sea or Lunan Bay. It is approached by a rough track. The houses are tucked beneath the brow of a steep bank and cannot be seen until you are virtually upon them. Few settlements on the east coast of Scotland are so comparatively remote, though no real distance from the towns of Arbroath and Montrose. Today, the Ha'en comprises holiday homes for the professional classes.

I arrived, then left. There was not a great deal to see. Doubling back along the track to pick up the tarmac road, I was now within easy striking distance of Auchmithie, the journey's end. In all honesty, the ride from Redcastle had been through largely uninspiring agricultural land. I was pulled once more to the coast.

From my map (OS Sheet 54), I picked out a track which looped round a small plantation and would take me to the east end of the seagirt village of Auchmithie. It is not the route which motorists take into the village. Just at the right-hand bend before Boghead this track can be followed.

In its initial stages the track was deeply rutted. Worse was to come. Shortly before the plantation the surface of the track had been churned up by tractor wheels and was extremely muddy. I was forced to dismount and walk along a grassy strip in the middle, wheeling the red machine through the thick, dark, mud which caked my mudguard, wheel rims and spokes. I was having doubts about the wisdom of following such a route until the mud gave way to a harder surface and I arrived at a lower stretch where the track was more level. It was possible to get into the saddle once more and I enjoyed weaving between the potholes. The last section was stony, with ice-covered puddles which I crunched through as I neared the village. Far out to sea two fishing boats appeared as blots on the horizon.

Approached from the east, Auchmithie's cliff-head location is seen to good effect. A gap in a dyke at the end of the main street provided a dramatic view down to the harbour, framed by the sheer red walls of Meg's Craig. A line of small boats had been beached out of reach of the tide. Not a soul moved. The place was dead as a kirkyard at night.

In more distant times Auchmithie had been tied to an agricultural estate, the fisher toun being sold off as a separate unit in 1564 with its own crofts and arable land. In 1871 there was a population of over 400. By 1929, so greatly had the village decayed that there was no more than 10 small fishing boats, with 11 fishermen, the majority of whom were old men. A tightly bound fishing community had withered to the point of near-extinction.

Auchmithie and its fisherfolk are portrayed in Sir Walter Scott's novel, *The Antiquary*, the village being given the name of 'Musselcrag'. Rabbie Burns, the celebrated poughman-poet, breakfasted at the local inn while on his travels in 1787. The neat little fisher houses still straddle the main street. Many of them were built early last century but have since been upgraded, possessing a variety of modern roof types. Nowadays Auchmithie has lost something of its close-knit character. The once common surnames of Cargill and Swankie have been replaced by those of incomers.

I pedalled along to the local hotel, formerly a youth hostel, and leaned the bike against an outside wall without locking it. Inside I ordered a pint of McEwan's 80/–. My journey was at an end, just as all journeys must end. It had been a fascinating 17-mile jaunt down the Angus coast, a splendid interlude to the winter. There was no great cause for celebration but I was a content and happy man as my mind flicked over the quiet roads and places I had passed through on my various trips.

Cycle-touring had opened up a new, invigorating freedom and an attitude of mind, to accept the ups and downs of the road just as we must accept them in life. Travel has its own rewards. It is an intensely personal experience. Each turn of the pedals, every click of the gears, evoked the lure of the journey as I rode through the slowly changing Scottish landscape. No two roads were the same; each day was different. The constant shift of different faces and places enriched these journeys and led me into parts of the country which I might not have otherwise reached without the independence offered by two wheels, pedalling at my own pace, under my own steam.

As I slowly sipped my beer I reflected upon the various journeys I had made: riding east through the flatlands of the Carse of Gowrie, enveloped in fog; battling my way over the Corrieyairack Pass in a deluge of wind-driven rain; the joust with the Yarrow and Ettrick valleys; free-wheeling down the 'Committee Road' in North Uist with my eyes rooted to the interplay of light and shade on the Vallay Strand; forgotten Smirisary; some rough-stuff on the upland tracks of Highland Perthshire. These were just some of my thoughts. These journeys had been akin to journeys of self-discovery. Faces and places change with the passage of time. Would I do it all again? No, I thought. It could never be the same. My train-hops had been part of the experience as well, but now British Rail was treating cyclists as third class citizens. Many of the people I had interviewed had gone to their graves. It would never be the same. But I was determined to look ahead not back: the road goes ever on.

Glossary

Note: This glossary is intended to provide readers with a guide to the interpretation of Scots and other unfamiliar words used in the text. The narrow interpretation of certain words here depends on their context of usage in the text.

baa: ball
batter: the slope of the face of a wall that recedes gradually backwards and upwards
bide: stay
blackhouse: a Hebridean house of turf and rough stones with a thatched roof and a central fireplace on an earthen floor
blatter: the violent beating down of rain; a storm of rain
blootered: fiercely accelerated
broach: a roof covering the corner triangle on the top of a square tower having an octagonal spire
buits: boots
buttery: a flat, flaky morning roll associated with Aberdeen
carseland: an extensive stretch of low alluvial land along the banks of a river
cateran: a Highland robber or freebooter
chapman: an itinerant petty trader
chiel: a lad
clachan: a hamlet
clits: trotters
coble: a flat-bottomed boat used in salmon fishing
coggie: a bowl; a wooden container made of staves
couped: overturned
cruisie-lamp: an open boat-shaped lamp with rush wick
cuddies: young coalfish
dominie: a school teacher
dreich: dreary
drouthiest: thirstiest
dun: a small stone-walled defensive homestead of the Iron Age

fank: sheepfold
faulds: folds, pens
fee: a half-yearly engagement as a farm servant
feeing market: a fair or market, usually held at Whitsunday and Martinmas, where farmers engaged servants for the coming term
fermtoun: a group of dwelling houses of the tenants who shared a farm
fisher touns: fishing villages
flitting: the removal of a thing or person from one place to another
fowk: folk
gangrel: a tramp
garrons: small, sturdy horses of a type used for rough work
gibble: a tool
hairst: harvest
harl: a mixture of sand and lime used for roughcasting
heeze: an abundance
heugh-heid: the top of a cliff
hirpling: limping
hoggs: young sheep from the time they are weaned until shorn of their first fleece
howe-dumb-dead: the darkest point (of night)
howff: a rough shelter or refuge
ingle-neuk: a hearth in a recess, often with side windows or a back window, and seats on two or three sides
Jeddart: Jedburgh
kail: cabbage
keel: red-ochre, especially as used for marking sheep
knowe: a knoll
kye: cattle
lazybed: a method of planting (usually potatoes) on undug strips of soil, using manure and sods from adjacent trenches as covering
lochan: a little loch
lum: a chimney
machair: a flat or low-lying coastal strip of grassland common in the Western Isles
mowdies: moles
Munro: the name for any Scottish peak of 3,000 feet or more
orra-beast: a horse on a farm kept for odd jobs
orra-work: general farm work
outby: away from the populous part of a district, in an outlying, usually upland part
pack-brig: a packhorse bridge
pend: an arched entry leading from the street into a block of houses
policies: the improved grounds surrounding a mansion house
pot-reenge: a heather pot-scrubber

rickle o' stanes: a loose assembly of stones as in a building that has completely fallen into ruin
rig: a longitudinal strip of ploughed land in a field
runrig: land-use system where the alternate ridges of a field are worked by different tenants
saithe: a full-grown coalfish
scaups: mussel-beds
sharn: dung
shennachies: storytellers
skarrach: a flying shower of rain
smirr: a fine drizzle of a type that leaves one very wet
smore: smother
sned: the shaft of a scythe, to which the blade is attached
souch: the sound of the wind, especially when long-drawn-out
souter: a shoemaker; a native of Selkirk (once noted for its shoe-manufacture)
sprots: rushes
spurtle: a long-handled, flat-bladed implement for turning oatcakes, scones, etc.
stathel stone: foundation of a stack of grain, shaped like a large mushroom, to protect from vermin and damp
steeket: closed
stells: open, usually circular enclosures of drystane walling, used as a shelter for sheep on a hillside
stour: flying, swirling dust
stramash: an uproar
swey: a movable iron bar over a fire, on which pots, kettles etc. can be hung
syne: from then, since, thereafter
tackety: studded with tackets; hobnailed
tattie roguer: person employed to lift potatoes
thrapple: the throat
thrawn-gabbit: stubborn, tight-lipped
tilly-lamp: a type of superior paraffin lamp that had a mantle instead of a wick
trap: any fine-grained, often columnar, dark igneous rock, especially basalt
tryst: a market or fair for the sale of livestock (though not one fixed by charter or statute)
vennel: a narrow alley or lane between buildings
waulking: fulling (cloth)
waulkmill: fulling mill
whaup: the curlew
wrocht: worked
wynds: narrow lanes leading off a main thoroughfare in a town

INDEX OF PLACES

Suggested Further Reading

John R. Allan, *North-East Lowlands of Scotland* (London, Robert Hale & Co, 1974)
Derek Cooper, *The Road to Mingulay: A View of the Western Isles* (London, Futura pbk, 1988)
Edward J. Cowan, ed., *The People's Past* (Edinburgh, Polygon pbk, 1980)
Alexander Fenton, *Country Life in Scotland* (Edinburgh, John Donald, 1987)
Ross Finlay, *Touring Scotland: The Unknown Highlands* (Henley-on-Thames, G.T. Foulis & Co, 1970)
Duncan Fraser, *Highland Perthshire* (Montrose, Standard Press, 1971)
Lewis Grassic Gibbon, *Sunset Song* (London, Jarrolds, 1932; Edinburgh, Canongate Classics pbk, 1988)
Lewis Grassic Gibbon, *The Speak of the Mearns* (Edinburgh, The Ramsay Head Press, 1982)
Lewis Grassic Gibbon & Hugh MacDiarmid, *Scottish Scene* (London, Jarrolds, 1934)
Will Grant, *Tweedale* (Edinburgh, Oliver & Boyd, 1948)
James Hunter, *Scottish Highlanders* (Edinburgh, Mainstream, 1992)
Margaret Leigh, *Spade Among the Rushes* (London, Phoenix House, 1948)
Michael Lynch, *Scotland, A New History* (London, Pimlico pbk, 1992)
Douglas S. Mack, *James Hogg: Selected Stories and Sketches* (Edinburgh, Scottish Academic Press, 1982)
R.F. Mackenzie, *A Search For Scotland* (London, Fontana pbk, 1991)
D.D.C. Pochin Mould, *The Roads from the Isles: A Study of the North-West Highland Tracks* (Edinburgh, Oliver & Boyd, 1950)
Edwin Muir, *Scottish Journey* (1935; Edinburgh, Mainstream, 1979)
F.G. Rea, *A School in South Uist: Reminiscences of a Hebridean Schoolmaster, 1890–1913*, ed. John Lorne Campbell (London, 1964)
Robert Smith, *Grampian Ways: Journey Over the Mounth* (1980; Aberdeen, Keith Murray Publishing, 1991)
Alan Spence, *Discovering the Borders 1* (Edinburgh, John Donald, 1992)
William Taylor, *The Military Roads in Scotland* (Newton Abbot, David & Charles, 1976)
Tocher: Tales, Songs, Tradition (Magazine of the School of Scottish Studies, available from the Subscription Secretary, *Tocher*, 27 George Square, Edinburgh EH8 9LD)